Memory's Orbit

❧

Film and Culture
1999–2000

JOSEPH NATOLI

State University of New York Press

Published by
State University of New York Press, Albany

© 2003 State University of New York

For information, address State University of New York Press,
90 State Street, Suite 700, Albany, NY 12207

Production by Marilyn P. Semerad
Marketing by Michael Campochiaro

Library of Congress Cataloging-in-Publication Data

Natoli, Joseph P., 1943–
    Memory's orbit : film and culture, 1999–2000 / Joseph Natoli.
        p. cm. — (SUNY series in postmodern culture)
    Includes bibliographical references and index.
    ISBN 0-7914-5719-2 (alk. paper) — ISBN 0-7914-5720-6 (pbk. : alk. paper)
        1. Motion pictures—Social aspects—United States. 2. Motion pictures—Political
aspects—United States. I. Title. II. Series.

PN1995.9.S6 N375 2003
302.23'43'0973—dc21
                                                                2002029180

10 9 8 7 6 5 4 3 2 1

For my mom, Mary Natoli,
whose death this spring has
put me into parallel orbits of
grieving and remembering
with a smile

Contents

After September 11, 2001

It's ten days after the destruction of the World Trade Center towers and the attack on the Pentagon. I'm writing a preface not only to this last installment of my history of the American cultural imaginary in the 1990s, *Memory's Orbit,* but to the previous three volumes: *Hauntings, Speeding to the Millennium,* and *Postmodern Journeys.* They each had a preface but now that both the decade and this writing project are over and the "cultural imaginaries" we live in as Americans have so drastically and suddenly been interrupted, I need to bridge millennia. Our Y2K, that cataclysmic millennial event we anticipated, has happened. A belated millennial metamorphosis. We're in a post–September 11th world now; it's different. There has been a cultural sea change in America.

I think we all surmise that regardless of how well we come to know the causes of the September 11th destruction of the World Trade Center towers and part of the Pentagon, or how closely we can see ourselves as our attackers do, their crime remains unmitigated. We can say we don't care about the whys; we only care about bringing them to justice, bringing justice to them. And we care about how we will be able to charter a safe passage through the troubled waters we are now in. We can say that it doesn't really matter what our peace of mind was before; what matters now is that it's gone and we must learn to live in a world where threatening dark shadows always follow our steps. It never made much of a difference to Americans that most of the rest of the world has always lived in such apprehension. This is new for this brave, new world. We don't know how brave we can be in a world where surgical strikes can strike everything but the cancer.

∾◦∽

Whatever we imagined ourselves to be, whatever our 1990s psychic mind-set was, is now no longer. How to answer this question that has been raised again and again these past ten days?

1

Why this unspeakable, unthinkable, inconceivable act of terrorism against the United States, against a people who pride themselves on lending a hand all over the world, who provide more aid in every form than any other country in the world, against a people who welcome to their shores the downtrodden and oppressed, who impose no religious, racial, ethnic, gender, social, or political barriers on those who live in this country, who live in the most successful democracy of the modern world?

Are there reasons behind this attack or was it simply madness? What are the reasons? Who are our attackers? What do we look like through their eyes? What have we done to provoke this horrific response? How do we eradicate the evil of terrorism? Can our intelligence networks ever get to the root of this tragedy? Have we entered a new world of intermittent calm and madness, with a darkness never quite dispelled? How can our "love of freedom" vanquish this new devil, Osama bin Laden? Do we have the right team of problem solvers in Washington now? Do we have the best strategists at the Pentagon now? Or should we be looking to our corporate world and its brainstorming entrepreneurs to "creatively destroy" this recent threat to global capitalism?

The questions come out of different mind-sets, different reality-producing styles. The naïve realists deal in Cold War dualities, Boolean binaries of black and white, good and evil, true and false, right and wrong, just and unjust, win and lose, and so on. They don't ask the question that lurks behind this attack: Who are we? They already know. "We are the virtuous; reason, right, and God are on our side." The problem solvers whip out the durable Enlightenment Project, apply a rigorous system's analysis, isolate fact from fiction, and come up with a solution. But the optimism of that approach has already and most recently in the United States been riddled by Viet Nam and Robert McNamara and General Westmoreland's unswerving application of the approach while the North Vietnamese and the Vietcong remained steadfastly resistant to it. That Nam world overspilled the approach.

The darkness of twentieth-century modernism continues to seep into our country, leaving its impression in the 1990s on the Clarence Thomas–Anita Hill hearings, the O. J. Simpson trial, the events surrounding David Koresh at Waco, the Rodney King riots, the fight over Elian, Clinton's impeachment, the 2000 presidential election, the Seattle riot, and now this, what CNN calls "The Attack on America." The steady erosion of Enlightenment presumptions in the 1990s and our resulting sense of standing on shaky foundations run into that nationwide chatter of supreme confidence fabricated by Reagan's infectious nostalgia for an America that never existed. It did exist in Walt Disney's mind and he gave it form in Disneyland; you might say Ronald Reagan's reality frame came out of his frequent visits to Disneyland. At least, from a postmodern perspective.

The angst-ridden vibe of twentieth-century Modernism also runs into rationality and realism's new spawn: the Third Revolution, the Computer Revolution, the digitalizing of time and space. After our dramatic loss of confidence in technology both in Viet Nam and in NASA, we are, thanks to the likes of Bill Gates and Microsoft, back on the road to progress through technology. The road ahead is filled with computer screens; people are even supposed to be wearing them on their sleeves. The new e-world has us dazzled. But there have been other signs. There have been throughout the 1990s clear signs that America is having a hard time dispensing justice in the courts and social justice in the streets; becoming more and more class divided; becoming more and more cynical and cold in regard to the plight of the "Losers"; scornful of the unionized working class; turning with the new Bush administration toward a global concern limited to return on investment; becoming more and more in the control of a limited and privileged discourse, and, tied to that, increasingly forgetful of powerful American narratives of value that had nothing to do with our "show me the Money!" attitude.

Our world has also been shifting from the uncertainty and nervousness and always-looming darkness of twentieth-century modernism into the aimless playfulness of the postmodern. A good part of that playfulness extends to whatever we've inherited along the lines of traditional values and meanings, firm foundations, and reachable eternal verities. The market has found its port here, jacking into an attitude that buries the old and has us rushing for the new. New realities require new fashions, new homes, new cars, and new looks. In this new postmodern world, nothing has lasting, intrinsic value; value is in the newest line, the most recent innovation, and the new technological advance. If you're not always shopping, you're losing hold of this new digital world. You're doomed to be remaindered, discontinued, obsolete, dead in the water, your mind yesterday's product. But just as there are counter-currents dispelling dark Modernism's darkness, there are postmodern countercurrents to what I've described here and what Fredric Jameson calls "Postmodernism," or, "the cultural logic of late capitalism" in his 1991 book of that title.

Here are the countercurrents, with varying voltage, as I think about them in a way—a post–September 11th way—that was not mine when I set out in 1997 to present, facetiously, "The Ten Basic Tenets of Postmodernity" in *A Primer to Postmodernity*. Here are the post–September 11th tenets:

1. No rendering of reality can justify its supremacy, therefore we must recognize the legitimacy of multiple renderings of reality, multiple reality frames.

   In his account of the Palestinian/Israeli conflict, Perry Anderson points out that Churchill's "long-standing Zionism was based on racial rather than religious convictions." He quotes a chilling comment made by Churchill in 1937:

   > *I do not agree that the dog in a manger has the final right to the manger, even though he may have lain there a very long time . . . I do not admit, for instance, that a great wrong has been done to the Red Indians of America, or the black people of Australia. I do not admit that a wrong has been done to these people by the fact that a stronger race, a higher grade race, a more worldly-wise race, to put it that way, has come in and taken their place. (Quoted in Perry Anderson, "Scurrying Towards Bethlehem," New Left Review 10 [July–August 2001], p. 3)*

2. No rendering of reality is safe from countering, since postmodernity denies a privileged foundation to any and all. We're closer to Whitman's camerado equality, his "we're all blades of grass" than the market's need to have us "celebrity worshipping."

   We're not safe. The post–September 11th resonating thought here. We're not safe. Terrorism is a form of countering? Weren't we receiving "Bomb-o-grams" from the Unabomber?

3. Nothing grounds our preference for our own perspective; money and toys and the power that come with them cannot justify the superiority of one's observations, one's narrative of "truth and reality."

   Money, toys, and power. . . . Is this the "modernity" we say bin Laden has set himself against?

4. We have no license to impose or project our own values and meanings on others.

   But do we need a "license" to fight for our survival?

5. There's no external reference point which can validate one truth above another; there's no universally accepted universal moral arbiter: we look to our own cultural framing to see how we see.

6. We can't reason our way into the seeing of others; and yet, paradoxically, we can't ignore or negate the seeing of others; realities intersect and are interdependent.

7. It's conceivable that what we see as a just act may be seen as unjust from the perspective of other cultures. And vice versa.

I can still see the TV news coverage of Islamic fundamentalists celebrating the destruction of the World Trade towers. It wasn't perceived as an atrocity but some deeply yearned for victory.

8. At any given moment, we are living within a hierarchy of stories regarding who we are, what society is, what Nature is, what success is. We act relative to these mediations and make decisions relative to hierarchies in play at that time, in that place.

Are we indeed caught in a way of seeing from which we can't break out?

9. A metanarrative or master narrative is the story at the top; number one privileged story to which every action and thought and interpretation and valuing and meaning refer. We can live at a time when there is no Numero Uno Big Story but a lot of rivaling stories: 1960s is a good example; the Renaissance another; late eighteenth century and the last decade of the nineteenth are others. Prominent examples of master narrative with accompanying Master Voices: Third Reich in Germany, China under Mao, Soviets under Stalin, Europe under Roman Catholicism, Afghanistan under the Taliban.

"-isms," like Postmodern-ism, are too complex for thirty-second TV news coverage. Without personalities fronting stories there are no stories now.

10. The Number One story in the United States since Reagan has been free play of the global market, or global market capitalism. It's been opposed by stories on behalf of workers, consumer protection, the environment, and egalitarian democracy. Thus far "Show me the Money!" has trumped these counternarratives.

The attack on the World Trade Center and the Pentagon are like Kaczynski's "Bomb-o-grams": actions against narrating itself and paradoxically narratives against which we can summon no narratives. The message is in the action; the response in the name of survival is preventing, both defensively and offensively, future actions. Survival is the truth and reality to be reached. And that metanarrative has now, after September 11, replaced all other metanarratives in the United States.

If you adopt the postmodern perspective in regard to September 11, you do ask yourself, who could have been behind such a horror? But you also ask yourself, who are we? Who are we in our own eyes? How many ways of seeing did we find at the moment the votes were being counted, and not being counted, in Florida as we awaited the result of the 2000 presidential election? What accounts are we getting of how we see ourselves as Americans? Are we represented in think tank polls? Do the numbers reveal what we see and how we see? Who are we in the eyes of the rest of the world, and most specifically, the eyes of the Islamic world?

We can sidestep or hurdle all these questions by simply saying we're the greatest nation in the world; we're the ones who represent freedom. We can thusly adopt the naïve realist attitude. We can also take the high ground with our analytical reason; or we can fall into a pit of fear and despair, vainly trying to bring all realities under the umbrella of one true reality. I get e-mails and phone messages that end with the mantra "One." I'm not on this road to Oneness; it's a road that implies we can find that one story that will fit and accommodate everyone. It's a vestige of the Enlightenment. I take the postmodern view: we have to review the dominating American cultural imaginary we are in, and the one that has taken us up to the moment of the disasters of September 11. I set out in *Memory's Orbit* to continue to write an account of how I, like you, have been in play within our American cultural imaginaries

∾✧∾

For those interested in seeing a darkness that others see in us, for those who want to make an effort to understand and perhaps alter our attitudes, beliefs and policies, the "old" imaginary framing is now evidence, just as I find, at this moment of retirement, the "old" imaginary orbiting of my life stands as evidence as to what I am now. Both the cultural history and the ways I have inveigled myself into this cultural history I have been writing are from the "left," simply because market and cultural conservatives have established a master narrative on the "right." I'm committed as a postmodernist to finding the road not taken, the view from the margins, the view profit doesn't want to bring to the table, the view already declared extinct, the view left over after "creative destruction" has done its work, the nonhelpful, supplemental view, the view of the writer of a crank letter to the editor, the view taken when you don't take your *Brave New World* soma tablet, the view you don't have to "cost in," the view that sees "mutual aid" and not "self interest" at the bottom of our nature, the view, in short, of the fool. And, lest you think I should go back and revise everything I have written about the 1990s cultural imaginary in the light of September 11, I present the view not updated, the view not revised to accommodate new facts, the view that stubbornly refuses to detach itself from the place and time of writing.

I wrote *Memory's Orbit* during the years 1999 and 2000; I put the place and date on each piece. This was a particular consciousness situated in a particular place at a particular time responding to this or that event. But the past perforated the present; pieces written in 1999 or 2000 are often of earlier dates as those earlier times filled a present consciousness. I followed through with what I had begun in the three previous books: I wasn't writing unchangeable truths and I wasn't pretending to be free of the mood of my own mind or what I saw and felt and thought to be the spirit of what I was attending to. But I did make every effort to show that my perceptions and my consciousness were interwoven into the fabric of that time and place, as well as of the past. Only the dead are truly passive voiced; the world is never neutral; the mind is never without its intentions, its disposition; no pass of the magic wand of reason can disperse and disband this incestuous relationship. We are always and forever in the arms of the world of which we are part. I could pretend to distance myself but deception has never been a game I could play. I only wish I had more spectacular and dramatic and absorbing accounts of this imbrication of self and world to impart; so much seems so transparently prefabricated.

My life is partially off the rack at the local Goodwill. But then again that's my point: we're all off the rack of socially and culturally prefabricated sale items. Some from Goodwill, some from Bergdorf. In a way, in the last decade I've not only been trying to describe the play of cultural imaginaries we live in as Americans, but also trying to find the "personal" in my own life. I do that after sorting through the ready-to-wear and the play of Chance. I also hope that I have added a freshened-up story to be put on by others. In truth, I can't say what I hold to be more important: working into a part of our American cultural imaginary that overspills the sound bite, or looking to find that personal, not prefabricated self, or, adding to our inventory a memorable and adoptable narrative and way of narrating.

ᘒᘓ

Some time just before the beginning of the 1990s, I decided to bring my postmodern theoretical interests to bear on cataclysmic headline stories of the coming decade. I had been a fascinated student of the *fin de siècle* as it played out in England and in Europe. The decadence of Baudelaire, Rimbaud, Verlaine, Huysmans, Swinburne, Wilde, and Dowson in

Europe and England and the Gilded Robber Baron Age of the United States had filled a dramatic last decade of the nineteenth century. I suppose I felt that the mystique of the *fin de siècle*—in totally different form and substance—would fill the 1990s.

Two presumptions: that I would be alive, fiery, and *compos mentis* for the whole decade and that culturally convulsive events would pop up. I also had some uncertainties: Would my postmodern bent provide me with a hold on this stuff worth reading? Could I, without original theses, well-researched arguments, faddish hooks, manifesto intentions, or a sterling English prose style dare to call my fractal meditations "books"? I got over both humps. What Reagan, followed by Bush the first, had done to what idealists like myself call our "egalitarian democracy"—I mean begin its conversion to oligarchy—would certainly produce a very dramatic decade.

I had bloody expectations on the eve of the new year, 1990. What lay ahead would certainly be a bit more social unrest, a bit more riot in the streets, a whole lot more problems with "labor," a slow awakening of a seduced underclass, a sharp awakening of the middle class that they were working twice and three times as hard as their parents to keep up that suburban status, and an equally sharp awakening by college bound hopefuls that in this country education was now for the wealthy. Throw in my "silent spring" nightmares, surely to be realized in an America where le ROI—return on investment—meant playing fast and loose with the environment, and what you have, by my prophetic reckoning, was a coming decade full of sound and fury. And I was set up to say what it signified. Or, more precisely, set up to deconstruct what Washington and Madison Avenue and Hollywood *said* it signified. Or even more precisely, set up to overburden, overwhelm, overdetermine signification so that what the Dow Jones said was winning, success, happiness, progress, and just plain wonderful would be shadowed by darker thoughts.

Besides all the Have Not classes jumping up and pointing out the sham of Reagan's trickle-down nonsense, I anticipated Carter's malaise kicking into real psycho overdrive in all those same Have Not quarters. Could you conceivably put all the Disaffected now threatening the picket-fence worlds of the 1980s Yuppies in prisons? Could you hire enough private police officers to protect the newest upscale suburban housing tracts? Could you install enough electronic surveillance systems to really do the job? My thinking was Shakespearean: rot of Denmarkian proportions will produce personal pathologies. I was set up for serial killers, random slaughters, cultist escapades, teenybopper vandalism, post office shootouts, mass suicides, sociopathic drive-bys, urban "wildings," celebrity kidnappings, headline terrorism, and neo-fascist rampages.

With a glass of champagne in hand that eve of 1990, I'm thinking eye-watering toxic planetary environment, every wage earner out on strike, every person of color on the march, every prison in a state of riot, every trailer park seething, every university student protesting, and every night time in the possession of the possessed.

Did the 1990s turn out like that? Not quite. Or sometimes, almost. Bill Clinton's two presidential terms did a typically Clintonesque kind of thing: they fractalized cause and effect, truth and consequences, action and reaction. What I mean is that he didn't remedy the damage Reagan had done; he didn't end our increasing desire to define democracy as whatever was good for corporate profits. He didn't lessen the gap between rich and poor, but it didn't expand as much as it would have, I think, if we had had another eight years of a corporate presidency. Global warming got worse, but not as bad as it could have gotten; unions still had a tough row to hoe, but not as tough as they could have had; welfare was supposedly ended in our time but as it turned out, only the checks to those on welfare ended; Clinton took us into places where there was no return on investment but he did so tardily; we continued to support despotic regimes for corporate reasons; blacks could feel a breath of fresh air after twelve years of "tough love" and a strong intent by the Haves not to "reward the bad behavior" of the Have Nots. In short, Clinton put a loose and permeable lid on the America I thought was ready to explode in the 1990s. But all this wasn't happening in 1990 when I began *Hauntings*.

∽∾◌∾∽

"What were you haunted by?" a no-nonsense, laconic Midwesterner asked me when the book first came out. By my own past. What was I taking into the 1990s with me? What baggage, what issues did the 1990s inherit? And since I held that the legacy of the previous decade was a darkening legacy, I felt that the 1990s would be haunted by the 1980s. The 1980s were a psychic retreat from Vietnam, a retreat turned into an advance once the presidency, with the help of the Congress, put all the gathered fruits of our two-hundred-year-old democracy at the disposal of the Viet Nam profiteers. While one-third of my working-class Bensonhurst neighborhood buddies were destroyed one way or another by Viet Nam—as were one-third of the working-class youth of every American neighborhood—the "elite entrepreneurs" with every variety of wartime contract were starting Swiss bank accounts until the "investment climate" of the United States improved. And improve it Reagan did. For the top 1 percent of the population. Trickle down occurred when that 1 percent then paid fees and commissions to brokers, lawyers, financial consultants, bankers, accountants, agents, managers, doctors, shrinks, architects, interior designers, and others in the professional classes. I was haunted by that; we were all haunted by that. I remained haunted but once the Soviet Union collapsed in 1989, most Americans were looking forward to the beginning of something new, something beyond the Cold War. My attention was drawn to the murder of Yusef Hawkins in my old Bensonhurst neighborhood. I watched the Rev. Al Sharpton march through Bensonhurst, determined to show the whole world how racist this neighborhood was. My old neighborhood, the place I had been brought up. The past had a hold on me. And as we all sat and watched the Rodney King beating, our American racist past showed that it still had a hold on us.

At the outset I was haunted; the next three years only justified that feeling. I went to the movies to see our cultural fears played out; everyone else was there for the entertainment. They could do the popcorn-and-Coke-we're-at-the-movies thing and then go home and get "back to reality." My mind was crisscrossing headlines, digging up the past, running by a film's own defenses, finding the fear at the heart of everything. Eros and Thanatos were now brought closer together by AIDS; Hannibal Lecter's real world counterpart, Jeffrey Dahmer, was scarier than Lecter; the moral insensibility of the young in *The River's Edge* was just a premonition of what was to come in this decade; the Wall Street message that "Greed is Good!" was the haunting legacy of the 1980s; watching the Rodney King tape over and over again evoked yet again that birth defect we Americans couldn't seem to erase from our conscience: the life of blacks in America. Of course, the very fact that our national "conscience" had also dwindled to cold unconcern for Losers—not fellow Americans, or fellow human beings, or fellow citizens, just Losers—was like a solar eclipse. The surround of *Hauntings* was notable: Saddam's invasion of Kuwait in 1990, the Persian Gulf War in 1991 (a war that left a residue that would continue to haunt the 1990s), and the south central Los Angeles riot and revolt in 1992. I ended *Hauntings* with Bill Clinton's election in 1992. For me his election meant that a man who understood we were in a postmodern world and who would therefore act within the new premises of that world was in the White House. While George Bush the First knew clearly that he was not to do anything as president that would hamper return on investment, Clinton was a mess of utopian intentions with a too flexible conscience, an erratic hardball strategist, a truly divided man filled with his own hauntings, hauntings which were eventually to lead to an impeachment trial. And yet a man of his times, a man who clearly represented the deep division in American culture: let the market rule and damn the losers or let us try through governmental adjustments and interventions to equalize the winnings, correct the abuses of social justice in the wake of market rule, and maintain necessary political equality by keeping America from becoming another Brazil, with rule and power in the hands of the Haves and the bulk of the population disenfranchised Have Nots. Clinton went back and forth across this divide; so did every American not deaf to stories other than their own.

ↂↂ

In 1993 I began to write the second volume in this cultural history, a book that had the working title *Speeding to the Millennium*. Although the book would only go up to 1995, I felt the tremors of the coming millennium. Once again the headlines in the next three years seemed to respond. Most notable were the bombing of the World Trade Center and the FBI stand at the Branch Davidian compound in 1993, the beginning of the interminable Whitewater investigation in 1994, the Oklahoma bombing, the O. J. Simpson trial, and American peacekeeping troops in Bosnia in 1995. In my view, Newt Gingrich's "Contract with America" mapped our journey to the new millennium: we were to avoid wrong turns such as we had made in the countercultural 1960s and renew America by downsizing government and allowing transnational market principles to run our democracy. I saw the clash of mind-sets played out in the films *Forrest Gump* and *Pulp Fiction*, the former rewriting American history the way Gingrich wanted it to be told in the classroom, and the latter demonstrating how we in the postmodern world tell our tales and live out our histories within multiple, intersecting realities, with time and meaning narrated by those realities.

It didn't seem to me enough to draw upon my own experiences in order to mark our never-ending mediation of the world. Millennial enthusiasm and fears were in lives all around me. In order to give some sense of the way we were imagining ourselves and the world in these years I interspersed fictional vignettes between my headline/film/theory pieces. Discursive explorations took me only so far; I needed to create characters and plots and dialogue—fictional life-worlds—that were immersed in the feelings and fabrications of these years. I'm sure it looks like a strange book, with its long, monologic political rants, its sudden dips into arcane theory, its conversational wanderings into movies just seen, its fractal attentiveness, and, finally, these seemingly disconnected fictional pieces that don't follow the protocols of "the well-made story." My defense? I was after an allusive quarry: the divagations of the American cultural psyche in those years. I couldn't bring out what Blake called "weights & measures" or even what my dissertational advisor so long ago had called "a pointed argument, well-laced with examples, authoritative footnoting, and driving with the force of John Henry's hammer to closure." Instead, I had the reader entrapped within a mazelike world of too many exits too like just as many entrances.

The third volume, *Postmodern Journeys: Film and Culture 1996–1998,* found its structure in the real life and dream journeys I found myself on as I headed toward my "double nickel" birthday. In the middle of life's journey I suddenly found myself in a dark wood. In this country. My travels to Europe with a different group of students every year had made it clear to me that unless I journeyed away from the cold devastations of America's "profit to shareholders" priorities my "edge," that slight edge of anger that pushed my writing and my teaching, would turn into bitterness and cynicism. Not exactly the spirit you want to be in when you reach the age of fifty-five. And besides, Elaine didn't want to hang around "negativity." But there was nothing astoundingly personal about this. The whole country desperately needed to journey away from its own cynicism and meanspiritedness, inspired, if that's the right word, by a philosophy of short-term investment and huge returns. I needed to go on one of those aboriginal walkabouts, the kind of journey that's not planned, that has no goal, that seems totally disconnected from what you're doing at the very moment you walk away. America needed to do the same thing. And at the very moment the Dow Jones was breaking ten thousand, apparently realizing the American Dream in its finest form. The call to go on a postmodern journey was a call to walk away from all our toys and toward . . . what? What we had left behind along the way, which in my view was considerable. It was everything you couldn't put a price tag on, which meant nothing in the eyes of those born into a culture that had already stopped giving airtime to "everything you couldn't put a price tag on." What are you missing when you've never had it or known it? But I believe our forebears had it and knew it.

The surround for that book was Clinton's against-all-odds re-election and a welfare reform that ended guaranteed federal subsidies to poor people with children in 1996, the Heaven's Gate mass suicide, the death of Princess Di and the conviction of Terry Nichols and Timothy McVeigh in 1997, and the capturing of Ted Kaczynski—the Unabomber—Monicagate, and the impeachment trial of Clinton in 1998. The decade and the century were not ending well.

In *Memory's Orbit: Film and Culture 1999–2000,* I traded the journey forward for the journey back, and once again I returned to stories and their times and places that haunted me and in some way revealed the circling orbit of our own cultural memory. I went back to my working-class neighborhood in Brooklyn, to memories of a neighborhood where Italian was spoken as much as English, to a time when the road to becoming a full unhyphenated American was the road of education, of degrees. I orbited back to a world where there were working-class heroes and bad guys wore black hats, the Mafia style in all things ruled, and indeed the farthest you could travel in the world was the last exit on the BMT Subway. I saw again a time when Viet Nam set the mood of the country, where I was when JFK was assassinated, confessing eye to eye to a Jesuit, sitting awkwardly at a "literary tea" in Brooklyn Heights, a Thanksgiving dinner fifty years ago with my grandfather Benjamin at the head of the table, the years on my West Virginia farm when I tried out my Thoreau, my stay in a naval hospital under observation for the draft, my faculty unionizing and the consequent termination at the very beginning of my academic "career." And other memories, all keyed by headlines in these two years, 1999 and 2000. My cousin Billy's long, hard death triggers my Viet Nam memories; JFK Jr.'s death triggers my 1963 memory; an invitation to speak at an Indiana college triggers my Brooklyn Heights memories; and it doesn't take much to put me into the orbit of my Oxley Hollow days. Perhaps it's because I'm so far now from what I was then.

I know it's the early retirement offer made to me that has me thinking of where my "home" might be. It doesn't take much to bring Brooklyn back to me; it's where I was young. It only takes a trip to southern California to see my parents who are in their late eighties, for me to both wonder where our "home" is and wonder about that place where we were altogether living in a way that even Hollywood cannot restage. And not for a moment do I lose the sense that right at the moment when the year 2000 ends, and we are in a new millennium, that all of America is caught between forging ahead and returning to the orbits of our own past.

Oxley Holl'r, West Virginia

April 1976

> *My mind is like a space module or an asteroid never
> quite touching the present as it shifts in time within
> the inescapable trajectory of memory's orbit.*

I stood on the crest of a knoll and felt the April morning
breezes—a presence I should have kept in mind just a short time later.

A stand of tall spruce high on the hill overlooking the house
were moving in headier breezes, as they did even on what seemed to
be the stillest days of summer. I walked through what I called the
house garden, past the toolshed, and along a path that skirted the
cornfield. Lines of husk corpses, some dwarfed, some still standing
tall, all desiccated, filled the field. I headed for the dam separating
the pond from the cornfield. The U.S. Soil Conservation people had
built this dam, at no cost to me except for two hundred dollars for
an overflow pipe.

The idea behind that pond was to help me revive the property,
turn to arable land the eroded soils on the hills that surrounded the
hollow in which I lived. Hidden springs had been developed to fill a
marshy bowl of land and then the Soil Conservation folks had come
in and with dozers scooped out a sizeable pond. The pond would be
filled by the spring they said. They would supply me with breeding
trout and I might be on my way to "fish raising."

The dam last fall had been nothing but hardpan soil, cement-like
with so little give and porosity that you couldn't drive a nail into it.
"Scratch it over with a rake as hard and deep as you can, pepper it
with 10-10 and 10 and put down so many pounds of tall fescue and
set back," they had told me. The grass, miraculously, had come.
Grown and died. And now the dam sported a combed-over look of
dead, dry, tall fescue.

I stopped at the toolshed and pulled out a long-handled spade and took a box of Ohio Blue Tips out of a cabinet. When I got to the top of the dam, I looked around. I often would stop whatever I was doing and just do a 360, turning slowly and surveying the contours of Oxley Hollow, always pronounced "holl'r." A narrow gravel road that hugged the hill face was below and to the left of me. That switchback road snaked up along Mt. Jackson Hill for about a mile and a half until you reached the entrance to the Holl'r, which was invisible if you didn't know it was there. Even if you knew that road was there and below you but out of sight until you committed your front wheel to a left turn into empty space, you had to muster courage, you had to be right off as tough and faithful as the folks who had developed that road centuries before.

There were only seven families living in the Holl'r, and Elaine, my three-year-old daughter Amelia, my newborn daughter Brenda, my two dogs Dickens and Cissy, and myself occupied the original Oxley homestead, the first house you came to when you reached the bottom of the Holl'r.

The pond was about three-quarters filled and it looked cold and brand new. I thought about swimming in it, about getting a little row-boat so we could all, dogs included, float lazily back and forth on summer eves. I walked to the middle of the dam and then straight down toward the cornfield. When I got to the bottom, I pushed the spade into the ground, took the box of blue tips out of my pocket, bent down, then raised my head to feel the movement of the air; I judged it harmless, struck the match, and set it to the dry fescue grass.

The burn went both right and left at once. To the right was my two-hundred-year-old house with Elaine inside with the girls; I had left her in the kitchen feeding the baby, while Amelia drew pictures at the kitchen table. To the left was a huge, equally old, dovetail notched barn that was my big hope for solvency: here I would raise chickens for the Purina Company. After, of course, I fixed the barn up to meet their requirements. And I had no money to do that.

I never saw the fire actually touch the ground. The spade was useless; the fire wasn't below me and vulnerable to dirt thrown on top of it. Fireballs were moving in quick spurts a couple of feet above the ground, raging upward to the height of the grass and leaping forward so fast that within ten seconds a circle of blackness was at my feet and the air temperature had gone up thirty degrees and was still rising.

Once the burn on both sides reached the dried corn husks of the field below there would be two paths of conflagration heading in opposite directions: toward my home, my wife, and my children, and toward that barn, my hope to make a go at farming, living off the land, living far away from a past that haunted me.

I look back and to my left and see Elaine below me with the baby in her arms and Amelia holding her hand. Elaine has no free hand to wave to me; I can't see her face. She can't move toward me. I wave her back. There's only death of my own making up here. I attack the fire heading toward the house but I seem to always be behind it. I can't get in front of it. It's like fighting a headless contender and in a matter of minutes I am on the ropes, scorched, sapped, breathless, losing the fight. I drop to one knee . . .

෴

In dreams for the next thirty years, and still ongoing, I see myself bowed down to the fire, breathing hard, my lungs hot crusted, a black, ever-widening circle of burnt ground shimmering before me. I can't see the sky, just the fire's charge of energy in the air above me. The barn in these dreams is to my right as I am humbled there, old hand-axed logs, most dried and hard like iron, some rotted and sloped. These will have to be replaced I think. That's an old edifice, a dead place, distant that I can't reach, that I want to rebuild but I can't reach in these dreams.

And I know it's my past.

Martha's Vineyard

July 17, 1999

John F. Kennedy Jr.'s plane has nosedived into the sea off Martha's Vineyard, taking him, his wife, and his sister-in-law to a murky grave.

I go to Chinese astrology on the Internet to find some meaning in this tragedy. "The Goat and Rabbit combine with the Pig in his month branch to form a WOOD FRAME. This is detrimental . . . we can expect real danger, and it is life-threatening. The tragic accident is no coincidence."

If you want to know more about how to figure out what's life-threatening in your life and not life-threatening, contact Master Joseph Yu, a man who would now be worth more than the Kennedys if the whole Kennedy clan had been contacting him on a regular basis. Starting with JFK Sr. back in 1963.

Jacqueline wouldn't have married Onassis, the guy with all the money in the world who nevertheless had to use plain old Band-Aids to keep his eyelids up so he could see what there was to buy and to use and to marry. JFK Jr. would then have been raised by the Old Man. Robert Kennedy would have served his presidential time after JFK's two terms because Master Yu would have alerted him to danger in that kitchen back in 1968. He wouldn't have gone into the kitchen just as JFK would have stayed away from Dallas on November 22, 1963. So in 1968 Bobby would have become president and JFK Jr. would be eight years old. Eight years later, after two terms for the Crusader Against Shades of Grey, JFK Jr. would be sixteen and his uncle Ted would have ascended to the presidency. (Ted had been duly alerted by Master Yu and had not only not ever gotten into a car with Mary Jo Kopechne but had stayed clear of Chappaquiddick.) So two terms for Ted, which brings JFK Jr. to the age of twenty-four. Twenty-four and apprenticed into life under three presidential mentors: his dad and his two uncles. Would he wend a course toward starting a celebrity political magazine named *George?* I mean, is he irreverent and fearful when it comes to realpolitik because his dad and uncle were assassinated?

More likely he would see the presidency as his to claim. He wouldn't have to go through a dark night of soul searching, of casting a sidelong glance at the possibility of political life, as does the JFK Jr. who winds up nosediving into the Atlantic. No, I think he would have gone straight for the hoop and, at the moment his historical self was on another "self-proving" flight, he would have been occupying the senatorial seat vacated by Bill Bradley and thinking of taking on Al Gore in the primaries.

But hold on. Why should the Kennedy tragedy begin with JFK? Why not with his older brother Joe, the source Junior, junior to Joe Kennedy, the patriarch of the family? Joe Jr. pulls a Clinton and doesn't serve in the Second World War. Instead, in 1960, he runs for president. Which leaves his younger brother John free to philander at will. Why marry Jacqueline Bouvier? Who needs a debutante with cultivated manners to show a TV audience around the White House? Jack doesn't. Jack's spending his time swapping Jackie Campbell with Sam Giacanna and hanging out with Frank Sinatra. He has a kid—with somebody—but the birth is concealed and the kid, who might have been named JFK Jr., is named after his mother who takes the kid and some hush money and disappears. The kid grows up to be as handsome as Prince Charming; he goes to Hollywood to be discovered, disappears in a crush of the anonymous seeking stardom, and finds only tough times. He dreams about flying his own plane but is driving a 1986 Nissan Sentra on that day in 1999 when his plane would have nosedived into the Atlantic had he been born JFK Jr.

I ask you—who has a personal life freer of social and cultural constraints: the JFK Jr. who actually crashes into the Atlantic or my hypothetical, unrecognized bastard son of JFK? Who is more liable to be played or be the player? Should JFK Jr. assume personal responsibility for crashing into the Atlantic? Should the hypothetical bastard assume personal responsibility for being swallowed up by anonymity and poverty? Change the context, change the person. What is seen as personal is defined by context. What is personal in my life? Or, what views of the personal have I gone through in my life? Am I heading for a crash? Are you about to pick up guns and shoot a bunch of brokers, or your schoolmates, or your fellow postal workers, or the president? What's our story of who's doing what and what's doing us?

Am I writing about times and places or have times and places already written me? I'm somehow at this moment caught up in JFK Jr.'s life and death. Did he succeed in having the private life his mother sought for him? Did he escape that profound legacy into which he was born, the always already thereness of being JFK's son? Did times and places write his life, or did he find a personal way, a personal time, a personal place?

What is this whole family doing in my memory's orbit?

❧❧❧

Nobody bothers to consult Chinese astrology to figure out who assassinated Jack Kennedy. We get our man: Lee Harvey Oswald, Communist incendiary. Then Jack Ruby gets him and the trail of personal agency comes to an end. Personal closure. He killed *him*. Until conspiracy theories emerge. First *Rolling Stone* connects Castro, the Mafia, and the State Department with the assassination, and then Oliver Stone, years later, puts LBJ and American Capitalism into the conspiracy in his film *JFK*. Slowly, in the American consciousness, the cult of personality, the charisma of "free to choose," the psychological necessity of belief in "personal agency," the mythos of "rugged individualism"—all are being troubled by the obscure maziness of "conspiracy theories," the nebulousness of the social and cultural, the impersonality of Chance, the un-Americanness of interconnectedness. You have to travel from 1963 to 1999 to witness how the faith in the Cult of the Personal moves from implicit recognition and acceptance to defensive discourse.

In 1999, we are bombarded by this defending discourse: we are free to choose; individual autonomy is all; we must assume personal responsibility; choose to become rich; individual choice is the supreme good; winners are entitled to their winnings; losers need to assume personal responsibility for their losing; Chance is an anomaly that can be overcome by making the right choices; Just do it! But clearly what was once "natural" and unquestioned—namely, that the personal precedes and dominates the social/cultural and can, by choice, break free of the social/cultural—is by 1999 in desperate need of a vigorous and constantly rejuvenated defending discourse.

It's rather like liberalism, by the 1980s, needing a discourse defending what previously had been assumed to be a "natural" agenda. That defense, ironically, finally cannot carry on without dropping totally the signifiers "liberalism" and "liberal." It becomes slightly easier to defend the signifiers "progressivism" and "progressive." But back in 1963, at the age of twenty, I could only connect any idea of the impersonal, of the social and cultural within Marxist palaver, and all the paraphernalia of that metanarrative. I couldn't step back and look at the vying market/political scenarios of the moment, the nuances of the play of power insinuated everywhere. I could only do that within the Marxist

drama of "class struggle" and that had no apparent bearing on JFK's
assassination, or in American society of that time. The middle class is
still an effective buffer zone between rich and poor. But when we all read
that Oswald had been to Cuba and Russia and clearly sought the over-
throw of our capitalist society, we haul in Marxism as a part of the personal agency mythos. "It was this Red son of a bitch that killed
Kennedy." End of story. After 'Nam, and the total mystification of the
"Good Guys/Bad Guys" Hollywood scenario, which even Duke Wayne
couldn't sell anymore, Oliver Stone, a vet of 'Nam and a man who has
seen the personal totally caught up in the impersonal play of market and
politics, of Chance and Power, revisits JFK's death with one purpose in
mind: to shoot full of holes the "One Man–One Bullet" theory. In other
words, he's after the personal agency mythos; and he wants to replace it
with a panoramic shot of American power distribution in 1963 with
reverbs right up to 1999.

　　If you go back and look at the wealth that put Joe Kennedy in a
position to position his son Jack for the presidency what you find is a
scam artist, a card sharp stacking the deck, only the deck is the stock
market. Maybe Joe's revenge on the Irish-hating Boston Brahmins is to
put a son of his in the White House. The Brahmins' power comes from
their inherited position and wealth; it resides in the signifier. There's no
aura to "Kennedy" until Joe creates it. Joe's propelled by the injustices
of an entrenched Boston hierarchy; his choices come out of that milieu.
He wants to make millions so that he can possess power too. He chooses
to be rich.

　　But does he? I mean positioned as he was, did he have another
choice? And, having chosen to be rich, what makes him rich? Is it, once
again, the way the chessboard he's on is already set up? Or, is it the gifts
he has as a player on the board? Certainly both, but isn't it essential for
one of his winning gifts to be an ability to accurately read the way the
chessboard is set up at that moment, rather than, say, a gift to imagine
another arrangement, or a gift that has no worth within that particular
chessboard arrangement? And if the board's power grid is not a display
of "sweetness and light," of "justice served and injustice quelled," of
"rightness and reasonableness," of "liberty, equality, and fraternity" but
rather what it always is—a power grid in which values and meanings are
hierarchically arranged by those who have the power to arrange them
and also arranged by the arbitrary play of Chance, what then? I mean
what exactly then is Joe Kennedy Sr.'s gift?

　　Why, I think it is his close study of that grid and his ability to find
a move he can make to his advantage. If you read any biography of Joe
Kennedy what you find is a series of smart moves, undeflected by

Chance. Later on, Chance will claim the lives of his sons, Joe Jr. in World War II and Jack in 1963, and of his grandsons, Michael on the ski slope and JFK Jr. in the air. But Joe Sr. reads the layout of the board astutely and has Chance rolling the dice in his favor.

Smart moves? Is this not personal agency? Individual choice? It seems to me that Joe's gift is to understand how he is personally wrapped up in context, in the social and cultural grid that envelops him. He doesn't so much choose to be rich as see what the possibilities are to be rich circumstanced as he is. He doesn't contemplate his own image in a mirror and tell himself he's going to be rich. He's busy looking at how everyone around him is looking at everything, and what around him is attracting attention. He has no preconceptions regarding his being a winner no matter what; he is a winner as the protocols of the moment define and make winning possible. And since those protocols produce and secure the arbitrary hierarchies of power, Joe has to put aside any ideals or moral imperatives if he is to play the game as it is laid out and make a winning move.

A winning move is not a move that ignores the present "surround," no matter how in need of alteration and amendment Joe Sr. might judge it to be. Christ changed the Roman world and ultimately destroyed it, but Christ is never held up as a model of entrepreneurial success. Christ was a Loser who elevated losing to a sacred status. No one in the Conservative Christian Coalition is willing to lose as Christ lost. No one gives their stuff away, gives their capital gains taxes to Caesar graciously, or shares their portfolio with the masses. Did Christ win in the way Joe Kennedy Sr. won? Would Joe have been a winner if he had taken the Sunday sermon into his work life?

Rush Limbaugh squawked at all the attention JFK Jr.'s death was getting. He might be in heaven right now but his grandpa Joe is surely burning in hell, Rush declared on the airwaves. Yet, Joe's a model of capitalist success. Do all capitalists who make fortunes wind up in hell? Do all your heroes, Rush, go to hell? What makes Joe Kennedy's sharp entrepreneurial play more hell-deserving than Mike Milken's or Bill Gates's or Rupert Murdoch's or Warren Buffett's or George Soros's or Ted Turner's, and so on and so on? Is it simply because he bred "liberals"?

When black conservative Republican J. C. Watts urges fellow blacks to choose to be entrepreneurial and therefore rich, he is urging them to not read the chessboard as set up, not see the grid of power. He wants them to look in a mirror and recite the mantra, "I want to be rich. I want to be rich. I want to be rich." J. C. doesn't tell them that on the American power grid, being able to play sports with phenomenal talent will make them rich and successful, as it did him, but that's a clear case of individual talent meeting market priorities. And that's one black man out of several hundred thousand. He doesn't tell them that on the present power grid professionalization will make them financially comfortable but professionalization is grounded in literacy, discipline, and degrees—so far a white man's game played on a white man's chessboard. Every child from the ghetto asked to read Shakespeare or Milton or Kant or Veblen or George Eliot's *Silas Marner* or Milton Friedman or *The New Yorker* or Emily Dickinson's poetry is being asked to hook up in worlds foreign to them. And since black kids from the ghetto have already assimilated a counterculture, a subculture in which all the requirements of professionalization are left out and replaced by "street" protocols, they not only cannot read the white power grid, but their own, which has no power on the white power grid, has their attention.

This substitution of one power grid by another is not restricted to blacks; I observed it in Southern California in the Chicano neighborhoods of Santa Ana and Costa Mesa and in East L.A. and I observed it in southern Appalachia among the poor whites. I observed it in my own Bensonhurst, Brooklyn, Italian-American neighborhood. Poor locales did not only not breed the necessary requirements of professionalization, but among blacks, Chicanos, and southern Appalachians there was in each case "a whole way of life" with its own power protocols that stood in for that white entrepreneurial world J. C. Watts and his Republican Conservative cohorts espoused for every American. Unless those living by other rules and desires learn to drop those subcultural games and heed closely, like Joe Kennedy, the rules of the game the white entrepreneurial First World has in play—learn, in short, how the personal is ensnared and shaped by the social and cultural hierarchies—there will be no "winning" for them. Or, all their "winning" will lead to imprisonment in already crammed prisons.

The Million Man March was a march to an "assume personal responsibility"—"You can be a winner and rich!" drumbeat. It's a mistake to think you can make the moves that will make you a winner on a homemade chessboard on the board set up at the moment "out there," out there in the "global arena." Homemade games are substituted for the game you can't reach, you can't get to, you can't play. But nonetheless that game you can't reach is the game that you're in, that you have to respond to, but can't. It's the game that throws the dice for you and steers you around the board. Or puts you in jail.

What's personal? You presume it's what's in your memory's orbit so you go and see . . . but it's not your play; it is, after all, memory's orbit.

Brooklyn

November 22, 1963

My father's 1954 Chevy passes slowly just before Nick pulls up and tells me that the president has been shot.

The night before my father and I went some rounds regarding the academic probation I'm now on at Brooklyn College. I have one term to make up for going below a C average the term before. If I don't recoup, I'm out. My father tells me that street life has got a hold of me and I'll never graduate college. I'll be just like all the other good-for-nothings in our neighborhood. So the next afternoon when he passes by and sees me hanging out in front of Ernie's Luncheonette and not in school or home studying, I guess he figures it's all over for me. And I'm thinking the same way. I'm thinking I'm Nick Romano played by John Derek in the 1948 movie *Knock on Any Door*, a movie based on Willard Motley's novel of the same name. I'm just like Nick I think; the dark-haired Italian-American who has a passion for the street life; in the 1970s he will become Tony Manino played by John Travolta in *Saturday Night Fever*, a movie inspired by a magazine article about my own Bensonhurst neighborhood; in the 1980s he will become Henry Hill, played by Ray Liotta in the movie *Goodfellas*, the kid who wants to grow and be like all the Italian-American "goodfellas" he sees on the street.

I don't find out until years later that Motley is a black man who knows the streets as a black man but can't make his protagonist a black man. It's too soon for that; so all his black characters and black street life become Italian-American; not WASP certainly, but passable. Sort of. In the movie, all the street characters are sort of nonethnic street characters. "Romano" is a signifier that connects with airy ether—unlike "Soprano," which in 2000 is hooked up with very detailed Italian-American street life. I never thought of myself like the "Tony" in *West Side Story* because I knew that the gang fights in New York City were between Italians and Puerto Ricans, ethnic specificity from which both the Broadway musical and the movie ran. There's nothing recognizably

Italian-American in Richard Beymer's "Tony." But it's the street and it
doesn't matter, not until Martin Scorsese and Spike Lee begin to etch the
differences, and universities jump on the fad of "cultural difference and
diversity" and "ethnic studies" works its ways into the curriculum. But
for all that, Italians, Chicanos, blacks, Asians in the street are from a
box seat view all the same: Losers, gangbangers, Jerry Springer trash,
people without private lives, and certainly not in "Cops" view entitled
to private lives.

On that afternoon in 1963 Nick and I just drive around listening to
the radio reports about Kennedy. When they announce that he's dead,
we just keep driving and don't say anything. We smoke cigarette after
cigarette. Camels, no filter. There are no filter Camels on the market.
Just Camels. Nick doesn't stay shocked for long; a presidential assassination is too remote, too much like school, too outside the neighborhood, too outside our lives for Nick to have thoughts about it.

Where was I when JFK was shot? I was with Nick. He had just gotten out of the Navy. He was transitioned out. In between being in the
Navy, he was in the stockade—he had run off to the Isle of Capri with
some lovely and was eventually brought back by the Shore Patrol. He
finally returned to the Brooklyn Navy yard where he painted ships and
then was re-assigned to the Isle of Stockade. When he finished his sentence, they dishonorably discharged him and he returned to the neighborhood, where he worked various "route" jobs. A couple of hookers
living in expensive digs on the Upper West Side introduced Nick to
designer drugs and snorting highs and he took to it like a retriever takes
to water. Maybe they showed him how his life would end. I escaped and
lost track of him.

No one had much to say about JFK's assassination. Nick leaned
against a car and set himself to review the female proleteriat heading
down the avenue from the Fort Hamilton subway station. According to
him he was renewing old acquaintances from before he went into the
Navy. I saw him countless times call out a hello to a commuter who
went all smiles and yelled, "Nick!" they'd hug him and ask him, "How
have you been?" and then go off with him in his Tempest. He was a
predator of the nine-to-five working girl, the secretaries, receptionists,
telephone operators, waitresses, strippers, bookkeepers who like Shirley
McClaine's Miss Kubelik in the movie *The Apartment,* served the Manhattan corporate maw. These tired ladies trekking from the subway station represented Brooklyn's tribute to the Olympus of Manhattan. Our
loveliest were perks for the Ivy League executive class, part of the upper
echelon, equestrian-class benefit package along the lines of that Winner's
koan: "First you get the Money, then you get the Power, then you get the

Babes." But Nick was our homegrown challenge to that: he had neither money nor the power that came with it but he got the Kubeliks nonetheless. And one better than that, he journeyed across the river into the stronghold of the equestrian class and took their women. He didn't have a vendetta against the rich, like Billy Cruddup's Jacey Holt in the movie *Inventing the Abbotts* does, but Nick's disdain for human nature was endless. He didn't respect the women he seduced or the men who lived with them or the men who fell apart because they couldn't hold on to their women. The closer women came to him, the more he sneered at their weakness; the closer men came because they admired him for his way with women, the more he mocked their desires and their incapacity to fulfill them. The rich were sorrier dupes than the working stiff because they thought their dearest possessions, their women, couldn't be taken from them.

On the night of the day JFK was shot, I wound up, as usual, at Skee's bar. There was J. J. Jerry, steel grey hair combed sharply back, bags under half-closed eyes, open-collared, starched white shirt, standing behind the bar. Rodney Dangerfield could have found his whole act in J. J. Jerry. The bar was blue back-lit and all the bottles were lined up under a mirror which ran the length of the bar. The rest of the place was dark, except for the jukebox, which J. J. usually pumped quarters into so Sinatra, or F. S. as he was referred to, played endlessly. Tonight the jukebox was silent and the TV over the bar was tuned to the assassination coverage.

Jerry had a greeting for everyone. He tagged you with a personality descriptive modifier, in the tradition of Homer; he was profiling before the FBI knew what profiling was.

"Hey, J. J. Rebel Joey. Stay out of Dallas."

"Don't start the kid off," somebody sitting at the end of the bar said without turning around.

"Rebel without a pause" is what Jerry called me. Nicky walks in and it's, "Hey, J. J. Nicky Armada. Take no prisoners," which I could never really figure out, but it had something to do with Nick's status with the ladies. With my friend Bull it was always "Hey J. J. Agita Bull. Tearing them down?" because Bull suffered from a pathological case of disgust with everything. With a guy named Crash it was always "J. J. Shoulda Bet'em to Show Crash," because Crash spent his days at Aqueduct betting horses that never came in.

Tonight Terry Actor walks in. You got it—"Hey, J. J. Barrymore. Break a leg." When Terry does have a part, he likes to come in the bar still wearing vestiges of his costume and maybe a phony mustache or beard or white powder at the temples so we all know he's off-off-off

Broadway. Last week he was Ronald Coleman heading for the gallows in the movie *A Tale of Two Cities.*

"Itz a fa fa betta ding I do now than I've ever dun befo."

Terry was either auditioning or rehearsing, always just that close to getting the part but most of the time losing out to somebody who was blowing the producer. I never saw him in any production but other guys did so I believe he earned his name. I see him now as he was that night, script in hand, wrapped in a black overcoat with the collar up and only a scarf showing. Pasty face always powdered, dark glasses, talc on the sides of his black curly hair. He was in mourning for the dead president. Grief had him by the throat. J. J. poured him a drink out of deep respect for his grief.

"It's a fucking shame is what it is," Jerry announced to all those seated at the bar. A choir of floozies perched for optimum bodily exposure mumbled their Amens to that. The more whores in the place, the bigger the bar take, was Jerry's maxim. A bar on a Friday or Saturday night without the ladies is like visiting a dead body at Cessa's Funeral Home.

I think I'm in a conversation very soon with Helen and Frenchy. Frenchy's conversation is all questions or puzzling quizzlers in response to anything you say.

"So who do you think killed Kennedy?" I ask, never learning.

"Who fluffed the duff on the puff and got out of the muff? See what I'm saying?"

I nod. Helen is an even more enigmatic interlocutor. She had a habit of making declarations in an unknown language, or more precisely, a prelanguage gibberish, and then getting angry and grabbing for your crotch if you didn't respond correctly.

What she was whispering in my ear right now sounded like "Gubook book book." What the hell was "gubook"? It was a private language all her own. Wittgenstein may ask the intriguing question, "Does God employ a private language?" which is unanswerable given the constraints of human language. But Helen had her own private language. Maybe she could use it to ferret out who really killed JFK. Maybe she was giving me the name of the guy behind the hit: "Gubook Bookbook."

There was a dance at the Cotillion that night, a private, sorority-run affair. We got in anyway because somebody knew somebody who knew somebody who had a cousin whose brother-in-law worked the door at the Cotillion. This was a future Daughters of the American Revolution kind of affair, more like what I had seen in the movies as a debutante affair. Guys were in dark suits and the ladies were in evening gowns. Maybe the death of a Democratic president didn't matter here or maybe this was too big a shindig to cancel or maybe youth drives onward over the bodies of the older generation. Including presidents. I should have gone home and spent the night watching the TV coverage, glued to the national tragedy, at one with all my fellow Americans. But no, I was at a dance where I hadn't been invited and didn't belong.

Nick's lines were hooking no fish; he sounded and looked too obviously like a guy from the wrong side of the punch bowl. There was no class at this time in Brooklyn; all the class was in Manhattan where you had to go if you wanted to take taxis or if you drove taxis. All the ladies here that we were trying to talk to had taken taxis from Manhattan. I try my special approach with a young lady all blonde and pink who tells me to go home and shave first before asking someone to dance. "I have a beard here," I protest, stroking my jejune chin whiskers. "This is a product not a process." Nick is standing not too far away, monitoring my approach, and I can see my retort impresses him. But not her. She sees the look Nick and I have exchanged. The look of mutual support, reaffirmation, and victory on the way.

"How pathetic," she says and starts to walk away.

I run after her and put myself right in her path.

"Christ, Shakespeare, Abraham Lincoln, and Cyrano de Bergerac had beards. You think they're pathetic?"

"Funny, you don't look like you ever opened a book."

"I . . . I'm at Brooklyn College," I stutter, wondering if I am going to be there long.

"I think you're in my way. I think none of those people looked like they needed a shower, shave, haircut, and a decent suit."

"Now what's wrong with my clothes?" I say, looking down at my black blazer and fingering my open-collared black shirt the way any preening street Romeo would do.

She starts to walk away again but then turns and says,

"Do you know that the President of the United States was killed today? Doesn't that mean anything to you?"

Before I can say anything, she is gone and Nick is standing next to me.

"Something's really over is what I should have told her," I say.

"Who cares? Let's get the hell out of here. We're too fast for this crowd."

∽∘◦∘∾

We were faster than speeding bullets then because we were twenty; of course, the magic bullet stopped JFK. We didn't get the message that mortality's destiny sent that day. Nick had to rush off to a life Terry Actor might some day play as tragedy and I was destined to fall back on time and redo it over and over again in my mind. Maybe the intent was that something be over with JFK's death, but as it turned out, it was the beginning of what Newt Gingrich would later call "the wrong turn in American history." The man was on a totally different orbit of memory than my own.

Totally different time/speed formula . . .

Inside the Matrix

January 3, 2000

> *Of all the new phrases that technology has sneaked into the language, "real time" is undoubtedly the oddest; it suggests that there is some other kind. But perhaps there is another, unreal form of time, and we were all living in it.*
> —Adam Gopnik, "A Long Time Coming,"
> *New Yorker,* Jan. 10, 2000

One bit of advice Morpheus gives Neo in the film *The Matrix* goes something like this: "You're faster than you think you are. The Gatekeepers can never be as fast and as strong as you can be. The Gatekeepers will always be in a world based on rules." The Matrix is a computer program generated by artificial intelligence and the entire Matrix is watchdogged by agents or gatekeepers, sentient programs that are programmed to have superhero abilities. The way I've interpreted that bit of advice goes like this: Neo is the chosen one who can, once he realizes it, deprogram himself and remain in reality unaffected by what happens in virtual or Matrix reality. At the same time, in virtual reality he can reprogram himself to do anything. After all, it's a made-up world and all he has to do is make it up. In other words, he's a free agent in a programmed world. He's the Second Coming, a Redeemer of the Real for whom Morpheus and his crew have been waiting. Sure enough, once Neo knows he's a free agent, he begins to not only move at unprogrammable digital speed but he can also interrupt and intercept, freeze-frame, any action performed in the Matrix.

The first time I see this film I am where I always am: in analog time, not digital time, so the film gives me a headache. It's like watching my TV monitor at home when either one of my daughters is in control of the remote control. Reality frames flip by so fast that they don't register. I'm busy trying to complete a scene already gone, busy trying to collate

31

one with the other, or finding some thread of continuity between this screen and the next twelve. I'm busy correlating, by which I mean I'm looking for a corresponding narrative frame within which everything I see on the screen has a counterpart; I'm interrelating or interlocking an unknown story in process with a story already known. Everything that is happening here is analogous to . . . kind of thing. As I gaze at TV, computer, or film screens, I'm always busy supplying a cohering narrative. A film like *The Matrix*, however, is trying to simulate not my old-timey analogizing mentality but the disconnects of channel surfing and mouse clicks. It's trying to go faster than we can in real time and take on the speed of digital time, of time in cyberspace.

It's trying to do this, I think, because human consciousness and perception are undergoing a revolutionary change: the young are not only processing everything faster but they are not analogizing; they have no need to fill in the connect between word and world as a book-reading generation is shaped to. Why should they when in nanotime a new screen offers new stimuli; a new screen seems to be supplementing the prior screen, but such is not the case because somehow the meaning of that prior screen was not an issue. If it was, then we would be back to analog time; back to a chain of connectedness and correlation. I'm not back to it; I never left it. But I'm "old awareness"; markets can only target me in synchronous time with a "message." And that takes time. In digital time, gigabytes are processed and, most importantly, not "vetted" but simply stored, retrieved, and responded to as "choices." Nothing has to be correlated; if you've got a lot of history in your head, or philosophy, or the classics, they're just stories you don't need when you're moving in digital time. You don't have to connect anything in the present to them in order to deal with the digital present.

I'm slowed down by my correlating efforts; I can't connect any pleasure with just processing random screens. But everyone I know under thirty is thrilled by the sheer speed of image in *The Matrix* and advises me to see it again. I rent it on video and, notebook in hand, try to speed up my own reflexive/response time while at the same time I try to put on hold my analog narrating approach. In effect, I'm trying to lift off from my experiential based narrative links to reality and just cut loose, going as fast as I can without anchoring or structuring thoughts. I begin to see that *The Matrix* is a visual experiencing of a digitalized, computer-programmed reality that the plot of the film itself tries to break us out of. And return us to—I guess—real time. But is "real time" slow time, time narrated by human storytellers, and not time moving in the Matrix, in cyberspace? I mean is it analog time? Or, do we never live in "real time" but always in some human mediation of time? My temporal awareness is being challenged by a cyberspace temporal awareness. We're presently caught in variant time zones. And the film responds to that.

If you don't plug into cyberspace time, you can't enjoy the film, a film which is about unplugging yourself from the dreamworld of the Matrix and returning to the Real World. This sort of confusion mirrors our present fanatical devotion to and immersion in cyberspace and our present fear of becoming fanatically devoted to and immersed in cyberspace. The virtual reality, and its movement of time, which ensnares us within the Matrix, is contemporaneously a virtual reality our technology is heading toward at full speed. We are venturing capital toward a creation of the Matrix and venturing emotional capital in the hope of holding on to the Real World. And we're worried we are going to lose track of "real time."

Who's "we"? You have to combine my old-timey analog generation and the new and upcoming digital generation and take into account that at this moment there's a lot of blending of the two going on as corporations and government move their workers into digital time. Or try to. The cyberspace entrepreneurs, the dot-coms, tell me that technology will inevitably move us into a totally new and different reality. Is it technology that is driving us or desire? Apparently Native Americans never picked up whatever desire lies behind the invention of the wheel. We want to say it's not a matter of "desire" but "intelligence," that is, intelligence would have perceived the usefulness of the wheel and intelligence would have invented the wheel. I supposed desire comes out of how we imagine the world and ourselves, and obviously Native Americans imagined the world and themselves in such as way as to preclude the creation of a desire for the wheel, of moving more easily, faster. They had desires for other things but not for this. So I don't think a technology has an aloof awesomeness that we cannot fail to obey: "if we build it, the future will come" sort of thing. Progress doesn't bring technology; and technology doesn't necessarily bring progress. But it does seem true that desire brings technology and different desires bring different technologies, or preclude technologies altogether.

Raised as I was in the radio days of the "Lone Ranger," I think going fast is going as fast as Silver could run. What I desire in the way of speed is to go that fast. What I desire in the way of stimuli is to hear those radio voices again and fill in with my imagination what the voices evoked. What I desire in the way of stimuli is to read Dickens and Shakespeare again; Raymond Chandler and B. Traven, Wordsworth and Gary Snyder, and fill in with my imagination what the words evoke. Marketing and advertising have made their pitch within this range of desire for a very long time; but both can be accelerated if our acceptance of marketing stimuli, marketing image, and spectacle is accelerated. And, if indeed, the analogizing is deleted and only a fast track exists between image recognition and purchase, then we are first and foremost in a new marketing reality. Does that matter in an "it's the economy, stupid!" world? Apparently, it's all that matters.

Desire is for short-term profits and that propels our technology creation; there is nothing inevitable, or innately progressive, or natural, or logical, or "winning" about this. Just as there wasn't anything innately stupid about Native Americans not inventing the wheel. Unless, of course, we look upon both ourselves and them from within *our* "world of desire." We can do this easily by not thinking of it as a "world of desire, created by desire and prioritized by that desire" but by thinking of it as a world which our Western tradition of rationality and realism has uncovered/discovered. We can spin ourselves into believing we are free of desire here, disinterested, objective.

Our market-driven desires are for accelerated consumption and this is achieved by creating a desire for the newest of everything, creating a mass psychology which attaches itself to the newest fads and fashions and detaches itself from what is no longer "in style." E-commerce can go on twenty-four hours a day; you can surf the Web at midnight for a VCR or a new housecleaning service, or an airline ticket. Paradoxically, our market/technological-driven impulse to speed time up also seems to stretch time out. Time must be expanded at the same time it is accelerated. If you're trying to succeed in business, you have to extend your hours. Those who leave at 5 P.M. and put in a forty-hour week will surely "lose" to those who work sixty, seventy, eighty hours a week. If you're not in contact with your e-mail or your voice mail or your Web site on a twenty-four–hour basis, you're a "loser." You have to move faster and for longer periods of time in this Market Matrix. You get used to long meetings, long trips, long hours, long films like *The Matrix*. Expanding one's sense of time means having more time to go faster, more time ultimately to spin others into consuming, and to consume within the seductions of spin. Expanding the time frame doesn't mean time will not be digital but synchronous; this is not a return to unity, coherence, and continuity; time frame can be long and time can be disjointed, fractured, disconnected, discontinuous. You just have more time to call up disconnected computer screens. You can get more in if you work a twenty-four–hour day.

Ever-rising stock prices depend on ever-rising profits which depend on ever-rising consumption which depends on constant technological innovation. Are we racing to something new, different, and better? How new, different, and better? That's not a question reason can answer because it's a perception that desire creates. You need to hire an advertising company to spin the answer, like gas-guzzling, oversized, real-damage-causing SUVs are new, different, and better . . . than the cheaper car you're now driving.

If you can imagine that the faster everything goes—the faster the computer response time, the faster your stuff is delivered to you, the faster new products come on the market, the faster you can go on the highways, the faster the jokes, the faster your stocks rise, the faster your waitress is, the faster your kid gets to college, the faster you get your new house, your new boat, your new plane, your new SUV—the better off you are, the better you are all-round, then your sense of time will coincide with the market's sense of time. The only trouble is that it isn't your sense of time at all; you've been rushed into it. At some point in time, when you desire to go as fast as the market story desires you to go, the joke is on you.

I say then that ultimately the reason Neo, the world's savior, has to move at digital speed is because the market needs a future in which we are all choosing products from a shelf, clicking on Web purchases, and phoning in catalogue calls at digital speed. We're working longer and faster to "grow" the "bottom line." And if we're in the business right now of imagining a future world like that—setting up the Matrix, if you will—then that world is only a couple of clicks away.

A week after I re-see *The Matrix,* I see David Lynch's film, *The Straight Story.* It's like leisurely strolling through a museum of great landscape and portrait paintings, or standing before one *tableau vivant* after another. This is time told without a remote or a mouse: We haven't clicked on to these screens; we've slowly paced through them on Alvin Straight's John Deere tractor. This is "face-to-face" time. We are moving in analog time, slow as snails, and so whatever there is in the world that makes up this Real World of ours meets our gaze. It's all already there and the seeing is a continuous revelation: this is it, this is it . . . you are here, you are here. You redo Alvin's five-mile-an-hour tractor trip in your mind in your own SUV. All the close-ups go; all the stargazing ends; all the countryside speeds by in one blurred rush. You've taken the "drive-through" window journey while Alvin's gotten stuck on the slo-mo lane where he's broken down and sits and waits and looks and thinks and remembers and responds. He has all the time in the world to fit into his life's narration everything he sees; he has all the time in the world to narrate his surroundings. He's consuming but he's not buying; the landscape is neither a product nor a service; he's not surfing the Web of Nature, and time only moves within the narrative pace of his responses to what he sees out there, recalls back then, and imagines up ahead.

   Bruce Chatwin in *Songlines* refers to the way the Aborigines bring
the landscape into their lives by connecting it with stories of their past.
To see a certain hill is to immediately recall its "song," its place in Aboriginal narration of the world. To journey in the world is to follow these
songlines, finding one's way in the physical world at the same time that
one brings that physical world into the human world. We humans narrate that world, most coldly and abstractly in physics and chemistry and
biology, and most warmly and imaginatively in our poetry, our music,
our dance, our paintings and sculpture.

   What's enormously refreshing about Lynch's film of Alvin's journey
is that it comes out in 1999 as we are all speeding to the millennium,
either toward some dystopia or utopia. Utopia is now an ever-rising
Dow Jones, an accelerating bullishness of the market. And dystopia is
now all the fear and anxiety, depression and mania, rage and distrust
pouring out of the cracks of this most shortsighted, most dehumanizing,
most mindless of utopic visions. Alvin's journey goes on at the end of
this E-decade, oblivious to new world orders and global free market fantasies. It's rather like the way Nature shows up in Terrence Malick's *The
Thin Red Line*: the camera moves to a bird in a tree, or comes in close
on a flower or frond, or pans the clouds floating by, or registers the mild
curiosity of a variety of fauna to the war we humans are waging. Time
here is told differently; it's only wartime time for those waging war, for
those caught in the Matrix of war.

   And, now, caught in the Matrix of Market, the Matrix of Money—
hard to ignore or escape. But I tried . . .

Oxley Holl'r, West Virginia

Fall 1975

If you went out the back door at night and climbed up the slope against which the house had been built just about two hundred years before, and looked up, all the constellations of the heavens lit up the sky. It could make you dizzy, looking, slowly turning to see what you could name, as if in the naming you got closer. There are no lights; the nearest house, Kell Petry's, is around a turn about a quarter of a mile further into the holl'r.

Kell had a beagle dog, maybe a year old, who came down the road hobbling because his front two legs had been cut off in a fox trap; one above the knee joint and one below so when he walked on the stumps, he walked unevenly. That dog was always cross, eyes kind of dazed with continuous pain. Elaine had to ask Kell why he didn't put the dog down because it hurt her bad to see that dog, or even hear it bark in the distance. Kell didn't understand the question. I mean he culturally didn't understand the question. The beagle had survived the trap; he was crippled and in continuous pain, but he was still alive. Kell wasn't going to shoot him. Or pay a vet in town to put him "to sleep."

I began to look at the dog the way Kell did: he was a defiant bit of flesh holding on to life. He was living the way you learned to live in the holl'r. That was *another* tradition and we had to learn it.

Still, after seeing that dog, Elaine had me tie up our dogs, Dickens and Cissy, tie them up on a big runner on the slope just behind the house. Their doghouse was out there and bowls of water. The dogs came in when it got too hot. They were brought in every night so they could sleep in the kitchen by the wood-burning stove. Dickens was named Dickens because when he was a pup and could fit in the palm of my hand, he looked like a Dickensian caricature of a dog, the kind of dog Dickens would describe: unusually big black rubbery nose with a spot of pink at the tip; long, thick beagle body covered in black terrier hair; short, stumpy front legs with big paws; longer, thinner back legs. A woman in New Hampshire, where he was born, remarked how distinctive he looked. "What breed is that?" she queried. "Pootergle," I told her. "I've never heard of that," she replied. "He's wonderful." Poodle. Terrier. Beagle. A hybrid in purebred Mayflower country.

No one asked about Dickens down in Oxley Holl'r but Cissy caught folks' eye. Especially when they saw her chase after squirrel, so fast she could get out front and nip at their noses. "That dog can hunt some I bet," somebody would say. Something accrued to my reputation by having a blue-eyed beagle whippet mix. Good nose, agility, and speed. But she didn't know how to hunt and she was neurotic and if we didn't tie her up she would have wound up in a fox trap herself. Or, following one scent after another in endless circles, she'd finally drop down dead of exhaustion, her nose still sniffing a scent.

Those two dogs would get loose and go on wild junkets, returning tired, dirty, and hungry. I would go after them and stay gone while they were gone because there was no being with Elaine when the dogs were loose. There was only that one dirt road that wound down into the holl'r and only the few pick-ups of the six families living in the holl'r that ever went in or out but Elaine imagined Lower East Side Manhattan traffic. It was where the traffic was in her mind. And in my mind, I ran with them; something about seeing them on the loose and heading across the corn field and then gone out of sight that had me running with them.

In my Oxley Holl'r constellations, Dickens and Cissy are always running, short bodies in tall pasture grass, making the sign of the Running Dog in the household of the Heavens where even now when I look up, I see them just breaking free.

There is a history to the house in Oxley Holl'r that came to us in slow increments, not all but a bit of it. The Oxley family cemetery was up on a hill on my property, gravestones under a very old oak tree. Up there, under that tree, among those graves, on a day that's hot below but always a breeze blowing up there, you could look down at the house and the dovetailed notched spring shed, tool shed, granary, and barn surrounding the house, and feel so unbelievably temporary, always just a matter of time before you would not be above and looking but below ground, dark and quiet, senseless, unseeing.

As long as time mattered, we wanted to calculate it but all I wanted to do was slow it down, put the brake on, and maybe, just maybe, put it in reverse. I was the presumptuous Ahab of Time.

᠎᠎᠎᠎᠎᠎᠎᠎᠎᠎᠎ᦞᦞᧉ

"There's a bunch of people going up the hill," Elaine reported, looking out the window. There were three men in black suits, escorting an old lady, hunched over and walking with a cane. They were slowly making their way up the hill toward the cemetery.

"Maybe it's an Oxley," I said.

I sat on the front porch steps waiting for their return.

I waved to them and smiled and they stopped when they reached the bottom of the hill. The old lady was Mrs. Dram but she was born an Oxley. In that house. She pointed to it.

"Not funny looking then," she told me.

She puzzled me.

"Why it was two stories high with big double chimmleys on both sides."

"That's a fact," one of the men said.

She was ninety-two and had been born in the house which had been built by her great-grandfather into the side of the hill with stone pedestals and hewn logs as a foundation.

They were all up there buried on the hill.

She didn't ask anything about me but I saw her looking past me to Elaine standing on the front porch with Brenda in her arms.

"I intend to work the land," I told her.

"Nobody has for a long time. It'll be hard."

I thought then that she meant me but she was talking about Elaine. What was hardest fell to Elaine's lot and the old lady saw that then and I never saw until I sputniked through it all countless times.

The old lady looked back at the house, maybe seeing what it had been. And more.

I asked them in but they declined; I had a lot of questions for the old lady but they escorted her back to the car and drove off. What had that big barn, now almost collapsed, been like when she was a child? What was the whole holl'r like and who lived there? I wanted to reconfigure what it had all been like back then.

⌒⌒

I had this idea that I was going to find the time to write about what I was experiencing but I never found the time. The Present was always rushing at me with its urgencies. But the Past did come by like Chance on foot.

We met Clarence this way. He had just gotten out of the army and was in his early twenties. He didn't talk much. He answered questions in a guarded way. If he hadn't been in the service, he might not have talked to a stranger like me at all. I think he had been in Viet Nam at the end but he wouldn't say. We found him roaming the property, walking the top of the dam with a dog no more than a pup scrambling after him. I went out to greet him the way I had greeted Mrs. Dram. Clarence's mother and father had owned the property when he had gone into the service and he hadn't known that they had sold it until he returned to West Virginia. They were living in a small place in Princeton, a town about ten miles away.

Clarence was tall and thin and the way he walked around, looking at what had been his home, the home of his youth, I could see that he knew every inch of it, knew what had been, and recognized what was still the same. We invited him into the house and he accepted in a sort of dazed way. He didn't know about us but he did know one thing: we weren't the ones who had bought the house from his parents. That had been the Martins, a family from the Northeast who had swindled his parents. How, we asked, but he didn't know. He was bitter and lost, betrayed. Wherever he had been, the thought of these West Virginia hills and this particular holl'r, this particular acreage, had been the future for him. And now it had been sold off. He couldn't stay with his folks because they lived in a tiny place. They didn't have a foot of dirt to plant a potato in. They were as lost as he was.

∽∾⌒∾

We began to dislike Todd Martin and his whole clan. He was a dean of students in a local college and lived with his family in a modern ranch-style brick home in a sort of suburban community near the college. Going there was like going forward in time, like coming out of an older way of life holl'red into the present. Truly, the holl'r was like a black hole in space, unseen and unknown until you dipped the front wheels over the edge and turned the wheel sharply and found the way down and in. I thought of that couple-of-mile trek in and out of the holl'r as travel across difficult space, especially in winter. But it was really time travel. And the Martin brood represented what living was like in mid-1970s America. They were regentrifying yuppies before the word. They were harbingers of both the 1980s belief that "greed is good" and its sanctimonious fundamentalism. The Martins were avid Roman Catholics. If they had arrived in Mercer County before JFK had shown the West Virginians Catholics were not devil sent, a cross would have been burnt on the Martin's front lawn. They introduced the concept of lawn to that southernmost part of West Virginia. Everybody else had pasture or garden or chicken yard.

They were what I had seen as the future of America and what I was trying to escape.

The way Clarence's family had gotten swindled went like this (and this from Buck, whose old John Deere I borrowed to plow my land). Todd Martin had gone down into Oxley Holl'r for a "look see." He had stopped to chat with Clarence's Dad, who was at that moment struggling a bit harder than usual. So when Martin had said he'd be willing to take the place off his hands and name a price—Clarence's Dad had named a price—five thousand dollars. Martin said he'd be back the next morning with the money. When he did sure enough come back, Clarence's Dad took the money and sold the place even though his heart wasn't in it. It was a Southern Appalachia way to be a man of your word and he had named the price and there it was. The man from up north had taken advantage of the honest ways folks had in this part of the country. No Appalachian would have held Clarence's Dad to that bargain. It was a bargain with the devil. Then I came along and bought half the property for twice the price. No wonder the folks down there thought I was some kind of a fool and for a long time thought I was a friend of the Martins. Another swindler from up north.

It was only by working my land and helping the other families down in that holl'r that I managed to get out from under that poor beginning. And I guess it was Pat Oxley who put in the good word for me that had turned the tide.

"Pat, his Dad, and his uncle are burning off the winter grass," Lorene Oxley said when she called that night about ten or so. "I think he might need you. Can you come on up?"

"Sure," I replied, happy to be included.

"Bring a spade in case the fire jumps the trenches."

With the shovel over my shoulder I went out the front porch, Elaine telling me to be careful. Pat had a hundred acres of land nestled back at the end of the holl'r.

As I approached the top of the hill, it suddenly looked like dark night had turned back to a rosy twilight. And then at the top I saw where the light was coming from: one hundred acres of winter grass were ablaze. This is fear: my first thoughts were to get my family out of the holl'r. I saw the whole holl'r on fire and the only safety up there at the top, at the rim. Otherwise, we would be swallowed up in this inferno.

I caught a glimpse of dark figures leaning on shovels in the distance and I realized that here were Pat and his family standing guard lest that fire jumped the perimeter they had burnt back. It was the hardest thing in the world for me to walk toward that burning world, with bushes and trees going up like torches.

"Hey, Joe," Pat said to me when I reached him, looking at me and then back at the flames. There was a stretch of blackened earth about ten feet wide right in front of him and then beyond the blaze roaring and advancing like some wild beast of the night.

"Lorene called and said you might need me," I said, trying to be as laid back about the end of the world as Pat was.

"You maybe might want to stand about fifty yards east of where Bob's standing," he said, pointing to a standing shadow swallowed up in flames to our right.

"Okay," I said. And it was the hardest thing in the world up to that point for me to walk toward a sure end like that, but I did it. I did it because I had faith that these folks knew what they were doing. I did it because being out like that, walking on the periphery of a firestorm like that in the darkest of spring nights with no moon at all, positioned me squarely and dead set in the world like I had never been in it before.

                    ☙

What was life like down there? I got asked any number of times. You don't remember when you say it was this or that. All you remember are scenes. Words come out of a far-removed present but the pictures in your head stay sharp.

I see myself standing in the snow, a solitary barn to my left and to my right, and in the distance, just coming over a hill, is a herd of horses. I've just pulled bales of hay out of the barn and am cutting the baling twine. "Hang the baling twine here," Pat had told me. "One bale, one twine. Any twine left on the bale will choke 'em." I pan way back in my mind and see myself surrounded by that herd of horses, and the hay bales, and the white snow in the holl'r and the surrounding hills.

Another winter and we've run out of wood, which is all we use to heat the house. I walk through the snow up to Pat's place and we load chain saws in the back of a dump-load truck and then drive it deep into the woods where we spend the whole day cutting and hauling to the truck. We drive it back to my place, back it up to the granary and dump the load of uncut timber right out in front. It's enough wood to get us through the rest of the winter, as long as I cut and stack in the morning and then in the evening. There's a lone hanging light in the granary and I cut in its soft glow.

Every two hours throughout the bitter cold nights, I get up and put wood on each of the three fires we have going: the kitchen stove, the laundry stove in Amelia's room, the Ben Franklin in the living room. On the coldest nights, I add hard coal to the hard wood and still I barely keep the temperature of the house above sixty-five degrees. Brenda is only weeks old and she has caught some kind of virus; a desperate, late-night call to her doctor in a town miles away. "Don't take her out of the house. Keep nursing her." See it through. There is nothing to be done. It's in God's hands, truly.

"How does she look to you?" Elaine asks me, as she gently unwraps the swaddling blankets.

Why, I see through her, I think; she's translucent. I see life on the cusp of death, barely present, her body somehow already where bodies don't go.

I say nothing.

"She's breathing . . . differently. That's what woke me up," Elaine tells me.

I know I have to put more wood and coal on the fires. I rush to do that. All night I go from one fire to another, keeping them all roaring. It's in the heat; in the rooms; in Elaine's body passing on to Brenda's tiny body, in our lives calling to hers.

I had done the worst thing: I had taken my family to the brink of disaster; imperilled their lives, made them vulnerable to the darkness that always accompanies the dreams of romantic fools who decide to escape their own time and place and live in another. What I had wanted was only telling me what I had become.

Brenda revives, survives, flourishes, comes back to life, but life becomes a suddenly translucent thing for me. I see beyond the movement and hear something in a bitter cold wind surrounding us. I see the end at the very beginning, the destiny of the orbit.

St. Albans Naval Hospital

1966

My draft notice came in January 1966: report on such and such a day at such and such a time to the Whitehall Street, downtown Brooklyn, draft office. There was a subway token, a fifteen-cent subway token, taped to the notice. I had to pay for my own way back; the government was just interested in getting me there.

I showed up on time; didn't see anyone I knew; listened to the sergeant rattle off the day's schedule; took some sort of IQ test. The test was mostly matching boxes unboxed—that you had to fold in your head—with pictures of what they would look like when they were properly boxed. I shouldn't say "box" because that already gives you a sense of a square box and most of the shapes you had to select from were not square or rectangle. Mentally I was leaving out pieces of box, or coming up with boxes with pieces outside the box.

"Put your pencils down!"

I dropped mine, and waited for the sarge to come around and grade what I had done. I watched him coming along the row, fat dark pencil in hand which moved rapidly down the line of answers. He had those memorized. He spent about fifteen seconds on each paper. When he did mine he lowered the paper and gave me this once-over look, which he hadn't given to anyone else. Was I a genius at boxing unboxed box configurations? Would this mean I'd go into military intelligence?

"Three," he said, working his gum.

"Three?" I repeated.

"Out of twenty-five," he told me, blowing a bubble.

"Three boxes?"

"What boxes?"

"I thought it was about boxes."

He popped his bubble and moved on down the line. If I had thought about the boxes as containers and the unboxed fold-outs as container fold-outs I might have done better. There probably hadn't been a box in the bunch.

Later on, I had thirty seconds with a psychologist with a small, pefectly round head and a uniform and I began to think about circles. I could have collapsed innumerable sides inward to form circles instead of boxes.

"You can't avoid induction by getting a low score on the IQ test," he told me right off. "You just get the lowbrow jobs is what happens."

I nodded.

"And don't tell me you're gay because I won't hear you."

"I'm not gay."

"You on any kind of medication?"

I shook my head.

"Could you fire back if fired upon?"

I nodded.

"Do you know why we're in Viet Nam?"

"To keep the Communists from taking over?"

"You're sane. Dismissed. Send in the next guy."

Stupid but sane I headed for the physical, where I stripped down and lined up with my fellow Brooklynites. I didn't get too far in that before I was given more transportation money and told to report to St. Alban's Naval Hospital within the next two hours. Meanwhile I could have lunch in the commissary.

"Why do I have to go to a hospital?" I asked. None of my test results jived.

"We think you've ingested something to screw up our test results. We're going to keep you at St. Alban's until you get cleaned out and we get some true readings."

I protested. I hadn't done anything untoward. I hadn't ingested anything.

"Yeah, just like you didn't try to fuck up the IQ test."

"Once you've got the word 'box' in your head you can't fold things up into anything else," I replied, having now thought this all through. "Like . . . like circles."

This sergeant just leaned close and whispered in my ear; "You should have just said you was queer. That would have kept you out."

☙

After a filling lunch of meatloaf and mashed potatoes, followed up with peaches and ice cream, I made my way to St. Alban's Naval Hospital out on Long Island. I got put in a ward where two lines of beds faced each other with about an eight-foot aisle down the middle. I was led to a bed toward the end of one of the rows. There was a chair beside the bed and I sat on it. A nurse gave me a pair of pajamas, a blue robe, and some slippers.

"Get these on," she said and walked away.

I threw the stuff on the bed and took out a pack of cigarettes and lit up.

There was a guy to my left writing at a small table placed at the foot of his bed. He looked over at me and I held the pack of smokes out. He nodded but didn't move. I got up and brought the pack over. I lit him up.

"I'm taking mail order courses for an associate's degree," he told me. He had a Tex Ritter twang to his voice.

His name was Buddy.

I looked across at a guy almost totally wrapped in bandages, head too, just lying there on his bed. The bed to my right contained a guy under the covers sleeping. All I could see was the top of his head. Another guy came out of these swinging doors in the middle of the room and he was carrying a bottle with a long tube attached to it that disappeared under his robe. Way down at the other end of the room there was a guy sitting on the edge of his bed, with his back to me. Maybe he was reading. Everybody else was in bed, either looking up at the ceiling or asleep. Except Buddy at his desk and me standing there.

It's hard to go back over this time so here's the shortened version: the nurse officer and I went quite a few rounds over my not wearing the official issue p.j.'s. I couldn't go to mess until I put them on, but with the help of a queer orderly I was able to sneak down to mess. The queer orderly named Cal would wake me with a flashlight in my eyes so he and I could hit the latrine and get a urine sample. He had to stand near enough to see me actually pissing in the cup because according to him, everyone thought I was doctoring my piss in order to beat the draft. Maybe Cal was getting a little voyeur thrill but like Burroughs said, "he was a perfect gentleman in every way."

After a couple of nights I didn't bother going to bed. What was I tired from? Maybe I was tired *of* rather than *from?* So I spent my nights in the TV room. There was always the same crew in there: Cal, in his whites, and everyone else but me in blue robes. I was still wearing the clothes I had come in with. There was one guy who sat in a rocker directly in front of the TV, eyes wide open, never blinking. He didn't smoke or drink pop, but the other guys did. From say 11:00 P.M. to 6:00 A.M. we—six guys—smoked a total of I'd say about five thousand Camels. No one ever drank water; I think they all pissed pop. No one but me was ever hungry. I was always hungry. At first I watched what they were watching, which was always the worst kind of shite. No one got up to change the channel except this one little guy and he liked Lawrence Welk, wrestling, Billy Graham, quiz shows, and cartoons. He didn't have any idea that the only thing to watch after 2:00 A.M. was old movies. So he'd have us all watching a buzzing channel signal. Third night in there I got up and flipped channels until I found an old Edward G. movie. I returned to my seat and lit up a Camel.

"What's this shit?" the little guy said in his Alabama twang. He got up and went to the TV.

"Touch it and I'll shoot you," I said from where I was sitting.

"He's already been shot," Cal said, giggling.

"I'll shoot him again," I said, realizing that being in there was doing things to me. I felt like fighting back. Or just fighting.

"I can report you for saying that," Alabama said to me.

"Report me," I said, "Like I give a fuck. I'm not in the army. Or the navy. Whatever."

"What are you then?" Alabama said, standing real short there by the TV.

I don't recall how it ended; I think Cal shut the TV off and told us to go to bed. I did, but everyone else just sat there in the dark, smoking and drinking pop.

A couple of days later I was released and a couple of weeks after that I got a 1Y classification—a temporary deferment—from the draft board. Temporarily deferred. I never did get called. I remember the head nurse, just like Kesey's Big Nurse, calling out to me as I walked out of that ward in the same clothes that I had walked in.

"I hope you got what you wanted."

Did I want to get out of the draft bad enough to want an illness bad enough to keep me out? She didn't like me; I had given her some back talk in front of the troops. I think she was pissed because she thought I might have beat them somehow on all the tests they had given me. But neither their tests nor my cunning were at play here: Chance had played a hand and slipped me through.

Outer-Six Theatre

August 1999

Like everyone else saturated in Bill Clinton's inconceivable life and times, I had forgotten about Nixon's inconceivable life and times. Until I went to see the movie *Dick*. I don't know why I thought the theater would be filled with former countercultural types still seething over Nixon—like myself. It wasn't. I had the only greying ponytail in the audience. I changed my seat three times to avoid flocks of what we used to call "teenyboppers" who had plopped down in front of me, doing all those giggly things that the seriously aging find enraging. I finally gave up. I couldn't distance myself from youth and frivolity; I let it surround me and capture me. I accepted that this positioning was my fate. I would have to see what box-office filmmaking had done to Dark Dick while titters and snickers engulfed me. It was the way the 1990s approached Nixon. I couldn't help asking myself what these neonatal twits were doing at a film about Nixon. And didn't they know that Nixon as a subject was like the Holocaust as a subject—that you couldn't approach it with enough tragic vision? Especially when you consider what a Noble Statesman Nixon became to all of us in his last years. It was all inconceivable to me.

But the neonatal twits around me were right and I was wrong. They set the tone before the movie began, and the movie confirmed that tone. Look at it this way: Nixon and his cohorts are inconceivable if you look upon politics as rational, moral enterprise, and our fellow human beings as explicable and predictable. But there's nothing more farcical than politics and nothing stranger than "folk." You take greatness and you bring it to a fall and you have tragedy. Or, is it more appropriate to say you take someone in a high position and bring him or her to a fall and you have . . . tragedy? Nixon's in the highest position in the land but he's consumed by the lowest of inclinations, the most twisted of desires, the strangest of logic. How else to approach that but in such a way that makes the distance between office and man, between image and reality, between expectations and what is, all come before us to reprove our own naive, self-serving expectations regarding what we humans are.

Treating Nixon as a tragic figure—what Oliver Stone's movie *Nixon* moves toward—places both Nixon and ourselves higher than he or we deserve. If you set your gaze on the play of low appetites and narrow vision, on logic driven by ungraspable desires, of a sense of right and wrong tied to self-aggrandizement—in Nixon and in the rest of us—you wind up laughing. Maybe giggling. The tragedy lies in our ever taking ourselves as creatures whose natures reach the same great heights as the offices and positions we may hold. Nixon was one of us, but he was the one raised the highest. When we mourn or moralize his fall, we assert our own capacity as humans to never fall, to rise above our strangeness and achieve praiseworthy and consistent nobility. Nixon had the chance to be noble, of noble nature, but he fell.

I'm not saying we all fell a long, long time ago; I'm simply saying we are more clearly dark, twisted, and strange than we are pure, noble, sweet, gentle, and rational. The idea that this pervasive profile has a common origin doesn't seem so very implausible to me. There is no tragedy when the impure show no total purity, when the irrational show no total rationality, when the desirous show their desires, when the irreverent show their irreverence, when the ignoble show no total nobility. We all run as straight as a ram's horn. If we merit the camera's attention, we can all show up on the screen like Nixon, or Jimmy Swaggart, Gary Hart, Rob Lowe, Pee-Wee Herman, Dan Quayle, or even Monica and Bill.

I've just read in the local paper that the human species deserves to be at the top of the food chain; we should plunge ahead without hesitation and celebrate our genius. I'm "old school" on this: Swift gives me the clearest view of our species. I don't giggle but I think one of the ways to sit there and watch Nixon is to laugh; and I should keep on laughing when I see those twelve-year old "Midriffs" giggling, but I don't. Somehow knowing that our species "genius" is still showing up in the coming generation makes it hard for me to laugh. But I do think we should reserve our sense of the tragic for those occasions when an innocent strangeness is swallowed up by a vicious one. Nixon didn't swallow us up nor did he ever have the capacity to do so. And his was perhaps less a vicious strangeness (although he did have a vicious epithet for every ethnic group on the face of the Earth) than a self-destructive one, more than the usual complication of ambitions and desires, of quirks and obsessions, of bad connections and recollected injustices, of personal identity swallowed up by image and spectacle. Then again the only thing unusual about him was the fact that he was always, through

the self-taping, exposing his crimes, in something like the way a serial
killer leaves clues behind so he'll be caught.

I don't think for a second the young gigglers were giggling because
they reserved their sense of the tragic for a more appropriate subject. I
don't think they saw the same strangeness in themselves as they saw in
Nixon and were laughing at themselves as they laughed at him. They
probably hadn't read their Swift. They are responding to another time
from where they are sitting in the present—and that time is clearly
laughable to them. They can make all the connections between then and
now, people today and people then—yeah, *as if.*

അാ

Nixon expressed his loss of personal identity more openly than,
say, Elvis, or Bill Clinton. He referred to himself as "Nixon." "Nixon
will have another drink," he'd tell a servant. Somewhere inside that
Nixon was the Nixon swallowed up by the spectacle of what he had
become. Bill Clinton is both Bubba Bill and Rhode Scholar Bill but he
doesn't say "Bubba, will have another cheeseburger." Or, "Bubba
would like to see Monica in his office." Or, "Rhode Scholar Bill says
we are facing the end of Big Government." With Bill Clinton the personal and the public are meshed on the public level, which was not the
case with Nixon. The cracks in the public persona showed. Different
times and cultures shape different arrangements. Clinton is more
clearly the product of the age of spectacle; what reality is can only be
represented and that is by it's very nature a political activity. Nixon,
Quaker-reared in a modern and not postmodern world, was obviously
haunted by the distance between reality and truth, and what politics
demanded and had made of him. There was always The Truth that
could be reached and recognized; it lay outside words. Words masked
that Truth, and in an effort to save himself and his presidency he used
words to mask the Truth. For Clinton, there is no separable Truth but
only truths localized and temporalized. From this perspective, at this
time and place, this is how we observe things to be. Nixon doesn't want
to glance over his shoulder and see that External Point of Reference,
that Outside Truth, standing there and judging his actions and words.
He knows he's distant from it, but has to be. Clinton knows that there
are no external points of reference and that we are engaged day by day
in negotiating our human reality and the truths we concoct within those
realities. He wants to do his part in creating that reality. Such license
makes him bold; he can find a place in his heart and mind for what at
this moment and in this place seems to him to be what his reality should

be. He presumes that words can make a place for this turn of events too; that what matters is the representation and that he can master. Nixon's ontology creates a darkened conscience; Clinton's ontology darkens the spectacle of conscience. The former is imperturbable and lasting; the latter blows in the sands of time. The former will create the sort of psychopathology Freud probed; the latter is post-Freudian.

This difference is there in our response to Nixon's tragedy and Clinton's follies. It's not just that Nixon's offense threatened the foundations of our democracy and Clinton's seemed to a majority of Americans to be nobody's business but his and his wife's. Nixon could be seen as a tragic figure, or the Watergate event itself or the threat to impeach as a tragic moment in American history—all within the mind-set of that period. Clinton and Monica were instantly transported to the realm of spectacle, and once there, we could only experience tragedy as spectacle and not as real. Therefore, we have lost our tragic sense in the sense that we once had it during Watergate. And I would surmise that the tragic sense we held then was not the same tragic sense that was felt when JFK was assassinated. And that wasn't the same tragic sense that was felt when Lincoln was assassinated. And so on. In other words, the tragic disposition moves with time and place. It is the special sense of the post-modern moment to be aware of this and to hope to shape what we feel as tragic, as well as what we feel is heroic, what we feel is winning, what we feel is losing, what we feel is progress, what we feel is retrogression. Clinton is aware of this and therefore cannot stop to feel the impact of his actions—a sort of review of conscience—but rather plunges ahead to concoct what reality the event is to hold for us and for him and to concoct what conscience is to mean and be at that moment. Clinton's "cover-up" efforts therefore are ontological efforts whereas Nixon's were moral efforts; Clinton remains on the positive side of "world maker" and "mythmaker"; Nixon on the side of sinner and penitent.

What happens when the present disposition, itself fashioned by the market reliance upon persuading spectacle, entirely elides former meanings and values? Or, the present simply evokes the past to serve the present's purpose, not the past "in itself" but a present arrangement of the past?

That's when you get the young gigglers surrounding me with their giggles in that movie theater. For them the film is about two of their peers, Michelle Williams and Kirsten Dunst, whom they know from the hit TV show "Dawson's Creek." In the course of the movie, these characters have the opportunity to talk like the gigglers and to do what the gigglers value highly—change clothes and make-up at a rapid-fire pace. The Watergate past, which they don't know, is not a problem for them because it comes to them through two peer role models and celebrities.

The past is a stage set. Nixon and his cronies represent the "adult" world always too out of it and ancient to know what's "really happening." With the gigglers you have the other side of the postmodern world: they are not the "mythmakers" and "world makers" but "myth consumers" and "world consumers." They respond to the packaging of things, perhaps a reason why packaging is a major course of study with the present generation. Reality is in the packaging; the most accessible packaging wins the day, wins the moment here and now. No one is more aware of this than Bill Clinton, who packages events, ideas, the past, the future, the economy, and himself to reach the biggest share of the consumer market. It fits then that the man from Hope was packaged in film as *The Man From Hope* by his Hollywood friends. And that the packaging would replace reality and be consumed as reality.

⁓◦⁓

Nixon wasn't a tragic figure but an absurd and farcical one; *perhaps* he exceeded the norm in regard to how absurd and farcical we humans are. I don't know how you can find out whether that's true or not. As I say, the spotlight was on him, not on you or me. I think it's best to reserve one's sense of the tragic for innocence defiled and destroyed by the darkest side of human strangeness. Everything else falls somewhere on the continuum of the rational and purposive, as well as the irrational and farcical that makes us the strangest creatures on the planet by far. It's only when we think that we can erase "human error," categorize human "sins" and implement "goals and objectives" toward progress, and systematize and bureaucratize Chance and the vagaries of Nature and human nature out of existence that we forget how our strangeness propels us in everything, great and small. Maybe this is the Enlightenment inclination to replace endemic strangeness with a perfecting Reason. If it is, it's fast dying out. Nixon may have been the last president to feel tragedy within that inclination. I correct myself—Jimmy Carter was the last. And this realization of a human strangeness not replaced by reason or method, morals or law, is not replacing the Enlightenment inclination. You can connect that with an existential mood and a sense of the absurd and before that a nihilistic spirit—all packaged today as "past."

The corrective and instructive rod of laughter only works if there already exists something already apprehended that is in need of correction, and someone who is engaged in juggling and contrasting different views that can be instructed in this way. If Andrew Fleming, the director of *Dick,* wants to send up Tricky Dick as more cheap farce than tragic figure, he has to do it for a dual audience: those of us who lived through the Watergate years and therefore can call up the historical moment as we watch Fleming's send-up of that moment; and those to whom Nixon and Watergate are already no more than spectacle now being brought to their attention in an ahistorical climate. The present climate only "markets" the past to meet present needs; it doesn't use the past as an external point of reference by which to continuously contrast and evaluate the present. Now you can have a send-up, you can have irony and satire, you can have parody, if the viewer is in possession of two realities: the one recalled and the one parodying what is recalled.

The young gigglers don't have that double coding; whatever depth is brought to the images of Nixon and his cronies either comes out of previous spectacle or it doesn't exist. Now if we were presently still in an Enlightenment mind-set, any representation of the past would be referred to an historical record or documentation, evidence outside the representation itself; there would be some guiding notion of the reality of what was and the present staging of it. Since my gigglers are not in that world but in one in which they have been brought up to feed on the most accessible images and representations and consume those as reality, they consume Nixon here as just here in this film, as Dan Hedaya's performance presents him. He's a foil for their Hollywood surrogates in this film; he's the source of much fun and laughter. He's a giggle a minute.

When your own past gets packaged in the present as consumer fodder, as just stuff to giggle through and at, you see this as a transgression, as the greatest injustice—not just to you and your own past but to human civilization. How can we pretend to any progress but technological if what happened last week is brought to us by marketing and advertising—or it doesn't show up at all? What indeed are the opportunities of countermemory? Perhaps the market will get interested in countermemories, if they can turn a profit. But surely some countermemories, some counternarratives set out to deprioritize consumption, devalue profit as the highest good and the absolute and universal criterion of judgment, and resurrect the past as not a foil for the present but a corrective rod. Surely, these gigglers will have less wherewithal to counter the ever-intensifying production values of glitz, of Debord's spectacle and Baudrillard's simulacra.

Postmodernity didn't destroy critical skepticism, it intensified it: no representation of reality is anything more than an observation made by someone at a particular time and place. This skepticism doesn't ultimately take us to The Truth nor does it take us to nihilistic cynicism or existential despair. The more narratives, the better the attitude, and the atmosphere is filled with creativity not constraint. But we live at a moment when market values have almost sole power in shaping our narratives of ourselves and the world, of the present, the past, and the future. The spectacle-producing power of marketing and advertising, enhanced astronomically by the Internet, add up, in this postmodern age, to ultimate reality-making power. Spectacle is propelled by the drive for profit, profit demands consumption, ever-increasing consumption demands consumers, consuming humanity replaces all other stories of what humanity is and can be. This is a virus in the postmodern carnival.

Maybe my baby boomer generation started spreading this virus; after all, the market "players" coming out of the Reagan years and feasting on an ever-bullish Dow in the present are not these gigglers. They are the parents of the gigglers; the gigglers are consuming at the heels of their consuming parents. Poverty, hate, brutality, injustice, suffering, and misery have only been showing up as part of "cross-marketing" schemes: get a look at this, and then buy this, invest in that, seek more insurance, more protection, more distance between you and the Losers. Loss doesn't show up these days so we can remedy it, but only to remind us to fortify our own gains.

The gigglers may one day stop giggling. Gutter balls thrown in their lives may make it harder to giggle. Countermemories could well up and flood a movie screen, drawing them away from *these* scenes and *these* voices, to clashing scenes and clashing voices. A global market grounded in a casino logic will, according to the indomitable Rules of Chance, spin like the roulette wheel. It will eventually turn against every Winner, and the laughing all the way to the bank will stop. Some time in a bearish future there may be a send-up, giggle-provoking film about the bullish times of the 1990s, and someone sitting there in the audience will project a countermemory up on the screen. Another past, their past, begins to play, and they sit there somewhere between a present telling and a past recollection, each a scourge to each.

I see profit in that.

Oxley Holl'r, West Virginia

Winter 1977

"That your geetar?" Troy Connor said, winking at my guitar in the corner. I told him it was. "I play geetar on the ra-dio for my church every Sunday." The way he said "radio" was like saying "radical" but dropping the "cal" and doing an "eeo."

One night, Troy, Tom, and I were standing outside at the corner of my house doing what we had to do to get the entrance cable around back in preparation for tying in my new hundred-amp panel box. Snowflakes, heavy, flat and dry, were wafting down and they made me nervous because here was Troy, with his buck knife open and a hundred-amp entrance cable in his hand. We didn't need water falling from the sky. A skeptic in all things, I wasn't feeling any better because Troy had told me the power company had turned off our service.

But Troy and Tom were matter of fact and jawing about a new revival coming.

"You going to that there revival, Tom?" Troy said, nobody looking at anybody but each only looking at the cable Troy had in his hand and was stripping. "Tom" was pronounced "tome."

"I might," Tom said. "We been thinking of getting us a new church over at Speedwell."

"I hear this fellar here is purty good," Troy said. I was aware that preachers fell in and out of acclaim thereabouts; I don't know exactly how they attracted folks nor how folks gave them up and started looking around for a new preacher. When they got a hold of one that got as hot as a rock star streaking across the Billboard charts, they started church building. Charisma bred church building down there and that church became the heart of the community that built it.

"You fixing to come to revival with us?" Troy asked me, catching me by surprise.

Now I had seen Kell Petry's wife's face drop to the floor once over such a question. She had come by asking us if we wanted to go to church with her and I had asked what church was that; she had said Mount Jackson Baptist Church and I had said we were Roman Catholics. That was a "non-starter." She had this big broad flatiron of a face and I could see her thoughts working across it. But she came out just fine. "We ain't gonna hold that agin ya," she said, solemnly. I laughed, but it wasn't wit. She was being dead serious. And she didn't hold it against us. Nobody burned a cross on our lawn because JFK had already made a trip into these people's hearts. Mrs. Petry had a crushed velvet "art portrait" of JFK in her kitchen. And he had been a "Cadlick." Of course this was before there was a lot of talk of JFK and Marilyn Monroe. When Cadlicks fell they didn't get up in the proper way; they didn't know how to get themselves revived.

"I just might," I said, "long as they don't expect me to handle a rattler to prove I ain't with the Devil."

Troy laughed.

"I don't know as that fellar there does snake handling," he said.

And he winked at me. Troy and his twin brother Coy had been born and bred in the briar patch and I don't think either one of them had ever been out of the state—and maybe not even out of the county. If you want to know what they looked like think of a paler Danny DeVito a couple of inches taller and with wispy thin blonde hair. Troy and Tom taught me how to say "wha-ah"; back in Brooklyn we would say "whyer" and Midwesterners would "properly" not contribute an "r" or a "wha" sound. When I lived in Oxley Hollow, West Virginia, the names of Midwestern states—Ohio, Michigan, Illinois, Indiana—came up in conversations as places you aspired to and couldn't get to, but when you got there you missed the Hollow and had to come back. Somehow they were better and if you were better, they were where you were supposed to be, but nobody really wanted to go there. Those places were too cold in every way. I began to think of the Midwest in that way, not knowing that someday I would wind up living there.

∽∘≀∾

Troy invited me to play on the "rad-io," too. I never did, but I did sing in the Reverend John's Stately Black Women with "Voices On'em" Choir.

What can I say about Reverend John? He was about six feet six inches of glistening blackness. His biceps were the size of an ordinary man's thighs. His father had been a sharecropper in Georgia and when John was a boy he had picked "him some cotton," picking bales while others struggled with one. He taught me how to farm southern style, how to field plant, and how "to have a hand" with the crops you loved. I had bought the most powerful tiller from Mr. Parker and as I tried to get it to plow in a straight line, John just stood there laughing. It was getting away from me. I looked back at the row only a drunk would have made, most of it not more than a thin scar on the surface of dirt. "I got to get this drag in deeper," I said, messing with the drag bar which would hold the tiller in place while the blades cut in. What that did was nail me to a spot so I didn't have the "umph" to get her out and going forward. Finally John just brushed me aside, bent over and pulled out the cotterpin holding the drag bar in, and tossed the drag bar aside. He shoved the throttle open to full speed and then with some fifteen horsepower purring, just stood there while the blade dug in, a big smile on his face. With both arms stretched out, legs braced, he walked the tiller forward. He ran a forty-foot row at just the right depth. I walked alongside. At row's end, he put it in neutral and looked at me. "You got to show it who's boss," he told me. "Das all." He pointed one long index finger at me. "See?"

His daddy had laid hands on him and conferred the title of "preacher" onto John and then John had gone off preaching. He was what he called a "supply pastor." You supply him with the vittles and other needs and he'll "get them rolling in the aisles" at Sunday service. And in the days when LBJ was in the White House, John had been choir leader of a church group that played at the White House. That was his crowning achievement. How he wound up in Bluefield, West Virginia, I never knew. But he was strikingly handsome, self-assured, poised for every possible contingency, and the biggest hit with the ladies. He marred Stella, a woman with a solid position at a nearby college. She was in her forties, I would think, and he in his early thirties. John had done some tailoring in Washington, D.C., and I expect that was how he earned his living, but in West Virginia preaching was his calling. The only clothes he made were for himself: polyester suits of various stripes, or vibrant colors, or pure white, or black as his own skin.

"I don't eat anything the color of my own skin," he once told me and Elaine when we were touting the benefits of whole wheat bread.

We had been invited to their house for dinner; it was a house on the other side of the tracks and like all the houses there, it hung off the side of the hill. The house was wood framed and rickety and there didn't seem to be anything on the first floor because all I could see was a staircase. And Stella standing at the top. The rooms up there were bright and exuberantly decorated. Reds, whites, and gold predominated. Every bit of the walls was covered with something and every chair and table bore some special treasure. My mother used to call things like that "dust collectors"; they attracted dust so you could spend your whole Saturday trying to clean. That's probably why our house in Brooklyn was just a step up from the digs the state gave you when they asked you to give them some time. I don't think the spareness of our home interior was all due to my mother's hatred of dust collectors. I don't think her or my father like to look at "clutter." Clutter was what they called anything that they couldn't eat or that didn't serve a useful function.

Stella and John's house stimulated every sense; compared to the clapboard cabin we were living in in the Hollow, this was like turning off a black-and-white TV and plugging in living color. It was festive. I thought it was Christmas and Halloween combined. But it was just their house. It was the confines in which their souls found peace; these were the colors that expressed their souls. You have to know what was outside, what surrounded that house: the houses falling apart, the unpaved streets, the distance from the "big houses" where the whites lived and where once Stella had cooked for the Shott family, the family that not only owned the newspaper but the only TV station as well. This home was a retreat, a refuge, a rebuke, a testament to what the world outside never gave. And I understood it as such.

"What you looking at that salad like that fo'?" the Reverend asked me. I was being obvious about being really troubled by my salad. I poked at it with my fork. The lettuce was wilted like it had been out in the hot sun for a few days.

"That's a wilted salad, Joe," Elaine said. "That's the way it's made. And it's very good."

"I guess I just put a real premium on fresh, crisp salad," I said, putting a forkful of the wilted in my mouth. First time I had been at Stella's for lunch she had served chicken and dumplings and had whipped up a cornbread in no time. The dumplings were out-of-sight delicious, but I wasn't well acquainted with these parts of a chicken: shards of the back, neck, last-to-go-over-the-fence, and wings severed like I would sever the thigh from the drumstick. While I sat there soaking up the dumpling stew part with cornbread, John and Stella were working every bone skillfully with tightly closed mouths. When John was finished he had a pile of micro bones on a plate in front of him while I had had two coughing fits trying to pry bones out of my esophagus.

"I do declare this man is having trouble with your chicken, Stella," John said.

"I'm okay," I lied, trying to suppress a lifesaving cough. It felt like all the micro bones that should have been on my discard plate were lodged in my throat. I didn't want to talk for fear of finding out the truth.

Though I was terribly reckless in the things I did on that farm, I never fell back on the terrible hypochondria that had plagued me for years. All told it was easier to put aside mortality down there in Oxley Hollow. There was so much to do and so little time to think about the doer. I was into an archaic, seasonal sense of life and death. Death was what you put in the ground for a rich crop in the future.

Staten Island, New York

March 1999

The casket was open and from the doorway I could see Billy's profile. Blue blazer he had on, hands clasped, rosary beads laced through
the dead fingers. I cued up with the rest of the immediate family and
waited to kneel before his casket and say my last goodbye. I got to the
kneeler and crossed myself and then rested my eyes inches from Billy's
face. The mouth lined downward like a wooden puppet's, held tight
with a string that you would pull to open and close it; the skin stretched
taut across his nose; the face was blushed but death's pallor came
through. I pretended I was interested in his hands but the truth was I
couldn't look at that face anymore because although I hadn't seen him
in a number of years I remembered what he had looked like. And looking at his hands didn't help because his hands were full of memories for
me. We had grown up together. He was my first cousin who lived just
around the block and was six months younger than me; my cousin with
the hands that could do things my hands couldn't, like straighten bent
nails we'd find in the Brooklyn lots and then use them to build racing
cars made of wooden crates on skate wheels; years later, those hands
drew sketches showing me how I was to build my deck, or how I could
replace a load-bearing wall, or how I could attach a shed-roofed porch
to my house, or, how easy it was to achieve three dimensionality in my
paintings if I just positioned a vanishing point ("Like this . . . with
extending lines coming forward . . . so that everything caught between
those lines . . .").

If I stand up now, close my eyes, and look down into the past, I can
see Billy kneeling there close to the ground hammering nails into his
crate-box scooter and then into mine, building a fire so we could roast
potatoes in the lots, painting a tropical scene on one living room wall of
his family's apartment, on the beach in Coney Island working sand into
sculptures that people would stop to admire, behind the wheel of his
father's 1968 Impala driving. I'm perched either on the back of his

Schwinn Black Phantom bike or sitting side saddle in front of him holding on to the handlebars. We're in junior high school then. I'm reaching across to see those hands at work on a math problem Mrs. Adelman has thrown at us.

I see those hands pushing aside those gang members who have decided to jump me on the way home from school in the sixth grade because I gave them some lip during phys. ed. I see those hands on a hot summer night when we are teenagers, trying to hold off vicious kicks as Billy lies there, another gang surrounding us. They're older and bigger than us, and high on something; this is their neighborhood, and we're trespassing. We had taken off, but Billy tripped behind me. I turned and went back for him, but they charged me. I ran between cars; I see Billy lying there, moaning, and his hands waving, I think at me. Somebody swings at me, another grabs my shoulder; I break away . . .

I see those hands gesturing something I can't understand. Come? Run? Years later I come home and Elaine tells me she's spoken to Billy on the phone. He can only speak in repetitive fragments. "How ya doing, kid?" he asks her. This inexplicable disease that's ravaging his brain cells is consuming him. I need to go there and see him now. I need to go back to New York and see him. But I don't. I go somewhere but I don't go there.

So many years before, after that summer night attack and while Billy is still in the hospital someone comes to my house—somebody from the neighborhood—wanting to know what happened. The neighbor wants to know if I got hurt. "I guess you made the best stand you could," he tells me and I don't say anything. I want to say there were too many of them, they were so much older than us. They were crazy high and yelling and I wanted to keep throwing the left Sonny Moore had taught me; but I wound up just using it to break free.

"You're always ready to punch somebody," Elaine tells me years later. At first I don't know where that is coming from but now I know. Seeing Billy's hands clasped in that casket gives me the key to the puzzle. I really don't do anything but fight now; I've been fighting faces I can't make out rushing toward me. I throw the left. Hard and fast, over and over again.

I've got a recurrent dream. It's so bad I repressed the recognition that it was recurrent until Billy's funeral. Some time since then it suddenly dawned on me that I have a recurrent dream. I had been telling the students that travelled with me around Europe that in the first couple of weeks of travel, they would most likely have dreams, maybe bad dreams.

"It's because you're in strange surroundings," I tell them. "And a lot of your home-base security gets tossed around. You can't handle what's happening to you but it's happening. And it shows up in your dreams. Get those down in your journal. Get them down on paper as soon as you get up in the morning. Don't try to figure out what they mean or try to put them in some kind of narrative order. Just get them down as they went on in the dream. Especially get down the recurrent dreams."

"Why?" Monica, one of my teaching assistants asks me. "What's so important about a recurrent dream?"

"That's the one that keeps knocking on the doors for admittance to consciousness but is too loaded for you to let it in. It's an assault you're not ready for, so you keep it locked out. But tomorrow night or the next night or the night after that it shows up again and knocks even louder. You need to get into that and sort it out."

"Sometimes locked doors are locked for a good reason," Monica replied. "Prisoners want to get out but we don't let them out. There are just plain bad thoughts just like there are bad people. You don't let them in your house."

"What comes in a recurrent dream isn't a bad thought like an illicit desire or a criminal idea that comes to you face up and you decide not to go with it. It may turn out to be driven by these but it comes to you masked, as something that can partially get through to your consciousness but only if it keeps its real message hidden. Yet it still comes through with some force, with some power because you have to wake up to break out of it. You know at that moment you've been experiencing some high drama, something dark and deep has come close to you but you can't quite make it out. And it's frightened you so you batten down the hatches and double bolt the doors, but that just feeds it and it comes again with even more urgency. Meanwhile, the effects of it are showing up in your waking life. But actually your waking life is already the cause of the recurrent dream; your waking life is already tilted in such a way that the water line in your mind's dark waters is rising. What I'm saying is that there's already a disequilibrium in the house of consciousness. Your everyday life is like a thin veneer of protocols and routines that is showing some thin line fractures. The door you think you're keeping locked isn't a door . . ."

It's a hand reaching for you. It's your left jab thrown at the threat rushing toward you.

In the dream I have that keeps rolling over these long years—sometimes disappearing so long that when it shows up again I have to wonder if there is something familiar about this dream—there is always incredible violence. I am swinging at faces to the right and left, picking up whatever is at hand and crashing it down on bent backs, on lunging heads, squeezing necks with my two hands, picking bodies up straight over my head and tossing them, kicking free of hands that are trying to pull me down, tattooing left jabs until the faces disappear. Part two of the dream has me sobbing uncontrollably over some loss I cannot quite understand. I can't see clearly my brother Pete getting into his car and driving away, never to return, or my mother lying in a coffin and at the same time sitting across the dining room table on a late summer afternoon telling me, "Don't you mourn for me when I die, Joe, because I had a good life and I know that where I'm going I'll be at peace. You remember that."

Sometimes the sobbing wakes me up; the loss is unbearable but ungraspable. Sometimes the violence wakes me up. My heart is racing; I can't take the bloodletting; I can't be a part of it any longer. I want to stop fighting but I can't in the dream. I have to keep swinging, so fast and hard and with so much noise that I have to wake up for fear the clamor will wake Elaine.

"Jimmy ran," the neighbor tells me way back then, referring to the other guy who was with us; seventeen at the time while Billy and I were sixteen. "But Jimmy wasn't his cousin. You are." I try to tell him I was overpowered, I couldn't get to him. But he keeps nodding without saying anything, looking me in the eye. Every nod was like a hammer stroke, pounding a nail into a piece of wood. A hammer in Billy's hands, those hands which could do anything, that once needed my help and I couldn't give it to him.

He always forgave me. He never brought it up, not once.

I'm leaving his house years and years later, having come to New York at Christmas time to visit family. We shake hands and I turn to go, but then he pulls me toward him. "Come here, cuz," he tells me and gives me a bear-like hug. "I love you cuz," he tells me.

It's hard now; and too hard to look anymore. I can't quite see him in that casket because the tears are in a rush now. I've got to get up and make a decent retreat; but I can't seem to because my knees are pitching me forward, toward Billy. And I'm sobbing loudly and I can only hear that and not see clearly and I've lost my bearings. But then I'm being hugged and moved. Toward the door; out to the foyer where there are chairs and couches and where people who want relief from the sight of Billy's body go to talk, to break away from the grief. I can't stop sobbing; it's big Vic's chest my head is resting on now and he's telling me, "It's all right, babe. Let it out. It's all right."

These are the four days that turn me around: Billy's funeral. It turns me back to my Brooklyn life. I see these faces now and I run them by the faces I knew then. It's as if I've been no place, although I have been so many places, as if I went to sleep and then came back. I was the one that got put into solitary while everybody else went on with their lives. I can't seem to remember anything I've done since those Brooklyn days; I can't recall how I filled those other days up. I'm anchored there, kneeling by that coffin, out of orbit, somewhere where time doesn't begin or stop or go on. It's a timeless orbit.

Sleepy Hollow, New York

December 31, 1999

Belief evokes visions; our millennial beliefs are wrapped up in biblical prophecies, most notably the revelatory visions of John of Patmos. "For the time is near . . . ," the last words of the first paragraph of John's Revelation. Is that time coming upon us as the second millennium after Christ's birth ends?

Our imaginations are ignited within a biblical "end of days" scenario and typically what fires our imaginations translates these days into market opportunities. What better transforming medium than popular film? Here what minds imagine as millennial meaning is given flesh and word, spectacle and sound, character and plot, heroes and villains, incredible obstacles and miraculous victories, certain beginnings, and certain endings. Popular film plugs into our millennial fantasies and makes a box-office profit in so doing. In turn, the way we millennial-imagine becomes shaped by what we see and hear on the big screen.

Deleterious effects of popular culture? Movies stepping in between us and the biblical message? But our awareness of the "end of days" has already been mediated by John's visions. Consider how enwrapped we are in the way John imagines our end:

> Behold, I am coming soon, bringing my recompense, to repay every one for what he has done. I am the Alpha and the Omega, the first and the last, the beginning and the end. Blessed are those who wash their robes, that they may have the right to the tree of life and that they may enter the city by the gates. Outside are the dogs and sorcerers and fornicators and murderers and idolater, and every one who loves and practices falsehood. *Revelation* 22:12–16, Revised Standard Version

Is this not a spectacle? A biblical movie that runs in one's own mind before the coming of Hollywood? Our imaginations are caught within stories we have already imagined. Hollywood is not breaking into our connection with God's Word; God's Word is already what the Bible represents it as. Is the Koran or the Bhagavad Gita or the Tibetan Book of the Dead or indeed the Old Testament rather than the New Testament a more accurate screening of God's Word? Or is the way of Lao-tzu or the Eightfold Path of freedom from suffering of the Buddha a more accurate screen? Or is the whole matter of the millennium more accurately portrayed by the scientist who tells his class that the last day of the second millennium has absolutely no meaning in science—it has only "voodoo" significance?

Is Hollywood turning to trash our millennial awareness? Turning the sacred to the profane? Yet again, and for a profit. Do we object to the profit making here? To the free play of the competitive, profit seeking entrepreneurial spirit? "No one is being forced to buy a ticket." "You can abstain." This is how the market defense goes. At the same time we feel that movies could be better; more ethically responsible; more genuinely educational, less fictive, and more practical; more serviceable to our order of things; more supportive of family values, more helpful in developing a social conscience in the young; violence- and nudity-free; less fascinated with the dregs of humankind and with the evil that men do and more fascinated by those who have assumed personal responsibility, gotten in there and competed and come out Winners. Let's have endless Disney naive realist tales that confirm our sense of our own correctness, enhance our awareness of our own self-worth, convince us that who and what we have cast out deserve to be cast out. And so on.

Fortunately, from my point of view, popular film continues for the most part to go where the profits are: into our fears, into what haunts us, into what we are blind to but which nevertheless provokes us, into what we can barely conceive but somehow know is there, into the nightmare worlds we spend our daylight hours defending ourselves against. Everything potentially electrifying is plugged into—not resolved or clarified or analyzed, just represented. Violence is up there on the screen because it is a hot spot in the American cultural imaginary. Why? I'm not a "problem solver" nor do I believe in our problem-solving methods, which are only useful within the ways we already know things, like what a problem is and what a solution might be.

For instance, not having invented the wheel wasn't a problem to Native Americans; nor apparently was owning slaves a problem to a great many Southerners; nor are ever-increasing profits and a continual "growing of the economy" a problem ecologically speaking to most economists and all of Wall Street. Workers and the environment may instead be the problems to be solved; reduction or elimination of workers' benefits, reduction or elimination of environmental regulations the solutions. "Violence" within our market-oriented way of knowing and valuing everything is a problem because it interrupts the social stability needed for business to go on. But, less abstractly, violence is clearly what the Have Nots may resort to against the Haves, something that the growth of gated communities and the expansion of the private security and surveillance industry confirms. Violence, like Chance, may rob the Winners of their winnings.

Sex is a hot spot in the American cultural imaginary because sex sells, and it wouldn't sell if Americans were able to represent sex and sexuality in some mature, nonstereotypic, open way to themselves. They can't, so the thinnest hook up between product and sex seduces the consumer and draws him or her into the act of consumption. No one in a market-driven way of knowing the world sees a tie-in that generates profits as a problem, and therefore there is no incentive to "solve" it. Ditto for the "war on drugs." Someone—and I'm not talking about someone powerless and addicted in the streets—is making a profit on keeping drugs illegal. It's profit making and not a problem; declaring it a problem is a front, an advertising campaign directed at the young. And it works.

We work through our always-circumscribed knowing to our imaginations by means of our imaginations. Vision evokes belief as much as belief evokes vision. And we have found in this last century of the millennium a pervasively popular medium through which and by which to represent and incite our imaginations: popular film. Put down as bread and circus, as mere entertainment, as escapist fluff, as vapid and mindless, as superficial and transient, popular film yet floats the balloons of our imaginings while making balloons of what we want to hold on to as indisputable fact. If we had no sense of a "popular," lesser art or culture, or lesser representation of ourselves, there would be no serious art, no greater culture, no more reliable representation of ourselves. Popular culture exists in the shadow of high culture; these are the moments when we put aside our profound investigations of things and seek comic relief, a few laughs, a few thrills, a respite for mind and method.

Everything in popular film is fictive, is not the truth but some make-believe concoction, not "things as they are" but *as if* things were this way. In this dichotomy, in this dualism, it doesn't pay to waste time thinking in the "as if" mode or taking fabrications seriously. What one wants to do is assume a real-world practical attitude, learn to see things as they are and not as you or someone else might imagine them to be. Ironically then, this disparagement of our own imaginings, even though we live within them (from gravity to flight) is a major feature of our American cultural imaginary.

∽◦∾

I want to talk about a recent film in terms of what and how it draws on the imagination and how my own imagination responds. A number of films now are all tied up with the millennium in one way or another, but they are also about imagination and vision, or call it hallucination and nightmare. If you observe Henry Fuseli's painting entitled *Nightmare,* what you see is a man in bed asleep with gargoyle-type creatures surrounding him. Is this the dark side of our imaginings or is it just that our imaginations naturally wander into the dark areas of our being, what we cannot see in the light before us, what we cannot bring to light, what seems not conceivable to us, and yet will not leave us alone? Is the act of wandering into this unchartered domain the act of imagining? In other words, in the words of William Blake, is what the imagination conceives necessarily true? Are we probing with our imaginations what cannot be probed by the instruments of science but is no less a thing that we do as humans?

Another view: there are no monsters by this man's bed except those monsters his own fearful dreams concoct. It's all residue from daytime fears, or repressed psychodramas, or a bit of undigested potato, or a misfiring in the neurofibrillary circuitry, a physiological effect of REM sleep. And yet, what evokes belief? Visions. What evokes science? Visions. Look at what happens when the electron microscope reveals a kind of activity on the micro-atomic level that we have not imagined going on. Here we have a clear case of scientific method entering what has previously been inconceivable. Do we adopt a new way of imagining the world, a new world picture, a new narrative of things, a new post-quantum world-view? Hardly. We are all living in the same model fabricated by classical physics; it serves our needs on the macro-atomic level; it produces new, functioning technology. We have a "quantum mechanics" and the math to go with it that preserves scientific method. Yet scientific method has been trying to represent what it itself cannot imagine: contradiction, indeterminacy, uncertainty, chaos. Strikingly, what it cannot envision it also has no method of revealing. I mean that the premises of the scientific method are confounded by what seems to be going on at a subatomic level.

What is going on there remains opaque to normal science; science must un-science itself in order to follow. But this it cannot do without becoming "voodoo science." We await a new imagining so that we can grasp what a technology that can overspill what we intended it for has revealed. Our imaginations evoke the technology, but our imaginations are constrained by what we have already imagined and produced. What, for instance, was the person who invented the wheel imagining it to be? Was he or she or they imagining a BMW in their future? Four wheels instead of two? Rubber tires instead of wooden wheels? Front-wheel rather than rear-wheel drive? Disk rather than cylindrical brakes? Brakes?

Cyberspace is a more recent example. I heard an interesting discussion on NPR's "Talk of the Nation" among those who helped create the Internet. Did it turn out now as they had imagined? If they could restart, would they do it differently? What didn't they foresee that has developed? What do they imagine now to be the cyberspace of the next hundred years? Did we imagine five hundred cable channels at the dawn of TV? A use for Bell's telephone?

We are limited and restrained by our capacity to imagine, and we live in times when everything that exercises our imaginations—everything from Shelley's defense of poetry to the art and music curriculum in grade school—we line-item veto in fiscal emergencies. We have bureaucratized and classified the domain of the imagination itself in a way that affects how and what we see and hear. Witness the intentful solemnity of a ballet, a concert, a piano recital, an opera, a gallery opening, a museum tour, a photographic exhibit, the unveiling of a new sculpture, a building designed by a great architect, and so on. Then witness your town's debut of Tim Burton's *Sleepy Hollow*. We cannot imagine on the level of what we can see and hear in that film; and I am not arguing that it is or isn't a great film, whatever we may mean by that. But we cannot see what we see on the screen as doing what a painting does, what music does, what the novel does, what theater does, what photography does. We are led always by what we can imagine and that is constrained by what we have already imagined and the priorities we give to what we have already imagined. As long as film is linked to the "popular" we imagine within the culturally determined boundaries of the "popular."

Let's imagine that when we imagine we're scratching around things that lie just past and outside our present conceivability level, and that in some cases we've been scratching around the same places for the past two millennia. I refer to the world of the dead, to God, to the devil, to magic, and to the "end of days."

I read a newspaper review of Tim Burton's *Sleepy Hollow* that finds the film to be spectacle without substance; Burton has nothing to say. When I see the film I find the same subject matter Burton has been drawn to in his *Batman* films, in *Beetlejuice,* in *Edward Scissorhands,* in *The Nightmare before Christmas,* in *Ed Wood*—namely, the confrontation between the conventional and the strange, the social order in its normative mode and what that social order cannot dream of: entrenched, stable identities running into disturbing differences. Burton's focus in *Sleepy Hollow* is on a clash between the ways in which we identify things and make the world identical to what we already know, and the irrationalities of conjuring, dream, devil pacts, legends, faith, and love itself.

Washington Irving's schoolmaster Ichabod Crane becomes Constable Crane; the schoolmaster's bookishness converted into a criminologist's methodical pursuit of hard facts. But it is not the scientific method itself that has led Constable Crane to this rigorous empirical investigation of the world; he is haunted by the horrible execution of his mother, condemned by a clergyman as a witch. He is beset by visions and dreams of his life with his mother, visions he slowly works his way into as he moves deeply into the world of Sleepy Hollow, a world shadowed by a headless horseman. His science, his methods, his reason, his fact gathering, and his instruments are his defense against the fear, the mythology, the irrationality that has Sleepy Hollow in its grip. The defense collapses when he himself encounters the Headless Horseman; "He's real!" he cries out from his bed. "You don't understand. I've seen him. He's real. He exists!"

The existence of what should only exist in the imagination, in nightmare, in legend and myth, upsets Constable Crane's self-assuredness, his presumption, his sense of being able to control the world through reason and method. The villagers now find him useless to them: they already knew his instruments would be of no avail. With this crack in his armor of rational invincibility, Constable Crane now is vulnerable to a steady seepage from the past. He too begins to reach into a hidden world of his own being through his imagination. He discovers how he comes to have those peculiar scars on his hands; he discovers a much younger self turning from a cruel faith that condemns and destroys the innocent to the clear light of reason. Belief, grounded not in facts and reason but in blind faith, has confused his mother's free-spirit nature with witchcraft. And belief is grounded in what we imagine but cannot prove; thusly, what the imagination produces is not only suspect in Constable Crane's mind but is deadly.

The imagination kills; the Headless Horseman is a creature of fantasy, of the unconscious. His reality then destabilizes the constable's whole being-in-the-world; not only is he not sure of the methods he uses to identify anything but he is no longer sure of the identity he sees as his own. He has only imagined himself and the world to be in certain ways. Once he rouses himself from his bed, where he has been hiding under the covers, and ventures forth once again after the Headless Horseman, he becomes increasingly more open to what the imagination reveals and to the imagination as his pursuing faculty. The opposite of rationalism and method is not invariably the fanaticism of the cleric who tortured his mother to death. There is also the "good magic" of Katrina, to whom Crane is attracted. Hers is a healing, protective magic, while her stepmother has practiced a dark magic in order to compel the Headless Horseman to do her bidding. There are serious limitations to Constable Crane's forensic approach to reality, limitations not placed upon magic, where connections unimagined by science produce results in a reality extended beyond what can be empirically verified. Magic, you might say, is an imaginative exploration of the unseen, and in this case the unseen includes a hell to which the Headless Horseman finally returns. What we can imagine is not constrained by the boundaries of Disneyland (although, ironically, the Disney version of *The Legend of Sleepy Hollow* transformed that dark tale into "fun for the whole family").

Crane's trip to Sleepy Hollow takes place on the last days of the year 1799, and when he returns to New York City with Katrina, he cheerfully proclaims that they have arrived just in time to begin the new century! There is more than this that parallels our own present millennial moment: there is still a place called hell working in the human imagination, and there is the visionary force of the human imagination still at work. The sorry part is that while we can clearly imagine the lineaments of hell, we can at this moment in America only imagine lives around us that come into range of our class and cash. Everyone else is faceless.

Moriarity's Pub

Fall 1999

Maybe the reason everyone around us is faceless is because, like John Malkovich in Spike Jonze's clever film *Being John Malkovich,* all we see when we look in someone else's face is our own face. We can't see beyond the limitations of our own life-worlds, our own being-in-the-world. You don't have to be traumatized in childhood, or in Viet Nam, or find out you have cancer, win the Lottery, or be a psychopathic serial killer or a sociopathic Hannibal Lecter in order for you to be hopelessly trapped in a perpetual projection of YOU onto the world around you, including onto other people. All you have to be is *Homo sapien.*

The premise of the encounter between the "real" Malkovich and a world of Malkoviches who speak only one word, "malkovich," is the presence of a portal into Malkovich's being-in-the-world, his brain, his consciousness, his soul. The portal is accidentally found by Greg, a puppeteer by desire, a file clerk in reality, behind the sort of very small door Alice found in Wonderland. The thing you have to realize about Greg, the puppeteer, is that he's our contemporary hopelessly romantic and idealistic young artist; and he's brilliant. Say he's the aspiring Keats turning to poetry to reach into soul and world; he's Mozart with his music; he's the young Dickens recreating a world of characters within his imagination; he's Cezanne, seeing only through the stroke of his brush.

It's another portrait of the artist as a young man, this time a puppeteer. Now in 1999, he has a hard time getting out of bed. "Nobody is looking for a puppeteer in this wintry economic climate," he tells Lotte his wife. He can't pursue his art; no recognition, no rewards, no income. We see him on a street corner performing "Abelard and Heloise: A Tragic Romance." He's a masterful puppeteer, but no one is stopping to look, except a little girl. Her father knocks Greg out when he sees the puppets simulating intercourse. "What are you, a pervert?" the guy says knocking down the stage to get at Greg. So this young artist goes through the want ads and responds to a "Looking for a man with fast

hands" ad. It's clever: a puppeteer has to have amazingly fast and dex-
terous hands. Where is the market value in this? In what corporate niche
can this gift find a place? Who will pay him for having fast hands? He
could perhaps become a pickpocket; or maybe a barber; or a cardsharp
with a three-card monte stand; become a file clerk.

"Tell me about yourself." Maxine, a fellow office worker, by whom
Greg is immediately smitten, asks.

"Well, I'm a puppeteer . . ."

"Check," Maxine calls out to the bartender.

And why not? This is 1999. What young person in 1999 has con-
sidered their career options, investment future, and the current corporate climate and has decided to become a puppeteer? Have I run into a
twenty-something anytime in the last ten years who wanted to be a puppeteer? Maxine, who is Greg's polar opposite—she's an entrepreneurial
soul, a cash-and-carry algorithm—lays her world-view on Greg and
Lotte: "The world's divided into those who go after what they want and
those who don't. . . . And those who don't go after what they want. Who
gives a shit about them anyway?"

I've been treated to the same world-view twice already in 1999.
Back home in New York, when I asked what was to be done with the
forty-odd million Americans without any medical insurance, I heard
Maxine's response regarding those who "don't want to be rich." On
another occasion I was referring to the bottom quintile of the population who were too soured and beat up to come to vote. Same Maxine
response. And I remember being present when a table full of twenty-
somethings discussed the fate of a friend experiencing hard times. The
verdict: he had given up the desire to be rich. They could no longer care
about him. One more on the discard pile, on the Loser pile.

Maxine is a cold piece of work; she scares me. She's a fatal attraction for Greg, but she scares the hell out of me. Maxine unrelentlessly
keeps her eye on the bottom line, on the profit margin, on what's in it
for her. She pursues her own self-interest like my neighbor's cat has been
pursuing a chipmunk who this spring moved into our garden. When
Greg, flabbergasted by his discovery and journey through the portal,
rushes in to tell Maxine, he loses himself in philosophical musing. "Do
you see what a metaphysical can of worms this portal is?" he asks her.
Maxine doesn't. She walks out. Later that evening she calls him; she's
had time to think, but not metaphysically. She's applied her one-track
entrepreneurial perception to what Greg has told her and she's come up
with this: "We'll sell tickets at two hundred a pop."

The young struggling artist agrees; his obsession with Maxine,
maintained in spite of her monstrous selfishness, pushes him away from

his art and toward a money-making business. If there is any value in this business besides cash value, Maxine doesn't go for it. You put your money down and you go through the portal—which she never does, and she has no interest in seeing what the experience might be—and you get what you paid for.

When their first customer, a fat guy with glasses, begins to sob out his sadness, Maxine cuts him off and says "Two hundred dollars." Self-interest knows its focus; it doesn't wander into an interest in others that goes beyond the two hundred you get from them. Does Maxine then see only Maxines around her? Maybe Malkovich's celebrity vanity has him see only his own face. Maxine might only see people on whom she could feed, people whom she could control for her own benefit. She might only see her "network" of potentially useful resources. And then again she might only see people whose eyes are filled with lust for her and devotion to her, what she says when she looks into Malkovich's eyes and sees not only his love and devotion but Lotte's, when Lotte travels through the portal into Malkovich.

Maxine gets to sound more and more like one of our entrepreneurial Winners of the 1980s and 1990s, while Greg, the artist, seems to be dumping his art and going into business. When Malkovich takes a tour of his own head, comes back and orders Greg to shut the portal down, Greg says he can't because it's his livelihood. He's making a profit here; he can't shut the operation down, even if he's messing with Malkovich's head. Greg's on the side of the short-term profiteers now: what does it matter if we mess with heads, with hearts, with souls, with our fellow creatures, with the whole planet, if profit is being made here? The young man who had chosen to downplay livelihood and pursue his art is now the young man who will hold onto his livelihood no matter what. Maxine has shown him the light: if you're not turning a profit, you're not doing anything.

When Maxine chooses Lotte and not Greg, Greg begins to see that Maxine's self-interest extends beyond money. "You're evil, Maxine," Greg tells her, but he can't free himself of his obsession with her. He enters Malkovich and begins to control him like a puppet. Maxine is interested in this new development: "So Greg can control Malkovich and I can control Greg." The first thing she realizes they can do is control all the money in Malkovich's bank account. Greg begins to enjoy working Malkovich. This is the supreme act of puppetry: pulling the strings on a real, live human being. Now Malkovich will give up acting and become a puppeteer, and all the "notoriety" of Malkovich will go into making this puppeteer a success. Behind that success will be Greg, finally a Winner in "this wintry economic climate." Thus, a little variation on an old cynicism: "It's not who you are but who you control."

I'm not reassured by this artistic victory; it's slimy. I agree with Malkovich: it's *his* head and no one has the right to enter it. Except of course Madison Avenue, the world of Disney, MTV, Hollywood, and the Fortune 500. We haven't escaped the dilemma of the young, struggling artist in 1999. To achieve recognition and success, he has to hide behind the facade of celebrity. In Greg's world there's already a celebrity puppeteer: Derek Mantini, the compromised, sellout, fraud of a puppeteer whom the world admires. It's as if when it comes to puppeteers there is room for only one celebrity. Any more than that would be too enfranchising and work against profits. In the realm of acting, a great many more can be admitted into celebrity status; sports figures, so many; models, so many; politicians, so many; writers and artists, so many. And so on. The portal to recognition and success, then, as an artist, is through the celebrity portal, and that is restricted.

Why? Because if we all designated ourselves as celebrities, whatever we were yearning for would cease. Yearning to be what we are not and to have what we do not have would cease. And if that sort of yearning ceases, the Maxines of this world would not be getting our two hundred dollars. I don't have "to be John Malkovich." I may be a windbag of cultural *memes,* or what I call prefab mental wear, but there's a struggle in there that's mine. I'm not dropping it and picking up something else off the rack with a "celebrity" or "role model" tag on it. If we're all equal blades of grass like Whitman visioned, then nobody can claim privileged ontological status, regardless of the way the manure is distributed. In order to forestall this *camerado* world, who and what a celebrity is must be kept as rare as the rarest butterfly, as impossible to reach as the remotest star, as awesome as beatification.

There's another reason why Greg's artistic success here, through the mask of Malkovich, is no real success for the artist: he literally becomes the manipulator who pulls the strings of other people's lives. He is not the artist as beneficent creator, as the imaginative interpreter of the world; he is not an artist at all but rather a Dr. Frankenstein, a Hitler, a fascistic dominator of the weak and helpless. Art has no morality, Wilde reminds us, but this is no art-for-art's-sake scenario. This is an artist who achieves celebrity by robbing another man of his soul. Art and the artist shouldn't be shackled by any creed if that art and that artist are to reach beyond what we can conceive, liberate us from what enslaves us, but the artist whose medium is enslavement cannot produce imaginative truth. Greg masked by Malkovich becomes the fraudulent artist, the sham artist he believes Derek Mantini is. Now they are joined in that falseness and in their celebrity status.

Perhaps it's the mission of the artist to get us to see not just our own faces in the faces of those around us but other faces, to see into the lives of other people, or begin to, to break out of our own tight framing of self and world and conceive of other ways of seeing, other connections, other realities. When I see Maxine up there on the screen reducing all human existence to a cash nexus, I cringe. I begin to look around me and wonder how many silent Maxines I am speaking to, who are reading what I write. . . . But of course they wouldn't read what I write for very long. "Check," I can hear them calling out. When I see the young struggling artist lying in bed, with no reason to get up in this wintry climate for artists in America, I know where my attachment for this puppeteer comes from. It's an orbit of memory from which I never travel far.

⌒⌒⌒

Like one or two who "majored in English" eons ago, I did it because I liked to read and think about novels. I also liked to watch movies, but I didn't think about making movies and I believed, like so many others, that a good novel came before a screenplay. By the time I was a grad student and inspired by Blake, I wanted to create. I wanted to be a poet; believe it or not it was a wintry climate for poets. Perhaps I could teach poetry, and write poetry when I wasn't teaching? Thus the Ph.D. My poems got longer and more character-driven and when I found myself with the kind of sabbatical that sudden termination gives you and a lot of anger regarding that termination, I wrote my first novel, a novel expressing my anger at—guess what?—the "injustices of academe."

After my failed but eye-opening stint as a farmer in West Virginia, I got a job in North Carolina. While on the job, I wrote another novel, a novel expressing my new nihilism. I called it, appropriately, *Giving It Up*. The country was in a mid-seventies depression: Ph.D.'s were driving cabs in Boston and mowing lawns in Los Angeles. Viet Nam had worn out our souls; the Ayatollah was burning us in effigy. My edge took on social and cultural dimensions. Do you think one giving-it-up gesture was enough for the times, for me? I wrote another novel about two guys coming back to Brooklyn after Viet Nam. I called it, *Get Ready to Run,* a call to those who, like me, weren't already running. Years later my mother-in-law told me something about the "over-educated" that made me think we were the only ones running. Read your contemporary history: some people were busy staging the "Show me the money! Greed is good!" Show that pushed Reagan to the presidency. Read your contemporary something or other: too much reflection, too much imagination, produces discontent. But discontents poke holes in a lot of balloons that need to come down. I find it ironic that we're now hoping that such discontents, nurtured and educated within a "free-market capitalism" environment will bring China, for instance, out of its "undemocratic" pit.

Just before I moved to the comfortable conservative environment of Orange County, California, I was seething with rage and raging with imagination in a North Carolina town that Tobacco had built. I went from running away to swimming away. I wanted to cross a great ocean that would separate me from the malaise that Carter had talked about and from which I was suffering. I started on yet another novel, *Going to Sea*. The novel was just as driven by the giving-it-up anger as the previous one, but I soon got a story in my head that wouldn't leave me. I folded 8 x 11 in. sheets in half and carried them in my back pocket. In between the questions I got while sitting at a library desk, I wrote a novel I titled, *The Sweetheart*, a title inspired by dedication the anarchist's anarchist, Max Stirner, wrote in *The Ego and Its Own* to his sweetheart. I went schizoid for that novel, dividing myself into two characters. Williams is a man who speaks only when spoken to and then only replies with enigmatic quotations from Bartlett's; he is otherwise occupied with a not quite clear vision of a woman he refers to as his sweetheart. She's the invisible force and meaning in his life, but she glows now and then like a firefly on a dark summer night. Moran is a man with one brown eye and one blue eye who's a mesmerizing con man and a forgiveable sociopath. He's the only one who can connect Williams's words to relevant and startling meaning. Williams is released from the mental hospital he and Moran are in; Moran escapes. They both work their way, in different ways, to the top of a large merchandizing company, introducing at every point that sort of anarchistic dadaism that filled my own soul.

I got that novel to Peter Shepherd at the Harold Ober Literary Agency in New York and he sent it around to publishers for the next couple of years. Encouraged by this—what my youngest daughter, Brenda, calls my "goofy hopefulness"—I began *South of Babel*, a novel about a guy who—of course—had given it up and was now living in a fictitious South American country accompanied by a loquacious parrot. Shepherd at first turned the novel down. I left it, reread it months later, saw that the venom had swallowed the comic absurdity, and rewrote it. Shepherd then agreed to represent that also. So in the late 1970s and early 1980s I had two novels making the rounds.

The recipe seemed clear-cut to me: you take years of reading every Romantic Radical who's ever written, you add a good dose of Old Left education at the City University of New York in the early 1960s, you add an unjust termination of job and career providing just the right amount of tart edge, you add to that a Sicilian sense of retribution and vendetta, three ounces of Brooklyn street rebel, two cups of the purest willingness to thieve time for the sake of your writing, one over-loaded imagination, and one agent who responds to your zaniness, and you get two novels making the rounds. If you follow a recipe antithetical to that you get two novels that actually get published. That much seems clear to me now.

While I waited for the publication of my novels, I read the most mind-boggling contemporary thought I could get my hands on. I did it the way some people do yoga and other people play bridge. I then thought that if I got totally into the contemporary theory debate, which I did find fascinating, I might be able to get back into a regular academic appointment that would give me the summers off, most of the week, and therefore a chance to write even more novels. When my agent wasn't able to convince any commercial publisher that my books would make a profit—editors thought they were comical but no one could say where they were going or what they were about—I turned to academic writing and swept the novel writing off the desk. I suspected that it wasn't the inability to see what the novels were about that was the problem but rather the fact that they smacked too much of a countercultural time that Ronald Reagan's crowd, now in power, was trying to bury. These were novels written for people with an edge, angry, discontent, negative folk who in a decade would vanish into their own portfolios or just vanish.

After about ten years I published some short, fictional pieces in *Speeding to the Millennium*. Postmodern ideas had allowed me to understand the form of my writing; my former techniques now had a name. I also tried to write some commercial novels but Shepherd didn't think I was up to speed in that game. I wrote a Western novel; I wrote a sci-fi novel; I wrote a murder mystery; I wrote a bit of detective-porn. I tried to rewrite *The Sweetheart*, sort of mellowing the tone, rounding the edges, bringing it into a post-Reagan world. I stopped that rewrite almost at the get-go. I wrote a giving-it-up–self-consciously-aware-of-its-postmodern-credentials kind of novel, *Flying Geese*. None of these passed my own muster upon a reread after six months or so.

In southern California, I met a struggling writer who was president of a writer's association. He was greatly impressed that the Ober agency had represented two of my novels. Almost is nothing I told him. I'm not a writer who believes he's writing for posterity; if something is still read decades later, fine. But I'm writing of this moment, out of this moment, for this moment. And, I think because I had gone too far to the edge while the publishing world had moved closer to a "mass market audience," I failed to connect with a marketable percentage of those living in my times. Another way of putting that is to say that *my* times were filled with an angry, anarchistic, dadaistic "giving-it-up" spirit grounded in personal experiences that thankfully few people shared or maybe too many people shared and didn't want to dwell on. While my imagination was feeding off my angry edge-ness, most folks were looking for escape, looking for escapist fare from novels and films. *Their* times were already in the future; mine were orbiting in the past.

This dude didn't hear any of this. I told him flat out that it never came to anything. The novels making the rounds, the New York agent, the goofy hopefulness. But he invited me to their next meeting. Dues were only so much a month. I also ran into a woman who said I should write a novel someday; I told her I had eleven in my basement. No, ten. I had lost one. These are pre-computer disk days. She told me her husband had written about a dozen novels and just last month had burnt them all. He said it was a purgation; now he could go on to do something else with his life. While those manuscripts survived he couldn't really have a successful career in whatever it was he was doing. And he had found a six-figure-salary career.

There was a lesson in there. I knew she was advising me to do the same, but I figured I could give up everything but the writing. I could, for instance, write about giving up the wintry economic climate. And besides, writing novels has done one thing for me I'm happy about: I don't see my own face around me but worlds of faces of other people. Is that good? Is that better? I think it is. My politics are the goofy-hopeful politics of Shelley: a well-exercised imagination brings us into closer orbit to those who share this planet with us. Shelley tried to restrict the imagination to a sympathetic role; unfortunately, a well-exercised imagination can breed paranoia, and politics, rather than becoming all wonderful and grand by means of the well-exercised imagination, can become dark and deadly. There's a Hollywood imagination lurking behind Reagan's "Star Wars" scenario; perhaps it's Dr. Strangelove's. Imagine all the gods animism does and then thank them that what the imagination conceives is NOT necessarily true, *pace* William Blake.

And yet I know that I am not a reliable reference point for my own perception of the world and that some people are conceivable because I've found through the imagination a portal to them and I begin to see.

On the Set of Oprah, Jerry, Martha, and Tony

Spring 1999

> *Everyone else is faceless . . . except for Oprah, Jerry, Martha, and Tony.*

I spend a lot of time switching from Oprah to Jerry and then from Jerry to Oprah. It's like the two extremes of American culture: Oprah's earnest "assisted psychological and spiritual care" and Jerry's nonchalant "exposé of Trailer Park Trash." What class is Oprah dealing with? Her audience doesn't chant "Oprah! Oprah! Oprah!" but there are frequent avowals of "I love you Oprah!" She certainly has her own following. Suburban housewives? Soccer moms? It looks to me like Beaver Cleaver's mom-types are in the audience. Even the "sisters" are not the "We hear you, sister!" kind of black chorus. This is a middle- to upper-middle-class crowd and the show, in spite of Oprah's occasional use of street Ebonics, is very white.

You might say Oprah's whole mission is to lead us all to a very civil society where we can work through our psychological hang-ups, fulfill our spiritual needs, and learn how to treat each other warmly. Along the way or in between, we would learn how to get rid of "psychological crutches," get total "makeovers," eat right, exercise daily, and appreciate fully the fact that Oprah has a nutritionist prepare her meals, a trainer work her body, and an entourage of personal "human resources" to meet all her personal needs. Her show is a daily education in civility, with a nod toward the spiritual forces which would fill our lives if we only let them. We are to be elevated and very often the Elevated, the Celebrities Oprah admires, will show up to converse with Oprah. She enables us to get close to them, to see how they can be role models in our lives. We also learn how to empathize with the rich and famous, who have to put up with "poor relations," their "public" (the rest of us), the burden their role model status places on them, and the general trials and tribulations of being Super-Beings in a plain old democracy.

I'm embarrassed about dissing Oprah because she's Good and her show is into Goodness. I can't take this daily display of Goodness, sort of like how Dracula couldn't take the rays of the sun. Forget that I'm White and she's Black; fact is I'm Dark and she's Light. The way I react to Oprah is different than the way I react to Martha Stewart. I can't stand to watch Martha Stewart blankly and "martha stewartly" showing us how to put a pillow into a pillowcase, stuff a turkey, sew a straight seam, or turn any old piece of shite into a useful addition to the home. She's got the television interpersonal skills of Mister Rogers; I think sometimes she is Mister Rogers in drag.

I'm really a Dark Being after a few jolts of Martha; I'm irrationally and prejudicially totally pissed off by her and her empire. And the way I want to strike back at her empire is totally personal, like a gang-bang scene in a homemade ghetto video. When I come to think of it, I probably don't like the people all nice and cozy hanging on Martha's every word with all that Martha shite in every room of their cozy soccer mom/Junior League/Yuppie/assortative mated/Birkenstock household—the kind of cats who would slice your throat in the middle of the night and throw your body in the city dump because you failed to trim your lawn and therefore jeopardized their "property values." I mean isn't Martha all about property? Handling property, stroking property, getting property, jarring and storing property?

Maybe I'm wrong about Oprah's real audience. Maybe she is targeting the Have Nots, the already economically disenfranchised who may soon wake up and smell the coffee brewing in Oprah's kitchen while their kitchen is bare. I mean Oprah's spiritual message doesn't seem to me to amount to anything more than a panic defense of property—her property. And she's doing this on behalf of the eight billionaires and ten thousand millionaires in Seattle, for instance. If she can bring a huge television audience of "We Wanna Be Like Oprah But We Ain't Got Shite" over to the spiritual side which reads "We Ain't Got Shite But We're In Touch With Our Spiritual Side," then you've got a postmodern-world/TV-pop-cult-celebrity retreading of that politically useful beatitude regarding the blessedness of the poor. In the long run—the very long run—it pays to be poor. That kind of thing. You have no cash but you can add up your spiritual assets and dividends—while Oprah's accountants are working on her multimillions. Cash makes the truly spiritual life difficult. You give it away, you write it off; you give it away, you write it off. Nobody needs it but the Celebrities, who are like Saints, daily tortured by the requests for cash handouts from poor relations.

I can go deeper into the way Oprah irks me: I don't like the way she sits there while one of her "hit men" works over some poor slob whose behavior needs some on-the-spot "sensitivity remodeling." The goal here is to bring the guy to tears. Until the tears are flowing Oprah sits there unappeased. She always expresses great difficulty in understanding how someone could have allowed this to happen or how someone can't understand that this is bad behavior. Pity the guy who makes a stand; he's taken apart piecemeal. Once he breaks down in front of the audience and on network TV and admitted he's a sorry son of a bitch, then he's free to go. But wait. First he has to look into the eyes of the person he's tormented, usually a wife or girlfriend, and tell her what the "sensitivity trainer" tells him to tell her. Then she tells the sorry son of a bitch what the "sensitivity trainer" tells her to say. Oprah gives out a sigh of relief, gives the audience a knowing look, and we go "to break."

Jerry Springer doesn't sensitivity train; he doesn't try to break his guests down; he's not hoping they'll confront their darker selves right there on his show. All he's hoping for is that one's guy's darker self comes out and tangles with another guy's. Or one guy who doesn't know how dark life can be gets a chance to hear his girlfriend tell him just how dark human relationships can be. She's sleeping with another guy, or another girl. The other guy is the sap's best friend; the other girl is his sister. When the girl shows up as the innocent sap, she finds out her boyfriend is sleeping with her mother and her mother is now pregnant. And then her father comes out in a rage and attacks the boyfriend, but then his boyfriend comes out in a rage and attacks him. Meanwhile, backstage, there's always a guy waiting to come forward to tell his girlfriend that he's really a girl; or a girl waiting to tell her boyfriend that she's really a guy. Already on stage there's a girl dying to have sex in front of a camera, or strip for the audience, or tell her husband that's she's been prostituting on the side. The males clash like bulls, each telling the other that the girl who has just told both of them that she doesn't know who she's pregnant by, is "going home with me"!

Jerry's role is to get all the stories laid out for the TV audience, get all the entanglements sorted out, and then stand back and let the antagonists duke it out. Instead of introducing a professional sensitivity trainer to his guests, he asks them whether they see anything wrong with whatever it is they've done. "So she's a minor and your niece and you got her pregnant. Do you see anything wrong with that?" "So she really hasn't done anything to you but he's slept with her, so why are you fighting with her?" "Doesn't it bother you that he's your daughter's husband and your granddaughter's father and you're having sex with him?" "Don't you think you owed it to her to tell her that you're a 'her' too?"

"Doesn't it bother you that your kids might see their mother having sex in a porno flick?" "If he says he can support you without your working as a prostitute don't you think you should give up that life?"

What Jerry always seems to be searching for is any sign or remnant of conscience, personal or social. He's asking for us. Do you think it's fair to her to do so and so? he'll ask. Or, doesn't it bother you that he's your brother and that's his wife you're sleeping with? Every afternoon he goes in search of an answer to a question that all those folks doing things as Martha would and all those folks "empowered spiritually" by Oprah have been asking for the last twenty years: "Just how depraved and conscienceless is the underclass?" "Just how trashy are the Trailer Park Trash?" And no one is asking this question in order to gauge how far our democracy has been plundered by its "profits to shareholders" creed. The questions are asked to discover how close to being a real threat to the Haves are these Have Nots. How discontented are they? And how far from cutting our throats and taking our property without any qualm of conscience are they? How well are our social deterrents to crime—prisons built, prisons privatized, prisons maintained as hell holes, folks fried in Texas, three strikes and you're in without parole forever, no appeals on death row, no budgets for public defenders and so on—working? Are the Losers busy ruining their own lives, or are they looking over at us in our gated communities watching the "Nightly Business Report"?

You can watch a show like *Cops* to see how effectively the cops are patrolling the public space that the underclass operates. That show gives us the impression that not only are the cops out there keeping the trash in check, but they're doing it with a great deal of patience and respect, the kind of respect that one citizen in a democracy would show another citizen in a democracy. But if you want to see the "way the Losers live" you turn to Jerry Springer. His show is both reassuring and nervous-making. It's reassuring to see that the trash are so involved in their own messy lives in their own messy little worlds that they can't step back and see how our American society has done a hell of a lot in the last twenty years to make their lives even messier. So narrowly focused are the trash in "maximizing" their own pleasure, regardless of the cost, and so ill-equipped are they to do anything but narrowly focus on anything, that any stepping back and taking a "broader view of things" is impossible. This is reassuring to the Haves. These folks probably won't make it to the voting booths, but if they do, they are just as liable to vote against their own best interest as for it. They're a very malleable bunch. The nervous-making part has to do with this clear view of the trash's lack of any moral compass. I mean, if they weren't distracted by their own crimes against each other, they'd be fully capable of trashing the lives of the Haves. They'd do it without a pang of conscience. By all the accounts Jerry brings to us, it seems pretty clear that there's nothing noble in the simplicity of this trash. The romantic allure of the peasant that Wordsworth, for instance, felt, has been replaced in our postmodern world with a fear and loathing of our trashy underclass. These people will commit any sort of bestial, incestuous, vile, adulterous act without a blink of the eye. No one here knows in his or her heart what it means to perform a criminal act unless they are arrested and charged; there's no notion of guilt or innocence, only a sense of "getting away" with something or not, a sense of being lucky or not.

I'm caught between two emotional antipodes: everybody should shut up about sex and everybody should keep talking about sex. I think post-1980s born-again America is getting a daily lesson in how and why no chocolate cake is better than sex and that talking about sex is better than not talking about it. I can't help but think that there's just as much lurid and stupid sexual exploitation going on in the lives of the rich and private as there is going on among this trash whose lives are a public project. The Haves not only value privacy but have the means to maintain it. They don't spend their lives in project apartments or die in public sanitariums. The Have Not underclass doesn't fathom how privacy could be of value, never having had any. Jerry doesn't have to pay them to show up and spill their innermost sex secrets because they have as little sense of an inner, private life and thoughts and feelings as they do of a moral conscience. They don't possess "privatized" lives; they haven't retreated to the manor house; they still mentally occupy the "commons," the public space. On the "Jerry Springer Show" they physically occupy it as well. And I think whereas we can all learn nothing from the secluded, gated, protected, fully privatized life, we learn something about our own natures by watching and listening to the Springer people. It's not simply "there but for the grace of God go I," but rather some exposure of the body's will and desire in an age of clever hacking, virtual dreams, and Dow Jones digits.

On the negative side, I don't admire the way the underclass is further demonized on this show at a time when the country is trying to justify its support of the rich and its writing off of the poor. Seeing these Springer people—both audience and "guests"—reconfirms the equestrian class's prejudice and stereotyping, which goes something like this: The underclass doesn't deserve to receive any help from government or philanthropists because they fail to assume personal responsibility. They have no "will to power," and seem genetically incapable of leading decent, civilized lives. In fact, they seem incapable of appreciating the spiritual and psychological counseling that Oprah provides or of appreciating the Martha Stewart way of living in comfy digs surrounded by comfy handcrafted things. What's criminal really about these Springer people is that they refuse to rise above their own lusts and "serve somebody," namely Oprah, who can arrange to have them cry over their sins, or rise above their own ill-appointed hovels and "serve somebody," namely Martha Stewart, who can show them how to needlepoint their couch and suck up the dust on their bric-a-brac.

⌒∽∽⌒

So who's involved in a more criminal operation? Oprah, Martha, or Jerry? By criminal I mean morally reprehensible, by which I mean socially, culturally, economically, and politically reprehensible. The older I get the more I lose patience with "private" sins. I want to know, who's affected by your actions? How many people? Is it just the present that's affected or is the future involved? So the cover-up of the savings and loan scandal during George Bush's watch looms big time in my moral directory while Bill Clinton's dalliance with Monica is a "social" sin only insofar as it harmed Monica's, Hillary's, and Chelsea's lives. And there's no way for us to register that. Lobbying for the continuation of the Viet Nam War because your company has a nice defense contract puts you right in the center of Dante's hell. "Downsizing" forty thousand workers and passing their salaries on to a few corporate executives earns a ring in hell. "Liberating" welfare recipients and their dependents because it's a good "conservative" action in "conservative" times is an earner too. Televising the lives of poor slobs just to get good ratings and attract advertisers is a real transgression, and not simply a private one. Presuming to tell people how to live their lives and on what side of the bread their spirituality lies is equally a transgression. Getting people to accept your recipes only because your name is "Martha Stewart" is a burn-in-hell offense.

Now where does Tony Soprano fit in my moral universe?

I'm at a dinner party with Kev, Barb, Clabberhouse, Donner, and Elaine. The talk turns to the HBO hit show, "The Sopranos." Kev is totally repelled by the way Tony and Pussy have pumped bullet after bullet into the young kid who was involved in the shooting of Tony's cousin Chris. The kid was thirsty and Tony and Pussy go back and forth about sugar-free and regular and then after the kid drinks, they shoot him. Kev finds that sickening. What kind of people would go from such casual conversation to ruthless murder? Barb agrees with Kev; you can dismiss the whole show and the people in it as being unworthy of any attention, sort of like the protagonist in a novel who is too small in every way for us to care about. "Why should I care about these characters?" I remember someone saying that about a novel I had written which was filled with Bensonhurst neighborhood characters, my version of "The Sopranos" world some twenty-five years ago. Forget about the presentation; we're talking subject matter. I want to say what's so notable about Macbeth? He's a general who murders his way into the kingship. Is this a finer form of murder? Why is the presence of violence palatable here? It's transformed by art? It has a presence among humans that artists cannot ignore? I'm not so dismissive of Tony or the show because these characters murdered this kid who together with another kid tried to murder Tony's nephew "on spec." The kids figured they could show Richie Aprile, another "made man," that they deserved his respect. They were hoping for advancement by shooting Chris. They took a chance and lost. The lesson is clear: if you try to kill somebody "on spec"—in other words in the hope of a promotion and a rise in your personal stock—you have to be willing to accept the consequences.

My own head is full of stories in which the transaction is not so clear and clean. In academe you run into any number of people who have been "laterally promoted," which here means they've been put out to pasture, most of the time because a new political regime has no use for them. So they mark time until they quit or retire. Or if somebody wants them out, they're given humiliating kinds of assignments and schedules. Their souls wear out. Slowly, without any sign that this is a terrible act.

I think of the guy who gets attracted to another guy's wife, a guy he knows, a guy with whom he's sat down and broken bread. Then he carries on an affair with the guy's wife; he looks the husband straight in the eye and still carries on with his wife. And that goes on surreptitiously until the two call it quits. That kind of deception goes on everyday and it repels me. Why should I have any interest in people like this?

Here are some life stories that I'd tune out if they showed up on TV:

A guy running for office knows that if he pushes for a state income tax all his wealthy supporters will stop supporting him. Or if he fails to "reform tort law" and stop poor people from hiring lawyers to sue corporations on a contingency fee basis he will lose corporate support. What's unclear here is the suffering these kinds of actions cause. This politician screws a high percentage of the population "on spec" and gets away with it.

A president of the United States knows that CO_2 emissions harm the environment but he says the "science doesn't support this." The same president urges a tax reduction that benefits the Haves and not the Have Nots but promotes it as "fair." The same president pushes for oil drilling in the Alaskan wilderness preserve because profits come before everything.

A corporation knows that one of its byproducts is toxic, but it goes ahead nevertheless and advertises that it is good for your health. It's an "on spec" campaign; if it gets shot down, then they'll try a new approach. No one is going to show up and pump some bullets into the CEO because his "on spec" has killed people.

An "organization" takes its "business" south of the border because then it doesn't have to pay its workers a living wage, or provide any medical or retirement benefits, or worry about paying workmen's compensation if a worker is injured, or worry about unions because unionizers get thrown in jail, or worry about environmentalists because there are none. It's a sweet deal; it's the way the strong feed on the weak.

When I lived in West Virginia in the 1970s I heard countless stories from miners with "black lung." They were trying to get the mine owners to acknowledge the link between the work and the disease so they could get their medical bills paid. The mine owners fought that just as hard as the tobacco companies fought the connection between cigarette smoking and lung cancer.

I see a film called *Rainmaker* with Matt Damon as a young lawyer who discovers the existence of "bottom feeder" insurance companies. These are companies who sell cheap medical insurance to the poor and when claims are made the companies routinely reject them. They do so because statistics show that only a small percentage of the Have Nots they insure will bother to go to a lawyer and contest the denial. In this film, an insurance company has rejected a medical treatment that would have saved the life of a young man dying slowly and painfully of cancer. When the kid dies and a court case ensues, the insurance company hires a "dream team" of high-priced lawyers to prove that they did nothing illegal and are not liable. The film ends with the CEO, a guy with a rich man's unctuous tan, and his wife (in a fur coat) being arrested as they try to board a plane out of the country.

When Zoe Baird, with an annual income of over a half a million, decides to pay her nanny about five bucks an hour with no benefits and no social security since the nanny is an illegal alien, she's just feeding on the weak and vulnerable. Clinton nominated her for attorney general.

I could go on as long as I had access to newspapers. So what then is so very differently repellent about Tony Soprano's actions? Does he retaliate too quickly and cleanly? It's a breath of fresh air in a society that poisons and murders secretly is my view. I'm not here arguing that Tony's "organization" is better than incorporated or limited liability organizations, only that it's really not doing business any differently than the legals are. Tony's "power play" is direct and personal: "I have a lot of reasons why you should let our trucks pick up your garbage" is Tony's approach. Or, "We can insure your shipment, or your inventory, or your place of business, or your harassment from the police." Power plays, extortion, a feudal arrangement rather like *le droit de seigneur*— and thus an affront to the "rule of law," to our democratic system of justice. At the same time, our democracy is already being swallowed up by a corporation-created feudalism whose overclass is more into "creative destruction" of people and planet than into a Tony Soprano–type philosophy of "if everybody eats, we keep on eating too." In the end, you can learn to live with a brigand like Tony because he feeds on the social nectar but doesn't destroy the hive, whereas there is every indication that our free market transnationalism feeds on and will also destroy the hive of this planet.

There's a scene when one of Tony's old school chums asks Tony why he let him gamble when he knew what the outcome might be. Tony first tells him, "Hey, you're old enough to make your choices and you were begging me to get into that game." And then Tony's eyes narrow and he says something like, "Anyway, I knew you had this here store I could feed on. It's like the frog who takes the scorpion across the river because the scorpion promises not to sting him but then the scorpion does and he says 'it's my nature.'" But while it's Tony's nature to feed on the weak, it's not his business to sting the weak to death.

Human nature, with all its paradoxes, is certainly on display in Tony. On the other hand, I don't see anything more on display in Microsoft, for instance, than the cold faceless will to power of competitive capitalism. As we are presently discovering, it's far easier to put the perpetrators of Tony's type of ruthlessness in jail than shackle our corporate destroyers. We are, rather, almost celebrating corporate ruthlessness throughout the world, with most Americans wondering why such an entrepreneurial hero as Bill Gates and such a dominating company as Microsoft is being hounded by the Department of Justice. When we want to see *real* villainy, we can focus our attention on Tony Soprano. Evil is with these alien "goombahs" and not in corporate boardrooms; animal cunning and barbaric behavior is on display here in Tony's family and not within gated communities or in corporate suites; *negative* destruction is what Tony wreaks while a *creative* destruction is what the Fortune 500 engage in.

I have a hard time imagining that I could like a world designed by Oprah and her gurus. Maybe she's right and only celebrities and professional sensitivity trainers have souls and the rest of us are waiting to be shown. But I doubt it. There are other problems people have with money—not having it for instance—than the problems the rich and famous have with importunate relatives. In holding off-camera big players like Chance and Money, Oprah is able to contract our world to just individual responsibility, listening to one's superiors, discipline, and spiritual healing. Oprah's our guide to an equal-playing-field world, our agent of spiritual change, our link to psychological rehabilitation, and our only link to the stars. If you throw Martha Stewart into Oprah's world, you add something in between having a maid and being a maid: you can *play* at being a maid. Martha probably does more for the soccer mom conscience than Oprah does. Opposing this Martha/Oprah world is an anti-world, sort of the bizarre world of Jerry and Tony. Jerry fills up his world with all of Martha and Oprah's rejects, dropouts and failures, purely for the disdain and amusement of the Martha/Oprah world. Now if Tony offered a "get even" service for all the losers and heartbreaks that show up in Jerry's world, went on Oprah and *didn't* cry, and showed Martha how to stuff herself—or a dear friend—into a pillow—then you'd have a world I could learn to like.

Robin Wood Trail

Winter 1999

> *People are going to tell you you're no good. Don't let them.*
> *—American Heart*

If you want a better view of what it's like to be down and out in
America at the millennium, turn off Jerry Springer and rent the film
American Heart. It's a 1992 film which didn't get all the attention it
deserved. Jeff Bridges's performance as an ex-con, Jack Kelson, trying to do it right this time and trying to learn how to be a father to
a fourteen-year-old son who comes looking for him, escapes all the
Hollywood patterns. You know them; you've seen them. You have
the tough dad hiding a melty heart; you have the ex-con going
straight who's really a soft, loveable guy who everyone gets wrong;
you have the hard, taciturn loner; you have the guy who really can
play that guitar Jack carries around; you have those unexpectedly
touching scenes between father and son; the sudden miraculous
worldly wisdom; the last man displaying a heroic "grace under pressure." Bridges avoids all the clichés. He fights for responses always
true to what his background story is: he's never fit in and was lost
from the get-go, he's run from reform school, a man without a skill
or an education who steals to stay alive, a man unfortunate in his
friends, a man who holds on to a dream where he can be free if he
can just get to Alaska.

I didn't write about this film in *Speeding to the Millennium*; for
some reason, I sped past it. But now two films in 1999—*American Psycho* and *American Beauty*—send me back to *American Heart*. I get into
a "name the top five" kind of mood after watching *High-Fidelity*, a
movie in which three guys working in a record store are always quizzing
each other on the top five this or that. What are the top five movies ever
made with the word "American" in the title? I ask myself. Memory

revives *American Heart* and I re-see it. But not until I re-see *American Beauty* and *American Psycho*.

American Beauty has made almost everyone's top ten films of 1999 list. Reseeing the film three times just confirms my first impression, when I saw the film on the big screen. It's a film that also could have been done in 1949, 1959, 1969, 1979, or 1989. The theme escapes the present cultural American moment: male menopause with a seven-year itch, suburban male crisis. It's a well-crafted, if hackneyed, banal, pompous, and reactionary film. But one scene intersects the present. The scene in which Lester meets with Brad, the new personnel head, has intertextual significance: Lester does exactly what Edward Norton does in *Fight Club* in his meeting with his boss. They blackmail these guys into giving them what they want. In both cases, they want to be paid and not work. Both scenes resonate within the downsizing mood of American corporations today. Brad is hired as a head chopper; he has called Lester in to fire him. Before he can do it, Lester tells him that he knows some stuff that would damage the company if it got out. So instead of firing Lester, Brad asks him to write a self-appraisal, a self-evaluation of his worth to the company. Lester finally submits an evaluation in which he states that he's tired of being a whore for the advertising industry. He threatens to charge Brad with sexual harassment unless Brad gives him a year's salary as a bonus. It's the only scene in the movie that fuels and plays into the fires of America now. Lester's victory here and Edward Norton's in *Fight Club* almost make one wonder if there are really any such victories occurring in corporate America today. Judging by the downsize lists that make the headlines there aren't. Heads are being lopped off without any resistance.

Because *American Beauty* has received such critical and box-office success, I want to at least say something about the significant meaning that has been argued as existing in this movie (though I'm not going to give it half the coverage I'll give *American Heart* and *American Psycho*). I call it the "paper-bag-blowing-in-the-wind" metaphysics. I paraphrase some of this metaphysics spouted in the movie: There's an entire life behind things, an incredible benevolent force that wants us to know that there was no reason to be afraid ever; sometimes there's so much beauty in the world I can't take it; I guess it would be hard to stay mad where there's so much beauty in the world; I feel like I'm seeing it all at once and there's too much and my heart is about to burst like a balloon. I'll say what a wise-ass critic said about *Being John Malkovich*: a lot of intellectualizing will go on about this film but nevertheless it's just a bubble. I also want to say a little bit more: this particular bubble wants us to feel good about ourselves, wants us to see the beauty around us *here in America at this millennial moment*. Paper bags blowing in the wind are not what I'd focus my camera on. Or my critical discussion. Maybe there's a benevolent force that will soon come into the White House and the traditional values crowd will no longer have a reason to be afraid. Maybe there's a lot of beauty in your neighborhood; and maybe you live in the kind of neighborhood where public sanitation just lets the paper bags and everything else blow in the gutters and sidewalks. This is a reactionary film, a film that people from Jack Kelson's world will never see. They are, after all, the paper bags blowing in the wind in which Oprah's and Martha's crowds are trying to find some good. Since they don't ever appear in this movie, we have to settle for the midlife crisis of Lester Burnham. His life is almost as hard as Patrick Bateman's.

American Psycho, perhaps tainted by the "bad housekeeping" seal given Brett Easton Ellis's novel or perhaps tainted by the "sick of violence" atmosphere in America since Columbine, remained unmentioned by critics and moviegoers. It was distributed here in the heartland, but really remained an unspeakable and unmentionable movie. Let's say *American Heart* has the Springer underclass in focus and *American Beauty* has the Oprah soccer moms in focus. Who's on camera in *American Psycho*? I think it has the Martha Stewart elite shopper in focus. Tacky underclass, suburban white-flight middle, honking upperclass. Though, as I've said, *American Heart* doesn't present the underclass as bread and circus for the equestrian class or as scorn and despise for the middle class. And although Patrick Bateman, the American psycho, knows his top-of-the-line brands, restaurants, watering holes, and business cards, has Harvard business degrees, lives on the Upper West Side in Manhattan, and works on Wall Street ("earning a fortune to complement the one he was born with"), I doubt if he shops at Kmart, which Martha Stewart now fronts. You're more likely to find a Martha Stewart magazine in Lester and Carolyn Burnham's home on Robin Wood Trail. The TV show that most represents Bateman's class is probably Louis Rukeyser's "Wall Street Week."

Wait a second. Bateman watches Rukeyser? The Bateman who sits in his office watching TV or listening to music or doodling? Bateman is no Gordon Gekko, Oliver Stone's workaholic megabucks Market player. Bateman is Son of Gekko. He's got the money, the social connections, the Wall St. job, a secretary to make reservations for him at places like Indochine, the Cornell Club, the New York Yacht Club. This is the next generation of "Player," the wastrel, Son of the Player, who experiences "sheer panic" when he sees a business card more elegant than his own, when one of his wastrel set gets a reservation at the Dorcia and he can't. This is the time-waster who needs continuous stimulation, stroking, fantasy time, time to keep up on what products and places are hot at the moment.

What Bateman does watch is porn; what he works at is arranging his orgies and bloodfests. He exercises to an S&M tape; he amuses himself with the Springer types he runs into on the street. In fact, he's on the prowl for them. He's a predator of the underclass. He interrogates a homeless man as if he were some talking specimen from Mars. And then when he finds they have nothing in common, that the man disgusts him, he stabs him over and over. Fantasy? Or, a literal enactment of what the Patrick Batemans have been doing to the Jack Kelsons throughout the 1980s and 1990s?

Okay, there's no TV show like Oprah's or Jerry's or Martha's which represents Bateman's class. I think the upperclass honk—you hear it most notably in the women—turns the Nelson rating viewer off. It has to be done for laughs, like Mrs. Drysdale in the old TV show "The Beverly Hillbillies." The Bateman class isn't around to amuse or to instruct; they own TV stations, not appear on them. You stay out of the parlors of the multitudes you're feeding on. They're there to amuse you; not the other way around. Were you to see Bateman's world close up, as you do in the first half of *American Psycho,* each week on a TV show, you might just begin to question the purpose and existence of this whole class of rapacious, self-indulged snobs. You might just become a Class Warrior at a very inconvenient time in American history . . . I mean inconvenient for those who want to keep economic inequality a non-issue, here and abroad.

Rest easy—there's no "Bateman's World" TV show. Forget about that critique forming in your mind after watching the first half of *American Psycho;* you will discover in the second half that there really are no more Batemans around. He doesn't represent a class; there's no Bateman world. There's just this one psycho who goes around chopping up people, a psychopath who hasn't taken his medication, who suffers from a chemical imbalance, who's an embarrassment to his friends and family. You know you can find these psychos in every class; it's not a class thing. It's never a class thing when a novel or film comes along that pounces on the excesses of the elite.

Regardless of the retreat the film makes from its own critique, the acerbic and right-on parody of Bateman's world, this world of well-positioned asses, lingers. It's too deft and powerful to just disappear. Even when you know Bateman is an insane murderer, you can't wipe out the memory of the excesses of this class of Winners. Take what Bateman says about himself and extend it to a whole class: "There is an ideal of an elite class in America. There's just some abstraction, no real elite class. No real entity. Something illusionary. We are simply not there." This film shows us that they are there and it shows us where they are; they are not psychopathic murderers, just beneficiaries of a disproportionate percentage of the world's goods and services who believe that they are not a class engaged in maintaining their privileges at the expense of the many. There are only wealthy and successful individuals who have through individual effort and talent earned what is rightfully theirs. You can add these individuals up; you can find them at certain addresses and in certain clubs, but you can't say they represent a class. Only the underclass is a class; and the working class and the middle class. You know where to find them. It's never a class thing with the elite; assessment here must always be of the individual.

If you pay close attention to the movie, however, you will find a brilliant and sustained attack on this notion of existing individuals in Bateman's world. The attack is devastating to the conservative ideology. Why? Because in order to blather about "personal responsibility," "individual accomplishment," "deserving all the rewards of personal success," "individual choice," and all the rest, you have to preserve the sovereignty of the individual. It's not hard in a post-socialist age; all those old, tired arguments about social conditioning and influence, cultural shaping, environmental determinants, and so on went out with the Soviet Union. We're all into "individual" everything, "personal" control.

But what's this? *American Psycho* shows us a world of people who don't recognize each other, who misidentify, who think they are talking to someone who is really someone else. Bateman is called "Marcus" and "Davis" and "Smith." And he conclusively establishes any identity in dispute by referring to who wears what and who doesn't. It can't be so-and-so because this fellow is wearing Polo by Ralph Lauren and the real so-and-so always wears Hackett of London. And most riotously, Bateman isn't found out as the murderer of a man he has murdered, Paul Allen, because of misidentification.

It goes like this: Paul Allen always misidentifies Bateman as Marcus Halberstram. Under that name, Bateman dines with Allen and then chops him up in his apartment. When a detective questions him as to where he thinks Allen might be, Bateman tells him London, because he's already run into someone who says he's seen Allen in London. The detective is really after Marcus Halberstram because that's the name in Allen's appointment book. But he finds out that Marcus has a good alibi. He was having dinner that night with a number of people, including Patrick Bateman. "That's right," a very relieved Bateman says. "I must have forgotten." We're left to imagine who the chap really was at dinner whom Marcus identified as Bateman. And then the *coup de grâce* of misidentifications: Bateman breaks down after a rampage of murders and leaves a message on his lawyer's answering machine confessing to all the murders. When he sees the lawyer, Howard, at Harry's Bar and approaches him, Howard calls him Davis. He tells Bateman that he thought his phone message was a rip, except he picked a very easy target in that fool Bateman. Bateman loses control. He is Bateman. He did kill Paul Allen. To which Howard, angry now, tells him that that is impossible because he himself had dinner with Paul Allen in London twice in the past ten days. Not only does not knowing who is who keep Bateman from being arrested as the murderer, but it also renders his confession nothing more than a joke.

Is this lethal stuff? Well, not only do we see that this elite class is a childish, empty-headed class—no rich inner lives to say the least—but they are so much the product of a class pattern that they are indistinguishable, both to us and to themselves. The rich may be different than the poor, but within the ranks of the rich, there are no differences. They're all cut from the same bolt of cloth, all consumed with the same passion for an elegant business card, an elegant facade, the appearance of, simply, being.

At the end of the film, we sit and watch Reagan on TV along with Bateman and his peers. It's the "I didn't know about Iran-contra" speech. One of the Bateman tribe is amazed that Reagan can lie without a blink, can appear to believe his own words while at the same time knowing he's lying. It's politics, and the essence of being a good politician is to know something rather like this: you can have an invading army formed outside the gates and yet tell everyone within that there's no army there but only a gathering of individuals pursuing individual goals, and you will be believed. There's not a class pictured here in this film, or in Ellis's novel, only one individual who went psycho. But because there is a telling parody of an empowered class, this film, like the novel before it, failed to attract the attention it deserves. Too violent and bloody to be published, and too violent and bloody to be critically recognized in 1999. And yet perhaps the blood and the violence is as true to the mark as the class attack, only prophetic.

It's only a class thing with a loser like Jack Kelson in *American Heart*. Let's deny him individuality. Jack's not unique; he's surrounded by people like him. This is a class of Losers. People who don't have what it takes to succeed. You can hear the Bateman crowd give their views of these Losers: they have no ambition, no talent, no brains, no morals, no wisdom, no facility in amassing a fortune, no knowledge of how to spend what they have, no taste, no refinement, no competitiveness, no desire to be rich. Any time a camera focuses on a Jack Kelson world it pans and tracks widely to give us a full sense of how wretched the wretched of the Earth really are.

The camera tracks this white trash world: Nick's girlfriend, Molly, winds up as an "exotic" dancer like her mother, Bubbles; Jack's partner in crime, Rainey, enlists Nicks in his thieving and then runs out on him; Jack gets drunk, passes out in an alley, has his pants stolen by another Loser, then dances in his shorts on a street corner playing his guitar; Nick's "support group" is a bunch of kids hustling on the street corner, as many transvestites and lesbians as heterosexuals. It's your *Springer* world, your trailer park trash. You're waiting for the good-natured, philosophical cops from the TV show "Cops" to show up and arrest them all for their own good.

Forget all that nonsense. Bridges's performance, which is at the heart of the film and the center of the camera's focus, brings that surround out of stereotype and makes us care for Jack, makes us understand or try to understand where he is and how he got there. We go from stereotypic generalization to unique individualization. Jack is a type and he isn't; and by the time the film comes to its tragic ending, you can as easily say Martin Eden and Jude Fanshaw were types and not individuals. You don't mourn the death of a type; you do mourn Jack's death. Long before his death you begin to think the guy should have had more of a chance. You see, you begin to orbit within Jack's memory.

When his son, Nick, finds him washing up in a men's room at a bus terminal, Jack's first reaction is to ditch the kid. What causes him to begin to take up the role of a father is the vivid memories he has of himself at Nick's age. The flashback is in black and white: boys walking in a bleak, snowy scene two-by-two, accompanied by uniformed guards. They all look the same; they are dressed the same in black coats and watchman's caps. The camera picks out a pale, thin, expressionless face—Jack's. It's a truly haunting memory, for Jack, and for us. The last time he orbits back, the young boy is making a run for it through the snow, officers in pursuit. He's fourteen and running for his life, escaping. I thought of Blake's design that accompanies his poem, "Holy Thursday": a line of young boys, with expressionless faces, processing in line, accompanied by the Church wardens. Jack's journey through the realm of Innocence is blighted; the adult Jack, now in the realm of Experience, is two seconds away from falling apart, two inches away from Alaska, where he can breathe free air, where he can escape his past.

You can feel how Jack leans more and more on the boy, while at the same time seeing that he has to be steady and reliable so that the boy can lean on him. We don't hear the uplifting song "Lean on Me," but the booze-soaked croak of Tom Waits, with a hard-edged defiant hope, sadness, and failure saturating his voice. "You keep me straight; I keep you straight," Jack tells Nick. "People like us," Jack tells Nick, "make a lot of mistakes." By the time he says that we're not sure what people like Jack really are. Somehow there's too much tragic, sad nobility in Jack to ever fit into the "Jerry Springer Show" format. How does Bridges maintain our interest in Jack? How does he keep us from just dismissing him, or laughing at him the way we do those hapless souls who show up on Springer? Jack's not going to suddenly come through as a man with a hidden talent. You have to accept what he tells his parole officer when asked what can he do: "Can't do nothing," Jack tells him. You want to see a glimmer of Jack working his way eventually to a nice life in suburbia on Robin Wood Trail, with a new wife like Carolyn Burnham. Jack has it wrong, you think; he doesn't have to keep running; he doesn't have to run to Alaska to breathe free air. He can stay where he is and "assume personal responsibility." He can get some ambition; he can do all the things Patrick Bateman urges the homeless man to do.

Bridges withholds all those possibilities from us; what Jack is and what Jack has will keep him two weeks behind on the rent, two hundred miles from freedom, too many dollars short of making big money, with eight thousand windows still to wash, too down to pick himself back up, already too lost to make it. You can't turn him into a Harvard graduate; you can't yuppify him; you can't find in him what the liberal imagination wants to find. For me, the saddest thing is to hear Jack when he thinks he and Nick are picking themselves up, they're coming back. He's going to start a "catch a meal/bring a reel" business; he's going to sell steaks and gas; he's going to make big money soon. It's the only thing the society holds out to him: become entrepreneurial, buy stocks, tend your portfolio, and there's your freedom!

"Perpetrating cons isn't the only business," Jack tells Nick. Somewhere on the other side of where Jack and Nick live there's no thievery and there are people who are good. You know Jack believes that, but you also know that somehow you can't be as brave as Jack, as driven by a dream, as good a father, as full of heart. "People are going to tell you you're no good," Jack tells Nick as Jack lays dying on the ferry to Alaska. "Don't let them. Things are going to be different for you. You won't have to keep running." As the camera moves back and we see the outstretched body of Jack with Nick clinging to him, and the two grow smaller and Tom Waits's lugubrious song fills our ears, we're not sure where Nick is going or whether he will have to keep running. He was involved in a robbery in which his friend was killed. The police will be looking for him. It's more likely that reform school or the penitentiary in these more modern times await Nick. A life of running, his own memory orbiting back to this ferry to Alaska scene, to his father slumped on a deck chair, to his father's words: "What do you know, kid? We made it."

Time Codes:
Brooklyn Heights, Henniker, Bluefield, Irvine

April 2000

The film *Time Code*, released in April, 2000, got more pre-release chatter going than any film in a long time. When I finally saw it, I made sure I took a seat in the back so I could get a panoramic view of the screen, which was divided into quarters. Hand-held digital cameras focus on four different characters in each of those quadrants for over ninety minutes. One critic wrote that we were ready for this multiple screening because we were already a "multitasking" society. We all apparently have four windows of Netscape open all the time. Today on my bike I was just about run over by a woman who was driving an SUV while talking on a cell phone, holding a cafe latte cup *and* a cigarette. Once we get a computer flat screen on the dashboard, multitasking can really hit the highways.

There's a problem that Hollywood has that TV doesn't have: you can multitask your TV-watching with the help of a remote. A fractalized, digitalized attentiveness then can pop from one station to another at a rate of speed that would accommodate the most restless ADD. The format of *Time Code* is an attempt to connect the big screen with the new digitalized attentiveness.

Does it work? I'm a postmodernist who believes in Borgesian gardens of forking paths, where each path creates a possibly different surround within which we see and think and do. That's an awareness, not a divided screen. It doesn't even have anything to do with a TV remote or a computer mouse. Postmodernity has no plan to technologically fracture our awareness, to "super-size" our perceptions through technological means, to "super-stimulate" us beyond the stolidity of "single vision." It seems to me that this multiscreening approach has been used by TV advertisers for a very long time. The more and faster we can absorb and respond to stimuli transmitted to us by our marketing machines the faster we can buy, the more we can buy. We talk about increased communication and speedy access to information, and isn't this wonderful progress? But we're not in Wonderland; we're knee-deep in globalized consumer capitalism. It's all about "being reached," about access into our homes, our lives, our brainpans; it's all about "privatizing" and "corporatizing," and "marketing" information which becomes nothing more than a 24-7 barrage of product and service advertising.

When the last of a pre-MTV generation is dead and buried there will be no one left to bear this particular message. Access will be what shows up on your Web "search" engine; if it's not there, it doesn't exist. My "byte" here will be "overwritten."

So really, what kind of great experiment in form is the film *Time Code?* Divide a TV soap opera into four screens and what do you get? My response to *Time Code.* The narratives weren't compelling and I saw the wizard behind the multiple screens' concept. Nevertheless, my memory began to go multiple-screen during the night. These were—weirdly—culinary memories as I orbited from one screen to another. Over here in the upper left quadrant of the screen, I'm a graduate student at Prof. Ruth Temple's Friday night Brooklyn Heights salon; Angela and Wally Parkinson's dinner party in Henniker, New Hampshire, is going on in the upper right; we're at Rev. John's and Stella's Bluefield, West Virginia, home for dinner in the lower left; a Halloween party at a neighbor's house in Irvine, California, is in the lower right. I spent one whole night running a memory-held digital camera on this split screen. I had been "reached."

Sound can come from all four quadrants of the screen, but it is only audible now in the upper left quadrant.

Brooklyn Heights
Fall 1967

I wasn't at the Friday salon yet; I was in Brooklyn College sitting in Prof. Temple's graduate something-or-other seminar—it was British—looking like one of Scorcese's "goodfellas." My fellow graduate students and myself sat at four tables formed into a square. Prof. Temple sat at a table by her lonesome. She was in her fifties and dressed in a way I had never seen women dress. Maybe I had seen it on the screen, but not in the same room with me. It was always interesting to see how she would show up for these once-a-week evening seminars. Dick Bratter told me that Prof. Temple was descended from Polish aristocracy and that she owned a huge brownstone in Brooklyn Heights and would invite students she thought especially promising to her home for her Friday salon.

Everything about her impressed me; she was what civilization and read-ing the best that has been thought and written and said led up to.

Everyone else in that class annoyed me. They fell into the three clas-sic categories. The Spinmeisters dressed and talked the part but were just con artists. Sometime in the early 1980s this group would take their spin to the corporate world, but now in the mid 1960s they were spinning the university as if bottom-line profits were here and not "out there." The Anal Retentives were students who thought organizing their notes would put ideas in their heads. They would be equally successful orga-nizing a blood drive or a nuclear attack. They gave you back word for word what you put out. The Deeply Intuitives were just too hip for the house. They understood art and literature genetically, biochemically; they had the cultural *memes* to see and feel what the rest of us slobs had to think about. The class was made up of both purebreds and hybrids; one of the more common hybrids was the Intuitive who was also a Spin-meister. The pure Intuitive didn't speak, or spoke only in creative rushes.

I was really representative of the type you found in graduate school back then: the Running Away From type. We only wandered toward the class we happened to be in. Most here were running from the draft. I was already classified "temporarily deferred for medical reasons" and had been told Uncle Sam would never again knock at my door, but I was running from a brief stint working for the Department of Health, Edu-cation, and Welfare. You look into the face of federal bureaucracy at too early an age and you have nightmares the rest of your life. Am I a liber-tarian railing against just the Feds? No, I was also running from the cor-porate sector. I had been bouncing around Manhattan from job inter-view to job interview, from one employment agency to another, from one firm handshake to another. I wasn't getting better at it; I wasn't improving my skills. In short, I wasn't wearing the right suit and my Brooklyn inflections hung in the air. I was developing an edge so sharp that I wound up doing angry, ranting interviews. They were firing me before I was hired. I retreated to graduate school and wandered into a life of reading novels, and finally into Temple's class. I wasn't Friday night salon material, but I was here nevertheless. I guess I was also the Street Guy from the different neighborhood with the ethnic name, which then was just foreign because the whole fanfare about the glories of eth-nicity had not yet kicked in.

Temple apparently wasn't rebuffed by my style, nor did she join in the chorus of sotto voce witticisms heard whenever I felt compelled to show my disdain and criticism. "You're a substratum thinker," she once told me. "She means a subway thinker, where it's all hollow ground," one of the class frauds told me later. "Whatever," as the veneer thinkers would be prone to say in the next century. I got the invite, though, to a Friday salon at Temple's. I was nervous all week. My partner-in-crime from the Neighborhood, Mister Rogers, doesn't understand why our usual Friday protocols are being interrupted. "You got a chance with this lady professor?" he wants to know. I look at him. I hadn't thought of it but, yeah, there's definitely something sexual going on here. Not the kind of sexual you run into at the Rex Bar and Grill at about two in the morning, but something. I'm in my very early twenties and she's maybe early fifties. If she's got sex appeal, I'm missing it.

Friday night I climb those brownstone steps and ring the bell. She answers the door, and I see right off that she's more alluring than in the classroom. There's a line of bright red lipstick and her straight hair is pulled back tight, as usual, but now there's some kind of flowered band as a ponytail holder. Best of all, when she sees me standing there, she registers the vibe that I get when I feel a connection is being made. Call it a blush, because she immediately lowers her face and puts a hand out. I think I'm supposed to take it, but she escapes my hand suddenly and points somewhere: "You can put your coat up here." She goes up the stairs and I wander into a room on the right. I don't see any coats in this room; I've never seen a room like this one. A piano room? A library? A sitting room? Didn't I see Joan Crawford in this room in some movie? I rush up the stairs after her; she's still talking as if I've been behind her all the time. I don't know if she's hip to my excursion—she doesn't let on. When we reach the top of the stairs, she passes a small room in which I now see coats hung up. I add my coat, go back into the hall, pass a small pantry with a sink. She's heading up another flight. We get to a large parlor where about a dozen or so people are sitting and talking. Temple points to a divan where there are a couple of people from my class already seated. I have a choice of either sitting on the edge of the thing or lifting my feet off the floor and sitting against the back. I go for one, feel awkward and stupid, and then go for the other, which is worse because I feel like I'm reclining and my pants legs are pulled up exposing my less-than-clean boots. Meanwhile Temple is comfortably ensconced next to a younger woman, who is also comfortably ensconced. This is the salon guest. She's writing a biography of Dorothy Richardson and begins to talk about the project. I'm having BVDs-riding-up-my-ass problems. I reach forward, lose leverage, fall back, and turn it all into a deft move for a book lying on a table in front of the divan. It's Temple's newest book. I leaf through it pretending to read. The chatter goes on; everyone seems to be fitting in nicely at this Friday literary salon. I was the substratum.

Listen in: A Spinmeister named Cleveland is dismissing Richardson as a worthy subject of a biography to the biography lady's face, to which an Anal Retentive, reclined next to me, disagrees. For her, the hard work of capturing Richardson's life is hard precisely because Richardson's work is profound. I turn and size up the student, who is really a startling beauty, the only one in this salon for sure. Her name is Arlene and she's got a long-stemmed red rose lying in her lap. A salon door prize perhaps? There's a mirror with an ornate frame behind us, above the divan, and the various lights from all the floor lamps in the room are reflected there and surround her like an aura around a goddess. I decide I came for her.

"I think biographers assume that genius is triggered by psychic dis-functioning," a Deeply Intuitive named Robert booms out from across the room. He has dirty, shoulder-length hair, and is dressed all in black. His vade mecum loose-leaf collection of his own brilliant poetry is, as always, on his lap. The difference between his sartorial bent for blackness and my own is the difference between the poet's black and the gangster's black, between the Beat and the Bad. Temple asks a guy named Randolph whether he's read any of Richardson's work and what does he think of it? "I prefer Virginia Woolf," Randy answers. "But it comes down to what was written and by whom and when, and whether what was writ-ten about them can be trusted. I personally think women authors of the twentieth century have earned their biographers, but who's to say if the age is worthy of its subject or the biographer of his or her pay or whether Richardson intentionally misled everyone concerned and what evidence of that sort of disingenuousness could there possibly be?"

Randolph was going to spin himself into academic glory; of that much I was sure. That much spin plus schmooze would ensnare tenure. I therefore made another camouflaging move, wrestled with my shorts, and edged a little closer to Aphrodite, my eyes meeting hers. She was struggling to structure Randolph's spin and find that appropriate spot in her memory banks for each and every revelation.

"What evidence can there be of horseshite?" I whispered to her.

She gave me a look that almost withered the rose on her lap.

Ah, beautiful young women and beautiful roses. . . . This is what, in a dying moment, there is left to rave about.

The scene goes on: The Spinmeisters spin; the Deeply Intuitives "evoke"; the Anal Retentives note and highlight. And I'm just as com-pelled to be "outside the frame." There's not a glob of "free to choose" in the room.

Timeless. Until Temple stands up and announces that there are refreshments in the next room.

She walks out in a way that I have only seen women on the screen walk out of a room. It's Scarlet O'Hara sweeping out of a room; it's Loretta Young sweeping into a room.

Needless to say, I'm not in enough control of my table manners to eat anything. Temple comes over to me and asks me why I'm not partaking. She coaxes me toward a line of cakes and cookies, sandwiches (probably cucumber), tea and coffee. It all smells good, but I hold my ground and don't eat. I want to, but I don't. It seems like I want to, but it is too hard to reach out. The table is too difficult to reach from where I am, and I can't move.

My memory here is like Bernstein's in *Citizen Kane*. You recall when Bernstein is asked to talk about Kane, about anything he remembers, and he tells that odd story about seeing a woman in a white dress on a ferry for just a brief moment. He never speaks to her and never sees her again, but not a month goes by in his life that he doesn't recall her standing there on the ferry. A month doesn't go by that I don't look down and see that buffet table at Prof. Temple's.

Sound diminishes and picks up on the upper right quadrant of the screen.

Henniker, New Hampshire
1974

In the early 1970s I was living in Henniker, the only Henniker on Earth: New Hampshire. You took this kind of trip: Hopkinton, Henniker, Hillsboro, Hell. I'm making up the town of Hell. Hell was just where I lived right after the college I was teaching at failed to pay us one day in the autumn, not too far from peak foliage season. Elaine and I and one-year-old Amelia were living on Colby Hill Road, right across from the Colby Hill Inn and right next door to Mrs. Wormhoe's open-by-appointment-only antique shop, where you could get a cloudy green bottle with a crooked seam for just about what we paid in rent to the college each month: one hundred dollars.

It was the fall of 1974, and Yuppies, Agents of Change, dot-com millionaires, Market Players, Symbolic Analysts, Role Models and Mentors, Winners and Losers, Celebrities, Martha and Oprah were then either unknown or inconceivable. Tough Love, Upscale Cataloguing, Co-dependency, Political Correctness, cell phones, SUVs, MTV, Walkmans and Palm Pilots, PCs, mouses and remotes, Web surfing and Reaganism were still floating signifiers or had not yet been invented. If you could at any moment describe what was inconceivable at that moment, you would have described most of what I've just listed. But of course you can't; you can only do it after the fact. Back then you had a lot that is almost inconceivable now to those born around Reagan's time. We still had a low-profile high-consuming class; the folks who stayed at the pricey Colby Hill Inn were still in the same category as Dagwood's boss and "Green Acres'" Eddie Albert and ZaZa Gabor: they had money but they weren't in your face about it. They didn't want you to show them the money and they didn't want to show you their money; they didn't catalogue or wear designer labels or sport two-hundred-buck cross trainers or forty-thousand-dollar Rolexes. Mrs. Gilbert who owned the inn was a patrician, but she wasn't a role model of the land; she was just an eccentric with a pissy attitude. It would take Reagan to make her and her kind the paragon of American success, the fulfillment of the American Dream because they had money, toys, and stocks. It was a time when working-class heroes were still celebrated and celebrities were pitied for their screwed-up lives, a time *before* "trickle down" economics would decimate the middle class and offer up the underclass as entertainment for the "gated communities."

ை

We had a dinner invitation to Angela and Wally Parkinson's, and since Frank Tuohy and Dennis Mulroney were visiting us from Dublin, they got invited too. The college was split down the middle over what the administration called a "temporary cash flow problem," but it wound up putting the college in the hands of the Bank of New England. The bank had stepped in and for fiscal reasons was trying to "downsize personnel" by about 50 percent. They had already terminated almost everyone without either tenure or some sort of contract, which meant almost all of maintenance, most of the clerical employees, and all the temporaries and part-timers had gone. Half of the people I knew were scrambling to join the ranks of the Saved—the administrators who promised to save them if they didn't join in forming a union—and the other half were scrambling to get enough people recruited into a union so we could have an official National Labor Relations Board (NLRB) election. Dean Baffle had just that week called me into his office to ask me to see Reason: which meant stop talking union and start supporting him and the administration. He had reminded me that I had a wife and a newborn daughter. I in turn reminded him that I had a wife and a newborn daughter.

I was with Frank and Mulroney that night and had Baffle's words like a melody in my mind. "It's a threat is what the fook it is," Frank told me.

"You answer a threat with one of yer own," Mulroney whispered, leaning into me. "Yer fooken mafia ain't ya? Don't tell me you ain't. All ye fooken Sicilians is mafia. Fooken put a horse's head in his sheets. That'll get'em to back the fook off."

"Where's the food?" Frank said, as we straightened ourselves out in the hallway of Wally and Angela's New England late-eighteenth-century, white-with-black-shutters, saltbox home.

"Mr. Colcannon is here," Angela told me.

"Who?"

"The AFL-CIO rep.," Wally said. "He's staying with us over the weekend."

Colcannon was in a small parlor where a fire was roaring in the fireplace. He looked like Walter's drinking buddy: big gut with a red face, except he didn't have Walter's crown of snow-white hair. He had a kind of Brylcreem part-on-one-side hairstyle that looked like a cap on his head.

I immediately threw some hypotheticals at him in regard to the scary future of our faculty winning an NLRB election. To each hypothetical, Colcannon responded with "Let's hope they don't think of that." To each of my fears, he responded with, "We'll get the Feds on 'em."

Now the Duck and Dr. Hick had arrived, the dynamic duo that I had teamed up with the previous January term in a program called "Death and Dying: The Psychology, the Literature, the Autopsy." I hadn't known what I was getting into. The guy I called the Duck was a psychologist; he was very specially suited to this career choice because he had absolutely no capacity to make normal human contact. He answered questions no one raised; he returned questions like "how's it going?" with a blank stare; he laughed when he was behind the wheel; he called everyone "Dr. Freud" and got a little color in his face when he was around dead bodies, which was part of what we did in this very macabre January term program. He seemed to come alive every time we attended an autopsy, and we attended a lot of autopsies. The Duck looked very ordinary: full tweeds, brown hair, tortoise-shell glasses, wooly tie. But Dr. Hick was the real eyeful: he was very tall, bone thin, and had the closest thing to a Death's Head at the end of his neck that I've ever seen. He was a cadaverous grey, lipless, fleshless, and, like the Duck, almost voiceless. He was a sculptor and did things in granite (which was plentiful in New Hampshire), and the color suited him. Everything he did turned out looking like him, or some part of him: those are his legs in that piece; those are his eyes; that's his whole head; that's his hand. Wally had commissioned him to do a sculpture for Angela for their twenty-fifth wedding anniversary. The subject was supposed to be something to do with Angela's passion: the piano. Regardless, they would be getting some part of Dr. Hick's anatomy entitled *The*

Piano. As soon as they arrived they hung back as far from the fire as they could and stood there like vultures shadowing the living.

"What's dis here now on the boofay table?" Mulroney asked, peering at the buffet table.

He put one dish down and pointed to an even larger dish.

"Don't ask me," I said, looking at it. "Probably a casserole. Everything served in New England is a casserole."

Wally bushwhacked us.

"Angie's looking for you," he told me.

As I left I heard Wally tell Mulroney, "That's a casserole."

I found Angela, but new guests had just come in.

"Oh, welcome! Welcome!" Angela suddenly cried out and ran to meet her new arrivals.

"Are we late?" Bunny Pace said, as if he feared they weren't late enough.

"You look so domestique!" Anne Pace, his wife said, bussing Angela in the French style.

When Angela hurried off with their coats, I stood there by the sink looking at Bunny and Anne. He was the heartthrob of every faculty wife, the dream romance of every coed, the quintessential New England patrician prof., six feet of the really right stuff, but appropriately casual and accessible to the common man—and even more accessible to the common man's wife. Everyone envied the way he mixed his Brooks Brothers with his L. L. Bean, his Harvard "a's" with his smirks and condescending syllabics, his *Yankee Magazine* with his family genealogy. The Cabots only spoke to the Lodges and the Lodges only spoke to God, but Bunny *was* God. How wonderfully disarming was the nickname "Bunny." It incited you over and over again to contemplate his real moniker: Montford Q. R. Pace. The "Q. R." stood for "Qualified Retard," I believe.

"It's Jeremiah, isn't it?" he now said to me—as he had every time I had met him for the last three years, except every time he gave me a different name.

"No, I've decided I want to be called Bunny, too," I said, but he was already speaking in low tones to Anne. The art of the cut made him a gifted artist.

We were all politely circumnavigating the buffet table in search of the edible.

"This is baked scrod," Martha, an artist and lesbian, was explaining to Greta, her lover and a filmmaker, who was pointing her camera at the baked scrod.

"What, dear?" Angela said. "No, that's the noodle and cheese casserole."

"And how do you make that, Angela?" Greta asked from behind the camera.

"Well . . ."

"Don't look at me," Martha told Angela. "Look directly into the camera."

"You boil water," Angela said. "You throw the noodles in, and when it's cooked you put it in an oven pan and squirt the cheese mixture on top . . ."

"What kind of cheese?"

"It comes in a little bag in the box, dear."

"What's this?" Martha said, pointing to a casserole.

"That's a tuna casserole, dear."

"Tell the camera."

"That's a tuna casserole."

"What's that on the top? The white stuff."

"That's a sour cream and marshmallow topping."

"Do you squirt that out of a little bag?"

"No, those are fresh marshmallows."

"Is there such a thing as fresh sour cream?"

"I don't know . . ."

"Tell the camera."

"I don't know if sour cream can go sour, dear," Angela admitted. "But then again, it is true that it's impossible for it to be fresh. If it's already sour, I mean."

"It can," Prof. Much, a three-hundred-and-fifty-pound colleague, said. "It can spoil if not kept at the right temperature which is around thirty-five to forty degrees."

Greta focused the camera on Much, who was standing on the other side of the buffet table holding a plate with grapes and cheese on it in one upraised hand.

"What's that?" Martha asked Much, pointing to a casserole.

"I can't be sure by the looks. I'd have to taste it."

The camera followed Much's free hand as it reached out and ladled some of the casserole onto his plate. It followed the fork to his lips.

"I believe it's mutton," he announced.

"What's mutton?"

"An old lamb," Much said.

"Edward brought that," Angela said, referring to the Duck. "I don't serve mutton."

Everyone looked over at the Duck, who was now in the corner of the dining room. Dr. Hick was bent over the table doing something with two knives to one of the casseroles.

The camera focused on the Duck, who stared at it blankly but said nothing.

"How did you make that mutton dish, Edward?" Martha asked him. No response.

"Where can you buy old lamb around here?" Martha asked.

"Edward doesn't cook," Dr. Hick told us, standing up straight and leaving off whatever he was doing to a casserole. "He doesn't shop either. The mutton was a gift from a farmer."

"Does he eat?" Frank, who was standing next to Damn's date, asked.

"This isn't mutton," Much now said. "It's mock mutton. These mutton pieces are lamb-flavored dog biscuits. The gravy fooled me."

"Dije eat any?" Frank asked the coed whose name was Jane, and who was about nineteen years old—about half the age of the administrator, Peter Damn, who had brought her. She had the long straight blonde hair that attracted Frank like flies to shite.

"What did you say?" Jane replied, giggling.

"Nobody has said anything about my chicken," Angela cried out in mock accusation.

"Where is it?" Martha said while Greta's camera stayed focused on the Duck, who remained mute and motionless.

"Right here," Angela said pointing to a large casserole in the middle of the table.

Much helped himself to some and did a taste test.

"Chicken breast with a couple of cans of onion soup thrown on top and baked at too high a heat."

"How do you know that?"

"The chicken is dried out. It's been cooked at about four hundred degrees for an hour. It needed a quick saute on both sides and fifteen minutes of covered cooking."

"How does a proctologist know so much about cooking?" Angela said angrily.

"I'm not a proctologist. I teach Faulkner," Much said, indignantly.

"Well, that's my chicken a la onion soup casserole," Angela told us. "And numerous people have asked me for the recipe."

"There's no recipe involved," Much insisted. "What's needed is a can opener."

"Since when has it become tactful to insult one's hostess?" Bunny Pace said.

"Let me guess," Mulroney said, putting a finger to his nose. "When she serves her guests dog food?"

"Who is this man?" Anne said, looking at me.

"A guest of a guest," Angela said, looking at me.

"He's a proctologist," I said. "I told him there'd be an asshole here."

"Hey!" Damn yelled. "You're giving Jane a wrong impression of faculty."

"She seems overly impressed with you, Peter," Anne Pace said.

"Okay," Martha said. "We're trying to film the food scene. Okay? What's this?" she asked pointing to a casserole.

⌒⌒

I went in search of Colcannon, our union representative sent all the way from Boston.

"Now here's a man who'll stand and fight," Walter said, pouring me some sherry. I took it and sipped it. The sweet not the dry kind. Even worse.

"What are our chances of winning?" I asked Colcannon.

"You got the numbers," Colcannon said. "You'll win the NLRB. Bargaining is something else. It ain't just numbers. It's knowing what the fuck you're doing. And that takes experience."

"What do we bargain for first?"

"You gotta get a round table," Colcannon said. "A round table equalizes the power structure. Otherwise, you go in there with your bosses and already you're defeated."

"Second thing? After we get a round table."

"You need the right chairs."

"The right chairs?"

"You need the kind of chairs that gives your side the advantage."

"And they are?"

"Okay. I know one of your deans has a bad case of hemorrhoids. So you opt for hard seat chairs."

"And then?"

"Whether you're going to break to go eat or have it sent in."

"After that?"

"Whether anybody can answer phone calls during the meeting."

"After that?"

"Everybody wears suits and ties or nobody does."

"Next?"

"Ice in the water or no ice."

"Why is that important? And what do we want? Ice or no ice?"

"You don't care. You're just doing this to aggravate 'em. Get them used to bargaining over every fucking thing. You wear them down. You get them distracted. You get them dizzy. Should windows be opened or closed? How high should the thermostat be? How long can somebody talk? Should somebody be stopped from telling a joke?"

"We tell jokes?"

"Whenever they get serious, you tell a joke. Throws 'em off. Believe me."

"Tell him what you told me about our deficits," Walter said to Colcannon.

"You got four major deficits," Colcannon said, holding up five fingers. "First, your union president."

"Dr. Fleishmann?" I said, referring to a well-published tenured sociologist. "He's a well-published tenured sociologist."

"He's got his head where the sun don't shine," Colcannon said, shaking his head. "When the point is whether the table is round or square, he's thinking about something else."

"And that's bad?"

"There's no thinking involved. They say square you say round. Square, round. Square, round. Round, round, round, round, round, round . . ."

"Okay."

"Second, your vice-president."

"Jimbo?" I said, referring to our most experienced political strategist and organizer.

"Useless."

"But he thinks politically. He's our most experienced political strategist and organizer."

"A good political strategist thinks about tables. This guy thinks about a workers' revolution."

"And the treasurer is our third deficit?"

Colcannon nodded.

"Flying. Never touched ground."

"But he teaches logic."

"The only logic here is to win," Colcannon said. "An 'If P then Q' guy doesn't know that kind of logic."

"And I guess I'm useless too?"

"You the secretary?"

I nodded.

"You fighting for justice?"

I nodded.

"Head is up your ass," Colcannon told me. "Nothing personal. You should be fighting for a round table."

"So how do we get beyond our deficits?" Walter said, standing up to pour me some more sherry.

"Nobody talks unless I told them what to say," Colcannon said. "Nobody says anything that's not in the script. Everybody memorizes

the script. No free-lance thinking, no gratuitous comments, nothing outside the script. Something comes up not in the script, I call for a break."

I knocked back a glass of Wally's special sherry.

"When I say 'I think the Feds might be interested in this,' everybody gets up together and walks out the door. When I say 'I can see
you don't want to bargain in good faith,' everybody gets up together
and walks out the door. When I say 'You have unfair negotiating
power,' everybody gets up together and walks out the door. When I
say. . . ."

I got up and walked out of the barn. I made my way back into the
house where everyone had abandoned the buffet table and the array of
casseroles and were now seated in what Angela called the "big parlor."
Greta and Martha were going around filming people in their little
groupings. I was surprised to see Frank sitting in a window seat next to
Anne Pace.

"I refuse to live in fear," Anne was saying.

"How do you do that?" Frank asked.

"I just look in the mirror and say 'Anne, you can handle any situation if you just realize your natural superiority.' And then I look around
at other people whom I'm not sure might or might not harm me in some
way and think 'These people are losers and losers can't hurt winners.'
It's as simple as that."

"What's that? The power of positive superiority?"

"It's in the blood is what it is," Mulroney said to me and winked.

"It don't help to think you've got the winning hand when all you're
holding is losers," Frank said.

"Could you repeat that for the camera?" Greta said.

I hadn't realized she was behind us filming.

"Let's say I got something somebody wants," Frank said. "Can I
keep them from getting it? All the time? What do I need to keep what
I've got? How can I sleep at night and still keep what I've got?"

"How do you do that?" Anne said, intrigued as much by Frank's
profane Irish accent as what he was saying, I suspected.

"I carry dis little baby," Frank said, reaching down to his ankle,
pulling up his pants leg and taking a nickel-plated .22-caliber pistol out
of an ankle holster.

Greta zoomed in on it. Anne stared at it and Frank held it out to her.

"Take it. Feel it."

Hesitantly she did so.

"With that you're safe within fifteen yards," Frank said.

"What if you have fears that extend beyond fifteen yards?" Anne
said in a low voice, her pseudo-Harvard accent suddenly gone.

"Then you gotta use this," Mulroney said, reaching behind his back and pulling out a .38 two-incher. "This will give you the kind of fire power dats made the IRA what it tis."

Greta's camera came in tight.

Sound diminishes and picks up on the lower left quadrant of the screen.

Oxley Holl'r
Spring 1977

Worlds collided: Bensonhurst and southern Appalachia, Rev. John and myself. A cultural divide. A postmodern clash of narratives? Mostly a culinary clash: southern Italian and southern black. We went at each other in our own inimitable cultural styles over and over again. Besides not eating anything the color of his own skin, the Reverend would not taste wine. He preferred Kool-Aid, and the man could drink Kool-Aid. In fact, it was his contribution to the meal to mix up a gallon of Kool-Aid, of which he drank the most. We could go on for hours arguing over "greens"—how to cook them, and how to eat them.

"You stack them collards like a deck of cards," John said. "Then you cut them neat, put some water in a pan, throw them collards in, cover them up, then get you some fatback or bacon drippings, country ham, and get it all working in there. You cook 'em slow and easy like that for a couple of hours and then brother, you got yourself something. You like 'em hot you throw in some of them hot peppers."

My version was to saute garlic in olive oil, introduce the collards, add a wine glass of water, and cover until the collards were soft, in about fifteen minutes. It did not go down well with the Reverend. I don't think he had ever heard of either garlic or olive oil.

"You got to get beyond them fences in your head, brother," John would tell me, speaking about my limited eating habits. Meanwhile, he ate from a menu of three items: country ham, sweet potatoes and collards. He'd eat pork chops, sweet potatoes, and collards, or fried chicken, sweet potatoes, and collards. The parts of the chicken not fried went into the chicken and dumplings.

After Elaine and I had dinner that first night at Stella's and John's, Rev. John's all-woman-choir came over for rehearsal and we all just about fit into the living room. Stella played an upright piano in the corner and folding chairs were set up in two rows for the choir. John stood in the middle of the room and conducted. Elaine, Amelia, and I sat in the overstuffed chair, pushed to one side of the room. When John cued

Stella and she started to play, and then that choir began to sing, it felt like a tidal wave of sound had flooded the room. It was magnificent, thrilling, rock and roll. Cut out the story of God and salvation, of singing to the lord, and mark the rhythm, mark the beat. They were rocking. A woman with a flat square face of the most wonderful ruddy brown stood up when John pointed at her and sang solo. She sang like her voice was on angel wings. It was the most powerful voice I had ever heard. In a small living room. She sang her heart out. When she sat down and the whole choir picked up on the rolling thunder of supreme testifying, I wondered why nothing had been so real to me before. Later, when I told John how much I had been swept away by that woman's voice, he said to me, "Brother, that's good, but I had better. I had me a woman once sang befo' the president of the United States and she had a voice on her ain't nobody ever heard."

Then that choir really got to rolling. John put a tambourine in Elaine's hand and said, "You go it, gal." Stella played the most soulful hymn on the piano and then she came in with her voice. It was the highest, sweetest, most crystal light and clear voice I had ever heard. Stella had the widest smile, the most compelling twinkle in her eyes, the kind of sweetness overall that comes back to me after all these years and makes me feel good. I don't know if I ever did anything of its equal for her.

I did give her back the managerial position she had had once I became the acting director of a library at which we were both working, but that wasn't hard. Just a little backtracking revealed that blacks had been knocked out of the higher ranks once the college had integrated. A slow but steady replacement of blacks with whites in the higher-paying positions had left Stella in a clerical post at the time I had assumed the directorship.

Mine was a profane directorship of that library, but still I think it was a slight improvement over the previous regime. My predecessor, the good ol' boy Billy Squat Squires, had hired me to lock up the place and flush the toilets. When I first met him, he had on what passed for proper attire in the 1970s in southern Appalachia for hot young management types on the way up: a Kmart blue-light-special polyester suit with wide cardboard-like lapels and bell bottoms. The suit was brown and white and he had on a pair of black plastic shoes with the extra-high heel that was so popular then.

"This here is Peggy Sue," Billy Squat said, introducing me to Peggy Sue, the homecoming queen and Miss Peach Pie of that year.

"I'm pleased to meet you," Peggy Sue said, standing up from her desk and holding out a hand. She was tall and shapely, with blonde curly hair and a Pepsodent smile. Where my "please" sounded like "pliz," hers sounded like "pa-leezed"; "meet" didn't sound like "meat" but "mate." She stood there dripping southern babe-ishness, queen of all the hillbilly hearts from miles around, shades of Elly May on "Beverly Hillbillies." In appearance. I later found out that beneath that sweet appearance was a slight intolerance toward "coloreds." When she became my secretary and I began to call upon her secretarial talents, I also discovered she typed with two index fingers at about ten words a minute with ten spelling errors. Let me do a dictation scene with her:

I call her into my closet-sized office. (I had turned Billy Squat Squire's office into the break room and the weekend movie theater.)

"To Marybelle Loadage, Presidential Assistant," I said, putting one of my boots up on the corner of the desk. Peggy Sue crossed her legs, pad on her lap, pencil in hand, and smiled at me. She exuded lusciousness.

"I understand what you're telling me about displaying the necessary tact and patience, but since my budget has already been slashed without anyone consulting me I don't see how anything but a quick and jarring response, like a blow from the champ to the chin, is going to get me you or the president's attention. There's too much at stake for me to roll over and play dead on this one. While I'm acting director, I'll act."

"Let me see it when you get it typed up."

Here's what she handed me about four hours later:

> To Marybelle Loadage, Presidential Assistant
> I understand that you are telling me about tack and pay cents. But since my buzzard slashed without anyone consulting me a quick and jar response. Like a bulb with a grin is going to meet with you and the president's attention. There is too much steak to roll and play dead with on this one. I am Yak Zing, The Director.

She had been Billy Squat's personal window dressing. I understood those entrepreneurial imperatives. My Ph.D. originally got me hired as public window dressing. So both Peggy Sue and I were where we were because we had a place in Billy Squat's climb to power.

Squat was a real "piece of work," as they say; you could have taken him apart and found all the wiring that would make a Gordon Gekko or Michael Milken in the 1980s or a Rupert Murdoch or Bill Gates in the 1990s. Only the play of Chance kept him from their league. He had the soul of a Yuppie before there were Yuppies, of a junk bond salesman before there were junk bonds; he could push product like a used car salesman; he was making cold calls down there in southern West

Virginia before I ever got a phone line down into Oxley Hollow; he was
like a hot, young Wall Street broker on the make; he played nothing but
hard ball on the job, pursued his self-interest like a basset on a scent;
he was plastic, he was polyester, he was fast food, he was slash and
burn, he was "show me the money" and fuck the other guy; he was sexually harassing in the workplace before anybody ever heard about sexual harassment, he used the line "Is that a pubic hair in this coke?" on
Peggy Sue before Clarence Thomas used it on Anita Hill; he had the
Dow Jones closings where his heart should have been. He believed in a
diversified stock portfolio instead of Jesus Christ, Buddha, Allah, or
Krishna. In short, self-interest and greed had materialized. He was the
future of the country. All that was needed was a president of that
kind—and in 1980 we all found him.

And in 2000 the same creed and greed that had given us Reagan
brought George W. Bush to the gate.

*Sound diminishes and picks up on the lower right quadrant of
the screen.*

Irvine, California
1981

A week or so before Halloween I had had a bike accident: concus-
sion, broken fingers, lacerations on hand, wrist, arm, and face, and a
cut that required stitches on my right ear. A head bandage keeps the ear
packaged; a sling keeps my hand rigid. It's a costume party at a neighbor's house. Elaine knows the neighborhood moms, I don't. My neighbors across the street gleam in the sun; the husband comes out in the
morning with a coffee mug, and waves to me as he gets in his Mercedes.
I roll my bike out of the garage and wave back. It's 1981. Ronny is in
the White House. He's just proposed cutting taxes for the rich and cutting the size of the bureaucracy, and will soon force the airline con-
trollers back to work, thus announcing to the world that workers'
unions will no longer be allowed to get in the way of corporate
progress. A little while later a stunning, tall blonde will come out of the
house and get into a Jaguar and go off on a shopping spree. The daughter, a younger version of the mother and a past Miss Orange County, is
off to campus in her foreign sports car. The son drives what looks like
a dune buggy, but I think it's a customized Jeep with a roll bar and an
extra-high-volume radio. He has tousled blonde hair and a shell neck-
lace. Is there a surfboard affixed to the back seat? Do bears shite in the
woods? On some weekends an RV about the length of my house is

parked across the street, trail bikes attached to front and back, antennae spouting from the rooftop. This is the weekend-get-away vehicle. In the evenings, husband and wife make an appearance, martini glasses in hand. They wave. Elaine and I wave back. Our neighbors. Nameless, but they do gleam in the sun.

We live in the only rental house in the neighborhood; no one is happy that this house was for rent and not for sale, but I'm "at the university" so my riding a bike to campus becomes an eccentric thing, as does my owning a Toyota Corolla. But it's a brand new one. We're renting the house from one of the first Yuppie couples in the United States. They've got only two or three years to make their first million before they're thirty and they have decided that buying and renting houses in "good neighborhoods" is their quickest path to that million. I'm shown the lawn-watering system, which handles to twist with this, the proper tool. (Impressive hydraulics.) The lawns have to be watered every night when the sun goes down. So I religiously make the circuit of the property with the proper tool and turn on the spigots. Water showers are arranged so that no square inch of grass is left unwatered. Years later I learn that the southern Californians have their eye on Lake Michigan. They want a siphoning system from Michigan to my lawns. Interestingly, when I drive around the Chicano neighborhoods in Costa Mesa and Santa Ana, I don't see lawns but cactus-filled front yards. Nothing to mow; nothing to water. These people clearly don't know how to consume. Because I agree to mow and water my own lawn there's a reduction in our rent. I don't cut and trim enough or water enough so the owner, the Yuppie Kid, takes on these tasks himself. Our neighbors to the right and left of us do not ever appear. For two years I never see them. They leave very early in the morning and return after dark. The neat little buzz code "24-7" means nothing here in 1981, but my right and left neighbors are on a "24-7" work schedule. You must assume that they want to be MULTImillionaires before they're thirty.

We have been given the keys to four pools in this gated community, and Elaine and my daughters take full advantage of them. What is the price of being able to swim in any one of four private outdoor pools with outdoor showers? Your soul.

My costume tonight is my head bandage and arm sling; I'm a patient. Elaine finds a white lab coat and a stethoscope and she is— voila!—my doctor. The house is built around an atrium, an open court filled with well-tended flora. Rooms sink within rooms; you are always going down one or two steps to another level of spacious room, filled with chattering, cocktail-drinking, costumed guests. I know no one, except of course my doctor, my wife. Oh, pardon me—my partner. Here we say "partner." To say "my wife" is to assert patriarchal possession of woman as chattel. I know only my "partner," so I can reach the buffet table without running into someone I have to play catch-up with. I pan the table: everything is "minimized." In the future Microsoft's Windows will have us all "minimizing" text and images; here the food has been "minimized." Not that there isn't a great assortment, a plentitude that impresses, a proliferation of edibles that mark our distinctiveness as top-of-the-line consumers. I can dip chips in salsa or in guacamole; I can kick it up a notch and dip chips in faux crab salad or spike boiled shrimp on toothpicks; I can ladle tiny Swedish meatballs into my dish or run Brie on a cracker; I can spear any number of pigs in a blanket, run a side of coleslaw or five bean salad in my dish; I can fork shaved ham and roast beef on tiny buns; I can serve myself a slice of quiche Lorraine; I can go totally "Oriental" with the tiniest egg rolls and fried dumplings or Italian with miniature pizzas with pineapple toppings. I move toward the end of the table where the desserts are laid out. These have been "maximized" and "Halloweenized." Cakes and cupcakes have orange and black icing. I am busy eating and staring into the face of a huge jack o'lantern that is the centerpiece of the table. There's a lecherous smile cut into the pumpkin and he's winking. I'm thinking about this when a woman whom I'm sure is my neighbor from across the street tells me, "It's too bewitching." I mumble something, my mouth full. I don't know what's bewitching. Maybe the food. Maybe she's telling me not to eat it. Her mouth is so close to mine that I think she's going to kiss me. Her skin shines like the inside shell of an oyster. It seems stretched across her face, her cheeks, her nose, her chin like a skin on a drum. It's an ageless face, the best that money can buy.

"Your costume is bewitching," she tells me in a nasalized voice.

"It's not a costume," I tell her. "I was in an accident."

She laughs like I've said something funny and moves off to my right. I go back to eating the minimized. From across the room I can see Elaine pointing me out to a group of women. See? I'm the doctor and he's my patient. I wave with my good arm. A woman who looks like my neighbor from across the street sees me waving, waves back, and comes over to me. She has a glass the size of a goldfish bowl in her hand. When she gets close I can see that she's not my neighbor. This woman seems to be crying. Her eyes are tearing but more noticeable than that is the fact that the lower part of her face seems slightly off tilt, a wee bit slack. And I'm sure she's drooling. Now she smiles and I can see she has a top-of-the-line set of braces on. She greets me by name. She knows me. I don't recognize her, and then I do.

"You anala gone get furs EYES," she says to me.

Don't ask. I haven't a clue. I say, "Nice outfit."

"Ima a PIG Z," she says working her whole face around the effort. Just then Elaine comes over.

"Isn't Julie the best pixie you've ever seen?" she says, squeezing my arm.

Julie? Oh, the one who had cosmetic facial surgery. I think she wanted more chin and less lips. Or maybe more lips and less chin. Anyway, it was a success, except some facial nerve or other had been tweaked and the result was tearing, slobbering, and slackness. But she looked years younger was what we were supposed to tell her.

"I have to show you something," a woman's voice whispered in my ear. When I turned to my right I saw a woman who looked like my neighbor from across the street.

"Hey, Elaine, it's our neighbor, ah. . . ."

"This is Susan. The hostess. You're in her house."

"Okay," I said as Susan hooked an arm around my good arm and led me out of the room. On the way a woman who looked like my neighbor from across the street pointed to me and said, "Love your costume!"

I started to say it wasn't a costume, but we were out in the hallway now, then down two steps and into another hallway, and then down two steps and then into a room filled with comfortable-looking leather chairs and sofas, a huge desk, and photographs covering the walls. Susan wanted me to see the plaque she had been given after working in Washington as a lobbyist for twenty years, and pictures of her with every prominent Republican since Lincoln. I was riveted on a photo of her and Tricky Dick seated at a table in what looked like a nightclub. They were both smiling for the camera. I don't know why but she thought I was a lobbyist for the Irvine Ranch, a purveyor of the will of Joan Irvine to the state legislature.

"You'll find in here something important that Joan doesn't know about," she said, putting a white business envelope in my hand. I looked at it.

"Maybe you should mail it," I said, not wanting to explain that I was temporary adjunct at the university renting a house I couldn't afford. I was just here because my wife wanted to come and I was making the best of it by sampling some of the tasteless minimized articles out on the buffet table.

"It would be far better coming from you," she said, pressing the letter into my good hand. "And you know in the end it's all for Ronny."

"Oh, for Ronny?" I said. "In that case."

I shoved the envelope in my back pocket and then we both went back to the party. Looking to erase the taste of the minimized I had sampled I went in search of the boozeteria. I had a glass of Jack over ice in hand when a woman who looked like my neighbor from across the street reached out and clicked her glass with mine.

"It's really absolutely too intriguing," she said to me.

"What is?"

"Your costume."

I started to say it wasn't a costume, that I really was hurt, that I was a real casualty. But instead I said, "No, your costume is really absolutely intriguing."

She didn't hear me. She and everyone else was listening to our hostess, my friend in mutual support of Ronny Reagan, Susan, declare the winners of the costume contest.

The third runner-up was a woman who looked like my neighbor across the street except she was dressed kind of like a slut, but the Irma La Douce version. The second runner-up was a woman who definitely looked like my neighbor across the street except she was also dressed like a slut, but more contemporary.

Then it dawned on me. Most of the women in the room were dressed like hookers. Up until then I hadn't been able to figure out where costumes began and ended and real life began and ended. Hey, but that's Southern Cal for you. Every well-heeled woman in the room was destined in the next twenty years to see her wealth "supersized" like a Big Mac meal to truly obscene levels thanks to Ronny's destruction of an egalitarian democracy. Only then could an oligarchy fed by an unconstrained global capitalism and hiding behind a pale signifier—"democracy"—flourish. When it wasn't Halloween they had to play the part their wealth had created for them. But now it was Halloween and they could dress like the working girls that mostly bad times had forced their sisters in south central and east L.A. to become. Money and status, reputation and respectability, leadership and propriety, Miss Manners and Ivy League schools, Junior League and the Christian Coalition kept the women in this room *on every other day of the year* from strutting their stuff dressed like models in a Frederick's of Hollywood catalogue. In about a decade that market niche would be filled by Victoria's Secret, the slutty tackiness of the Jerry Springer crowd made respectable by virtue of price tags that put these garments beyond the reach of anyone who would testify before a Jerry Springer audience.

I was heading for a Jack refill when I heard my name and Elaine's name announced. First place: doctor and patient.

". . . because he almost makes us believe he's in pain."

I raised my good hand, surrounded by prototypic Yuppies dressed as sluts. I was ready to say I was really feeling some pain, especially in my fingers, but first prize was a dinner for two at Jack's by the Sea in Santa Monica and I figured, why protest? Nobody there wanted to think about or see real injury, real hurt. It was Halloween. We were in costume. This wasn't the way the world was. We could hide things, keep a lot of stuff out of sight. Did I know then that that attitude was going to continue right up to the millennium?

"Marvelously tacky," a woman who looked like my neighbor called out to me when Elaine and I were outside and heading for our car.

And this woman got into my neighbor's Jaguar.

New Hampshire

February 2000

John McCain has just giving George W. Bush a trouncing in the New Hampshire primary, but George W. is supposed to make a comeback in the "states that really count." He's in it "for the long haul," as he tells journalists, and he has the treasure chest to back him up. McCain, on the other hand, is running on a anti–treasure chest campaign: call it "campaign finance reform." If you take the money out of politics, we can have democratic rather than oligarchic elections once again. But McCain needs money to get his anti-money campaign "out there," by which I mean on TV. McCain's in the same predicament the country is regarding nuclear weapons: we want to break free of them but we're already in a world very much shaped by who has nuclear weapons and who doesn't. We want to break free of money's influence on politics but we're already in a world in which who has money and who doesn't shapes politics. There's no incentive to alter a good thing.

I look to Oprah Winfrey's show to bring McCain's quandary down to the personal level; she had a show recently called "Take It Off!" in which people with various psychological and ontological "crutches" were "outed" and urged to give them up. A man who had been wearing a toupee for years had agreed on an early show to "take it off," but when Oprah paid an unexpected visit to him a year later, he had the toupee on again.

Now, in this show I was watching, he was back on the show without the toupee and swore up and down that he was "free" of it. He was convinced he no longer needed it; he was emancipated. Jubilant, fat, fifty-ish and bald, he was now ready to face a "you are how you look" world. Oprah, who has over all the years she's been a celebrity, fought her own "how do I look" battles and has a personal trainer, nutritionist, cosmetologist, and clothes designer, clearly knew that we were in a "you are how you look" world. She knew that this guy's problem was that he had a *cheap* toupee on his head and she could have easily hooked him up with a top-of-the-line toupee.

If the fat and bald guy can get the world's attention, maybe he can get them to vote against—in their own lives—the vicious hold that cosmetology has on our world. But since he's facing a world already predisposed to spectacle, to the allure of image, there is little chance that the fat and bald guy's campaign to reform our predisposition to image is going to reach anyone. There's no chance this guy is going to get our attention. Not without a good toupee on his head, at least.

We've sort of internalized this valuation by hyped appearance to the point that we buy what will make us resemble the hyped appearances we see on TV, film, magazines, and advertising billboards. And it's pretty clear that at the moment when TV game shows promising to make a millionaire out of a lucky contestant are proliferating—including one where a beautiful model can marry an unseen multimillionaire on TV—we've internalized the "money equals power and why shouldn't it?" jingle. Just as we're not disposed to "take off" our beauty masks and go around thrilled because we look fat, bald and fifty, we are not disposed to get the love of money out of our lives and the promise of personal "enfranchisement" that it brings.

Campaign finance reform has never played big in this country among the bottom 80 percent because they're too busy trying to get money *into* their lives, too busy trying to position themselves so that their money can be used to get what they want, to recognize the logic in freeing a democracy from the power of money. Why take the money out when you're already out of it and want it in your life? And, of course, if we didn't have such a glaring gap between rich and poor, the problem of money influencing politics would not itself be a glaring problem.

☙❧

George "Dubya" is the latest frontman for those whose money has already influenced politics and who need to continue to influence politics. Ralph Nader refers to him as a corporation in a suit running for the presidency of the United States. Although it is common myth to believe that Washington does not really affect what counts—the free play of the global market, or, more particularly, maximization of profits—it is not hard to project legislation and presidential agendas which would cut into profits. There are a number of essential domains which the oligarchy must protect. George W., for instance, defines campaign finance reform as getting the union bosses out of politics and liberating the worker so he or she can make his or her own decisions. You have to note the optimism that the oligarchy has in regard to the way the average worker will vote; the entire underclass and working class and middle class can be reached through greed, racism, selfishness, sexism, fear, and reduced taxes. It's possible for George W. to assert that if money is a problem in politics, it's not because the Fortune 500 wield it, but rather the unions, who are barely surviving at the moment. If we can stop unions from contributing to the Democratic Party coffers, then we have no problem with money in politics. It's merely a way in which every citizen can express their political preference. It's a constitutional right, like free speech, and should not be abridged, or regulated.

Regulation of any and every aspect of business may cut directly into profits. Right now the newspapers are filled with the Alaska Airlines crash, a crash caused by the failure of the stabilizers that keep planes level. Both the Federal Aviation Administration and the National Transportation Safety Bureau have since discovered "jackscrew damage" in a number of other planes owned by other airlines and have ordered all airlines to inspect their planes for similar damage. Rumors floating around right now regarding the Alaska Airlines crash suggest that that airline failed to carry out the inspections required by federal agencies. This question comes up: Why weren't these regulatory agencies doing their job? Why weren't they following through? It's not a hard question to answer when one considers we live in "antiregulatory" times. When Bill Clinton stepped into the presidency in 1992, he inherited a probusiness counsel chaired by Dan Quayle, whose goal was to get regulatory agencies out of the way of business.

Tort reform has been a major concern of Governor George Dubya in Texas. He has done everything he can to protect corporations from being sued by private individuals. Tort reform, in this view, amounts to preventing "contingency" payment of lawyers; only those who can afford lawyers will be able to have lawyers.

It would also be hard to imagine an antitrust suit against Microsoft under a George Dubya administration. Corporate competition has monopoly as its goal, but the government steps in and prevents this plateau of winning from being reached. If it didn't, then "incentive" and "innovation," what capitalism nurtures, would be threatened. Fantastical power mergers in telecommunications, banking, finance, brokerage houses, pharmaceuticals, and insurance have already been accomplished without government interference, so the stage upon which any future governmental action would take place is already heavily weighted against the possibility of that future action taking place, or against the possibility of any success if it did take place.

Particularly destructive to an egalitarian democracy striving at all times for social justice—and who dares say we should not be this sort of democracy?—are the oligarchy's bread and circus strategies. The infra-structure of this country desperately needs recuperation: something must be done to modulate business in terms of the finite resources and capac-ities of the planet; something must be done to salvage and allow recu-peration from the devastation already done to air, water, and land, as well as preserve our planet's biodiversity; something has to be done to extend medical coverage to the growing numbers who do not have it; something must be done to make sure that social security doesn't become commissions for brokers and market players; something must be done to educate the 80 percent of the young in this country who can-not attend the private schools and the Ivy League universities to be crit-ical thinkers and not simply future Mac job employees; family farms have to be privileged and protected; natural resources, wilderness, and national parks have to be kept off the global auction block; a serious effort has to be made to redistribute wealth and to reverse the unde-served misfortunes of the victims of global capitalism's savagery. "The new conflict," Christopher Caldwell writes, "is between the high-tech economy's winners and its declasses—neither of whom yet realizes (or admits) they constitute a class. When they do, each will try to clear some breathing room for itself at the other's expense. The WTO riots are the first signs of a losers' revolt. And the winners will want the losers con-trolled" ("Election 2000: What's At Stake?: A Symposium," *The Amer-ican Spectator* [Feb. 2000], 36).

In the face of this pressing need to detour the coming clash, Repub-lican and Democratic candidates are both into a tax reduction/tax rebate spin—to varying degrees. While George Dubya, for instance, wants to put the tax surplus in the hands of the people and keep it away from the federal government (which apparently will throw it away on useless pro-grams, such as extending Headstart, getting regulatory agencies up to fully functional levels, salvaging Social Security, and extending medical coverage), John McCain sees a need for spending the surplus on shoring up Social Security, extending medical coverage, and paying down the national debt. McCain opposes a tax reform which benefits the Haves at the expense of the Have Nots. George Dubya's reasoning is Reagan-ite: give the most money back to the people most productive at the high end of the food chain and they will be our champions in the competitive global arena, their winnings will "trickle down" to the people once again in the shape of jobs. Whether those jobs will pay increased wages, or whether GM's multibillion dollar profits will somehow reach work-ers are not issues to be looked at too closely. The "trickle down" is a sort of magical, sleight of hand redistribution of the wealth, but one that most academic economists, who collect handsome consulting fees, underwrite with their scholarship and reputations. If the Feds were to step in during good times and raise by law the minimum wage, they would be interfering with the perfect synergy of "trickle down" capitalism—which brooks no interruption in the beautiful and elegant dispensation of capital arranged by capitalism itself.

The People are a less risky gamble than the federal government in the view of those who advocate "democratic capitalism" because the People have now been almost totally packaged as Consumers. The federal government, on the other hand, could wind up with an executive branch with an "agenda." "The Democratic front-runners may be Dull and Duller, but both are capable of the 'laser-like focus' on policy that Clinton only talked about. Both share a deadly earnest belief that only liberals are righteous and that conservatives spend their days hugging smokestacks and burning black churches. Without the diversions that took up so much of Clinton's energy, they would relentlessly pursue a liberal agenda" (John J. Pitney, Jr., *The American Spectator* [Feb. 2000], 40). And again, from the same symposium of conservative fears concerning the 2000 presidential election:

> It's Gore that makes 2000 a potential turning point. . . . His general election will tone down the leftism of his campaign for the nomination, but do not be deceived. He would extend and expand Bill Clinton's aggressive governing that in defiance of Congress has increased intervention—and, yes, provided lots of help—in the lives of ordinary Americans. Indeed, without Clinton's personal encumbrances and assisted by a Democratic House of Representatives, Gore has a golden opportunity to expand regulation, add spending programs, and redistribute income. (Robert D. Novak, 36)

Part of the packaging that the People have undergone in the last twenty years at commodified computer speed includes a "politics is evil" component. What this leads to is a belief that a man who has made billions running a business and has no experience with democratic politics is better able to run the government than someone with political experience. Perot ran on this nonsense in 1992 and Steve Forbes has touted his "I'm not from Washington" credentials as if there was some brilliant logic in deeming inexperience a qualification.

I don't choose my doctors or lawyers that way; nor my car mechanic, butcher, shrink, broker, or guitar teacher. When asked in a *U.S.A. Today* interview who he thought would make the best president, Bruce Willis, celebrity icon, said "you," meaning the interviewer. He would rather have any ordinary American president than a politician. I have a feeling that more people read that response than saw any of the televised presidential debates and that there was more agreement with what he said than anything yet said by any candidate. Why? Because celebrities in America are powerful market forces; everything we don't own, they have; everything we don't look like, they look like. We wannabe them. And for this reason they're a tremendous marketing tool. And we all want Mr. Smith, the ordinary but honest American, to go to Washington and clean it up—as long as it's really Harrison Ford playing Mr. Smith.

In reality, however, the Know Nothing will be eaten up, spun, and propped up in front of the cameras by the Fortune 500. If you don't know anything and have no experience, you're not capable of doing anything, which is precisely what a nongovernmental interventionist capitalism wants from a president. If you don't know anything and have no experiences to counter your present experiences, you are prey to those who are experienced and who have made politics their métier for decades.

Dubya's backers are very much aware that he must appear to be an "outsider," not a Washington politician, not anything like Clinton who had political intentions from the get-go. Ironically, Dubya's stance as just a regular guy who just happens to be a "Natural Leader" but is not a politician, just a know-nothing when it comes to "the business of politics," has thus far come across as a know-nothing, period. The reporter who questioned Dubya regarding who was the leader of this or that country was touching exactly that Achilles heel: it's good politically now not to be thought of as a politician but at the same time you want a candidate for the presidency of the United States to know what's going on politically in the world. Dubya has been perfect for the part of a candidate who doesn't know politics because in point of fact, he doesn't. This revelation should sink him, but since the country is in such a "politics is evil" spin, Dubya can respond with, "What's the difference if I don't know that stuff; I know America and I'm a leader!" and hope to get some play.

Whether it's a fortunate or unfortunate turn of events, this country is more in need of the revisionary and recuperating powers of the federal government than perhaps at any time since the War Between the States. Quite clearly, big business has no such need: "the best government is the government which governs least" was a maxim, I think, based on a hope that the People would develop a civil society based on constitutional rights which would putter along with only a bit of fine-tuning from government now and then. A number of contemporary developments have made that truly a Hollywood B movie plot.

Ronald Reagan laid out a red carpet for those who came out of the Viet Nam War with money in their Swiss bank accounts; he did everything he could to get the government out of the way of making profits. And when he crushed the airline strike in 1981, he openly declared war on unions. They would not be allowed to get in the way of corporate profits. He took the "progressive" out of the income tax; went after capital gains taxes; instituted regressive taxes; put as much of our natural resources on the auction block as he could; put antitrust legislation in mothballs; put anti-environmentalists in charge of the Environmental Protection Agency; cut the budget of every regulatory agency (including the Securities and Exchange Commission); de-controlled everything from banks and airlines to telecommunications and agriculture; refused to raise the minimum wage; privatized as much of the government as he could; allowed insurance companies, pharmaceuticals, and HMOs to control medical care in this country; and allowed roads, schools, family farms, natural resources, workers' rights and safety, consumer rights and so on to make it or break it in a "free market play" environment.

The computer came along to accelerate and change the nature of financial speculation. It was now possible to simply exchange international currencies at computer speeds and reap enormous profit; the computer made global finance, investment, and just plain doing business easier and more reliable. But it also changed the plane of investment from real world to virtual reality, which means that something like stock valuation, which may have little or no relation to real profits, was an entirely appropriate and compatible enterprise for the virtualizing dimension of computer transaction. Now instead of brains and talent being the stuff of success, the possession of money itself geometrically augments the money you possess.

There is very little to keep the wealthy from getting wealthier and since the Have Nots don't have money, their chances of "getting on board" the money-making train, or downloading some of the profits into their own accounts, are very slim. No one, in fact, knows how to get them into the game, and a game it is indeed. Precisely the sort of game that leaves itself open, as all games do, to the play of Chance. I suppose if the goddess Fortuna turns the tables, the first to suffer will be those who don't have the volume of money to play the game well or long.

All around me couples making a dual income of around one hundred thousand are tending their new portfolios of stocks. Those stocks may collapse and stay collapsed for a long, long, long time; or they may continue to rise for the rest of the investors' lives; or the companies that issued those stocks may go out of business. Maybe three-fourths of the high-tech stocks now attracting every investor may go extinct while their investors are still alive. Who knows? Only the goddess Fortuna. It's a chancy game, but we've given ourselves almost totally over to it.

Who hasn't?

Look at the population demographics: the baby boomers are, money-wise, different than the generation before them. The boomers are the first generation of what Christopher Lasch called "assortative mating"—one person with a college/professional background marries another. A high percentage of the "regular," not adjunct faculty where I teach, are married to other professors, doctors, lawyers, accountants, executives, entrepreneurs, and so on. All this means that double salaries allow for time shares, stocks, the latest toys, and—most importantly—a politics of protecting investments. Despite what leftist ideologies these folks began with, the present need to secure and protect property and investments turns them quite naturally into market conservatives.

Lower the capital gains tax? That sounds appealing to a former SDS member these days. Unions? Strikes? Not good because they tend to lower the Dow Jones. Talk of raising taxes or interest rates? Not good because they tend to lower the Dow Jones. This is the professional class, the 20 percent who serve the top 1 percent, and who are more often than not shareholders. This is the class that includes the media power brokers, the journalists and writers, the intellectuals and consultants of all stripes, the think tank pundits, the Ivy League tenured professors, the gurus who get on the talking heads shows—and what they know of the other classes is getting less and less. Their ability to represent or even be interested in the other classes is diminishing in proportion to the growth of their own private fortunes.

Speaking of diminishment, let's look at the diminishing Middle Class, or more properly speaking, the work-twice-as-hard-and-are-still-diminished Middle Class. This is the class in which husband and wife, with no professional status or marginal professional status—read, they get paid by the hour—work a combined eighty hours a week and are able to afford what Ozzie—not Harriet—could afford working half the time. This is the new working class which calls itself the Middle Class and has its eye on becoming millionaires, through the lottery, game shows, gambling casinos, stock market, Web site entrepreneurship, second and third jobs, trading baseball cards, telemarketing for Amway—any way, any how.

Politically, this is the bread and butter target group for advertisers. In order to look like they are doing well and to distance themselves from the Underclass who show up on Jerry Springer, the diminished Middle Class has to buy the latest stuff. Consuming is also a relief mechanism: after working so many hours at less than "think tank" jobs, buying stuff is a quick psychological lift, a reward. Buying stuff, watching TV, surfing the Web, child rearing, house cleaning, cooking, laundry, eating, and sleeping are what's to be done when not selling widgets for a living. If this diminished middle class can buy enough stuff, including mortgaged house and car, they can sell themselves on their own image and repress any signs of how far each day they are falling behind the Wealth-Makes-Wealth Class. This Middle Class will vote against any concessions or benefits to the Underclass because it is vitally necessary for a lot of people not to be Middle Class in order for the Middle Class to enjoy fully the satisfaction of calling themselves Middle Class.

The Underclass, formerly called the Working or Blue Collar Class, and formerly loaded with Working Class heroes, now represents all those—probably about 40 percent of the population and growing—who actually make the widgets, or used to make the widgets, and now mostly work at all those jobs that the computer hasn't yet replaced. On the way to work, a professional may instruct the maid on what has to be done that day; or the cook on what should made for dinner; may tip the garage man where his or her car is kept, or the doorman; may instruct the gardener; may call up a restaurant for lunch reservations; may take a cab; may get his shoes shined; may tip a bartender or a waitress; may confer with his CPA or her broker; may get the mail from the mailman; may give the janitorial staff some orders; may call a mechanic to fix her car; may stop at McDonald's and make an order from her car; and so on. There are a whole lot of jobs that the computer won't replace and where professional degrees are not necessary. Unless the government sees to it that the minimum wage is high enough for a person to pay rent and heat, feed, and clothe themselves in today's world, there is no indication that market forces will supply a living wage. A counter person in the fast foods industry who demands a higher wage can easily be replaced by someone else at a starting salary. And that situation is true for almost all jobs at this level. This is the class without any leverage whatsoever.

Skilled jobs pay more, but not everyone has the skills, or can or wants to develop the skills, that are required. While computer skills of all sorts are marketable now, there may be as many people who want to sit in front of a computer all day as there are those who want to crawl under sinks and plumb, or those who want to wire a house, or those who want to build a house, or those who want to upholster furniture, and so on. Making "computer literacy" an essential and required part of a school curriculum seems to me confusing process or method with knowledge itself. We don't require everyone to learn how to use a stethoscope or an electron microscope; we didn't require everyone to learn to use a library card catalogue when it was around. But the computer now gives us accelerated access to all sorts of information, and most importantly about products and services we can buy. So it's a market tool, like the TV and radio and newspapers and magazines, and it's also the medium by which business on all levels is done. It should then be required in a business school curriculum. Otherwise, why make it a privileged form of instrumentation? The fact that it serves the market more handily than does a book is no reason schools should privilege it.

Clinton's notion that the entire working class can be trained to sit in front of computers and thus serve the needs of the global market is one of the top ten worst visions of the twentieth century. You can't train and force fit 40 percent and more of the population into a high-tech-market-constructed reality. It has to go the other way: you have to shape a working world that fits people, that puts people first. You have to ask the question, what sort of work would improve the quality of these people's lives? And you have to define "quality" as that which gives us a sense of accomplishment, of purpose, of contribution, of mutual respect and recognition, of love and not envy. And we therefore must be in a compact with a society that enhances our knowledge of the plight of others and our emotional ties to them. And if we believe there's some part of us tied to a lofty beginning—"trailing clouds of glory do we come from God who is our home" as Wordsworth writes—and aiming mightily to return to that spiritual home, then we must also add that which enhances our spiritual connection to the whole planet. And it's not clear to me that you can devote a five minute spot to "Your Spirit" in Oprah fashion—rather like adding another item to your Internet "shopping cart"—and establish a bond with others on this ineffable and variously interpreted level we call "spirit."

Goshen, Indiana

February 4, 2000

I'm surprised and then honored by the invitation I get to be the keynote speaker at the First Annual Goshen College Film Festival, which is part of that college's convocation. At first I'm reluctant to travel in midwinter the three hours or so from Michigan to Indiana. I'm hesitant not only because of the weather but because I don't really know what they want from me. It's the New Millennium and I've still got old interests. I think they were supposed to have been creatively destroyed. I've got interests in everything in fact that should have gone extinct with the collapse of the Soviet Union: socialism, deconstruction, poststructuralism, postmodernism. I persist in thinking that the culture wars are not over and that transnational capitalism is only at certain addresses good for planet and people.

There's no connection between the Soviet collapse and contemporary theory except the most important one: the one in people's heads. All the nightmares are gone in this New World Order of Global Capitalism. Deleuze and Guattari, Barthes, Kuhn, Feyerabend and Debord are in their graves, Foucault met his fate with AIDS, Derrida became laughably irrelevant to the market, postmodernism is now no more than a Web site called "What the Hell Was Postmodernism Anyway?" All of the disruptions to our market and technological progress went out like the fads they were. I myself and my thought and writing are extinct; I just don't know it. What faces me is an already existing hostile and antagonistic relationship with my audience. For years I've wanted to face an academic audience—or what I've made of them—do this long overture pause, and then "flip them the bird," as my students say. On that note, I figure it's best not to accept the Goshen College invite.

Then someone tells me that Goshen is a Mennonite college and my curiosity is aroused. A ludic postmodernist among the Mennonites kind of thing, like a Pharisee among Jews, or Bill Clinton at a 700 Club meeting. It's not like they don't know I'm a postmodernist. It's not a problem. They'd like me to speak on anything having to do with the millennium and film, and I can run postmodernism into it anyway I want to. I accept and e-mail them a few possible titles; they select "Ten Unconventional Ways of Watching Movies—and Some Results." By "unconventional" I mean postmodernist, so unconventional as to suggest that conventions make reality and unconventions unmake that reality.

Beth Birkin, who has invited me, fills me in on the differences between the Amish and the Mennonite in response to my question. She begins by saying, "We Mennonites . . ." and suddenly I am looking at her in a totally different way. Suddenly she's occupying her own office with me sitting across from her in a totally different way. I remember Elaine telling me once that one of her friends had remarked that she didn't think she had ever seen a Jew. An interesting comment. Had she not seen one because no one had been pointed out to her as a Jew? Or, had she not seen one because she had a certain image in her head of what a Jew looked like and she hadn't seen anyone around looking like that? Or, did she think she had never seen a Jew because the chances of seeing one in her town were as slim as seeing a UFO? Jews out in the heartland farmland of America are rare sights. I can't be positive I've ever seen an Episcopalian or a Lutheran or a Congregationalist, but then again I'm not looking for them. I suppose I might have an eye out for them if I had some image of them in my head, but I don't. Our culture doesn't produce ready snapshots of them. I guess because they're behind the camera; they're the subjects, not the objects. They're us. But Jews aren't. And Mennonites and Amish are what comes to mind in ready images when we think of what's not us. We put out clear images of the "unconventional." What we are goes without saying, or seeing. I mean if you want to talk about adjunct, marginal lives in this "show me the money" America, you talk about the homeless, the imprisoned, the welfare losers, Hale Bopp–type cultists, but you also don't fail to mention the Amish and the Mennonites and the hippies still living on the Farm commune in Tennessee. In fact, the creator of the Farm, Stephen Gaskin, is at this moment seeking the Green Party nomination as a presidential candidate.

In 1974, when I was rushed out of college teaching, I thought long and hard about joining a commune, and the Farm was at the top of my list. But my reading at that time of Max Stirner's *The Ego and Its Own,* the bible of an anti-communitarian, totally individualistic anarchism, moved me away from commune life. I eventually bought my solitary place in a West Virginia hollow. But once market conservatives and antigovernmental libertarians set their tents up in the "self-interest" camp, with no rule but the casino rule of the market, I saw that Stirner's "ego triumphant" over all the "isms" the world had to offer, his attitude that "nothing was greater to me than my own self," fit every fatcat fattened on the stochastic rising of the Dow Jones.

I became convinced that if Stirner were alive today he would not have called himself a libertarian, but that he also would not be living according to principles any different than theirs. What had become clear to me over the years was that while you could conceivably cut back the influence of the federal government by cutting its purse strings, you could not cut back the influence of the market. I mean, while you were marching to Washington to get "Big Government" out of your individual life, you'd be driving an SUV, stopping for a Big Deal Meal at McDonald's, browsing through six or seven merchandise catalogues, and thinking about a new generation of computer/DVD/cell phone/camcorder that you "needed." While we were all living individual, free-choice, ego as our own lives, the Fortune 500 would have been spinning and selling us every feature, every bone of our lives. If "self-interested" lives could be put in front of a home entertainment/information/ telecommunication monitor and kept off the streets, kept from joining together—as in the World Trade Organization protest in Seattle—then there would be little difference between people and chickens caged in an always well-lighted coop.

As I drove to Indiana that wintry day, I was thinking about my daughters trying to launch their careers, one in Tucson and one in San Francisco. Amelia in Tucson had been working for a private archaeological company for about three years and had now decided to give that up and go back to art. She had decided to make use of that degree in studio art she had from the University of Michigan. And she wanted to continue her studies in Europe. It was a big decision and an unusual one for this twenty-something generation. I knew because I knew what most of my students were intending to do: they wanted to be marketable and they wanted someone to show them the money. Amelia was detouring off that road. Brenda in San Francisco was surrounded by the suddenly super-wealthy dot-coms. They exuded overwhelming confidence in themselves and their future Brenda told me. It was hard to be struggling amid so much well-rewarded achievement. She was beginning to feel the pull of all that success surrounding her. Why couldn't she become part of it? At the same time she was critical of everything about this dot-com reality; she wanted to pursue her own path as an artist and writer. If that path turned out to be a detour from the road everyone else was on—a high-tech road leading to riches—then so be it.

So here I was with a dissident background of my own, with two dissident daughters on the way to speak at a dissident college. Things were more appropriate than I had first imagined.

∼◦∽

I've always associated the Mennonites and the Amish with a kind of utopian, rural, Bible-based socialism. Mutual aid and not unrelenting competition is the thing. Community has as big a hold on the individual as self-interest does. The Amish will never plug into cyberspace; the Mennonites are already there. That six-hundred-year-old decision by the Amish to choose to accept or not accept whatever changes came down the pike, while the Mennonites decided simply not to be conformed to the world "but should seek to conform to Christ in every area of life" (Mennonite Yearbook v. 77, 1986–7), turned out to be a momentous decision. I mean it was momentous by the time Edison brought in electricity and Ford the automobile, but now the Internet threatens to fossilize the Amish, while it threatens to rush the present generation of Mennonites away from the Bible and into cyberspace at digital speed.

Beth tells me they are given the choice to go out and live in the world or stay with the community. Maybe some nimble social entrepreneur will invent a Mennonite chat room so that those who have left the community can still have a virtual connection. Ironically, the Mennonites have in some five hundred years experienced a total makeover image-wise. Originally persecuted as deviants from the faith for their Anabaptist beliefs, they now are packaged as tourist attractions. Thousands flock every summer to this "plain people" section of Indiana just across the Michigan line. It's a buying trek for sure—Amish folkware of all sorts—but it's clear the attraction is comparable to the attraction Disneyland Main Street has for tourists.

This is time travel, back to a preindustrialized America where life moved along at enviable speed and it seemed that the quality of food, air, water was something for which we now only yearn. Now that we have a generation of folks brought up in an industrialized world being warp-driven into cyberspace, the plain people attractiveness will doubtlessly grow. It's an escape from digital time, the mindlessness of the NASDAQ, the groundless ecstacy of the dot-coms, and a world in which belief that "life can be lived simply" and people can be "mutually committed to each other" have vanished. Except perhaps here among these plain people.

These plain people may choose to ignore the new "innovations" or try not to conform to market values but nonetheless they are the "new New Thing" and the market has conferred value upon them. Fewer of the young are leaving the plain people life to live more worldly lives and find worldly prosperity, perhaps as dot-coms. There are indeed Mennonite Web sites. There's profit in being "plain." The more virtualities of cyberspace seem to be our future, the more we are attracted to face-to-face communities doing everything the "old way," and simplifying

their lives within that Thoreauvian vision which haunts the present consumer world like Scrooge was haunted by his ghosts.

It's the college's convocation: I clear my throat.

I am without a doubt attracted to the Mennonite preference for
"mutual aid" over "self-interest." But I know that "mutual aid" means
no more than socialism and that socialism in all its forms has proven to
be a fad that has seen its day. Socialism is a departed fad, but like all fads
it can come back into style. At this moment there are supposedly countless individual fortunes being made, especially by the dot-com e-commerce entrepreneurs. Presumably if everyone pursues self-interest in an
unremitting, unswerving, undeviating way, everyone will have a private
fortune. The Mennonites hang together with one purpose in mind: to
reroute the ways of the world toward Christ's way, if those two are in
conflict. In effect, they hold other than market values and goals and will
depart from those market values and goals as they feel called upon to do
so. We experience fewer and fewer examples of such variant ways.
When we find them, we look upon them as odd curiosities, museum
pieces, inexplicable mysteries. We no longer look upon our way as a
"way" or consider that we must dedicate ourselves to never deviate from
it. Our "way"—or the market way—has simply become the "natural"
way, something inherent and foundational, like the "self-interest" that
Margaret Thatcher proclaimed in the 1980s as not a choice but natural
to human nature. And we will not stand down from that view. But I, as
a postmodernist, see it as a story we've concocted and decided to elevate
as natural, as intrinsic in the fundamental "order of things." It's actually
a story we must work hard to protect from any "deviating" ways, while
at the same time marketing these "undeviating" ways.

The cover of the last 1999 issue of *Forbes* made a millennium's end
pronouncement: "Everyone Ought to Be Rich," and in an article entitled
"How to Build Wealth (And Not Lose It)," eight "rules were presented
that stand the test of time." The article began intriguingly: "You already
know the basics of investing. But how do you apply them in a market
environment where companies with no earnings carry 11-digit valuations?" (Dec. 27, 1999, 123). In other words, how are we to invest in
this new high-tech, e-commerce, dot-com world in which every fifth
computer geek in Silicon Valley is becoming an overnight millionaire,
and investment capital is flooding every cockamamy dot-com venture—
AND none of this is yet producing a profit? Do any of these players
think that this will all sort itself out in time within any domain other
than Chaos theory? I doubt it. But I sense the enthusiasm of the dot-
coms: they're like a whole new generation of explorer, boldly going
where no one has gone before. A new entrepreneurial excitement is in

the streets; not all the streets, certainly, but maybe we can all eventually be "networked" into e-commerce fortunes. And maybe the fate of some 80 percent of the population is simply to continue to be consumers with maxed-out credit cards selecting now with a mouse off a screen and not a shopping cart off a shelf. But the dot-coms have political aspirations and pretensions that a blue-chip generation raised on Forbes's "basics of investing" never had.

George Dubya represents the ideals of neither entrepreneurial faction but that's beside the point; what matters is beating a non- or anti-entrepreneurial candidate that the Democrats would come up with. George Dubya's "compassionate conservatism" is a Republican rewriting of Clinton's "moderate Democrat." Both signifiers are supposed to attract crossover votes as Reagan succeeded in doing in two elections. But here's Robert Novak on George Dubya's weak market conservatism: "Nobody will be talking about a 'Bush Revolution' by a candidate who seems uninterested in radical tax reform, real downsizing of government, or an end to racial quotas. Even the limited 1994 'Contract With America' seems a bit too much for this Republican" (*The American Spectator* [Feb. 2000], 36). But Novak's "revolution" is not what is managerially called "proactive." We are here not building a more just, expansive, liberating, fulfilling, democratizing, egalitarian social and political order, but rather only taking those steps which will make sure that the "free play of the global market" is not impeded by a government whose affiliations are not "transnational" but "national," and which is shaped by principles other than market principles.

Granted, what else this country is shaped by is at this moment not easy to define; if "you can't name it, you can't claim it," as an Oprah Guru of All Human Behavior is fond of saying. "Radical tax reform" means ditching a progressive income tax and therefore one of the means at the federal level for redistributing wealth; "real downsizing of government" means downsizing the only potential countervailing force to transnational corporate power; "end to racial quotas" is a diverting tactic which takes advantage of American racism and bigotry in order to get middle-class votes and at the same time distract the middle class from the ongoing drama of their own extinction.

The only kind of political revolution this amounts to is a reversal of the French Revolution and a return to a global market version of the *ancien régime*. I hesitate to say a reversal of the American Revolution because Thomas Jefferson's victory in changing "pursuit of property" to "pursuit of happiness" has proven to be both just a semantic switch and a real opening of the signifier "happiness" to hook-ups other than "property." Our revolution therefore has more nebulous and arguable foundations than the French "liberty, equality, and fraternity." It is therefore not surprising to find that the French have made greater efforts to maintain equality and fraternity—in the face of global market pressures—than we Americans have.

Dot-coms are politically proactive. They envision a real democratizing, individually liberating influence by our turn to cyberspace. "The average computer geek in Silicon Valley," Anthony Perkins writes, "believes that the rise in clever electronic devices tapped into global digital networks is inexorably shifting power from organizations to individuals, decentralizing authority, and accelerating innovation" (*The American Spectator* [Feb. 2000], 36). These beliefs are worth looking at closely. What "networking" does here is not merely confined to globalizing, and therefore maximizing, profits. What the Internet access does is to provide "individuals with all the information and power they need to communicate and operate around the world beyond the control of any particular government. Communities are now being formed around common interests, rather than physical proximity and citizenship. Big government has little relevance in this new empowered global society" (37). This is a startling political and social vision grounded in an even more startling "overwriting" of political thought and history.

Something out there is "inexorably shifting power from organizations to individuals"? How naive and simplistic is this? As Foucault points out, in our time there is an inexorable connection between power, discourse, practices, and institutions. And individuals are, if you will, "networked" within those exchanges. The feeling that Internet access has miraculously severed one from already existing realworld networks most likely comes from new fortunes being made by the jejune on the Internet. "Since June [1999] there have been ten initial public offerings that have climbed at least 1,000 percent. Upstarts you had no chance to own have produced a decade's good returns in a day" (*Forbes*, [Dec. 27, 1999], 175). Is it so difficult to predict that once these "upstarts" who have produced no earnings but have eleven-digit valuations are winnowed through the inexorable logic of the Casino they will either vanish, or become part of the global market transnational organization? Dot-coms now high on their entrepreneurial victories will either deflate or be absorbed into a market organization that wields more power over individuals and is a greater threat to liberty, equality, and fraternity than the Roman Empire or the Catholic Church ever were.

"Decentralizing authority"?—"Authority," or the power to most significantly affect discourse, practices, and institutions, is here limited to governmental authority. The connection here is with a libertarian focus on big government as a threat to individual freedom. But total bewilderment ensues when the Fortune 500 is mentioned as a controlling "authority" commodifying individual lives. What the dot.com enthusiasts need here is a good screen on Marxist critique.

"Accelerating innovation"? Talk about an imprisoning chain of inexorable laws! Ever-expanding profits require the creation of new needs which require the creation of new desires which require the spinning magic of marketing and advertising which require the creation of new products and services which require technological innovation which requires research and development which requires a commercializing of universities.

Internet access taking us "beyond the control of any particular government"? Only someone born into a Reaganite world in which life is all about being entrepreneurial, and who has been jacked into a computer for too long and who has dismissed history, politics, and everyday life—rather like Sandra Bullock in the film *The Net*—and who has no idea that power predicts what is information and what is not and that, in turn, what is deemed information supports power, and who has never served time in the military or in prison or been stopped for a traffic violation, would ever make this statement.

"Communities are now being formed around common interests, rather than physical proximity and citizenship"? I'm sure Mr. Perkins is thinking of "chat room buddies" and e-mail affiliations, but unless we have undergone a whole transformation in regard to human nature, virtual contact does not exactly enhance our facility and capacity to deal face to face with each other. Once again, I refer to the film *The Net*, which dramatizes what happens to a cyberspace-bound life when it gets ensnared in a real world dilemma. All the records of Sandra Bullock's identity on-line are altered and she is given a criminal identity. When she appeals to her neighbors to identify her, they don't know her. She's a "virtual neighbor," not an "across the backyard fence neighbor." And when she appeals to her "chat room buddies," all but one lives too far away to help her—and he turns out not to be the guy she's been chatting with on the Net for a decade. Her cyberspace "experience" is like an accountant's experience of two-column bookkeeping—it takes you further from people, not closer.

The "common interests" that are bringing people together have all to do with wealth. The Haves, regardless of race and ethnicity, are forming a community based on nothing more profound than having money, and having the latest computer technology—something the Have Nots will not catch up with. Meanwhile the Have Nots are afloat in a society in which there is no other notion of community but one based on money and possessions, or, to quote the title of a famous TV show, a community based on being rich and famous. You can have subcommunities within the Have community, but you have no equal community. All other communities are Loser communities, or "wannabe" communities.

The idea that we are a civil society of American citizens sharing a tradition of values concerning democracy, egalitarianism, social justice, mutual aid, and human rights is here replaced by a market determination of community. The Internet has proven to be a marketing superhighway which most likely over time will seal our fate as consumers, and all notion of what brings us together as Americans will be forgotten.

The dot-com political vision for America is even more fantastical. And ignorant. I mean ignorant of even an undergraduate-level understanding of pertinent historical background and already covered philosophical ground. And this ignorance too is the result of our delirious lust for wealth and our ecstasy in discovering a whole new world of e-commerce by which to make money at digital speed.

In an article entitled "The Kept University," Eyal Press and Jennifer Washburn point out how the new ownership of university curriculum by the corporate world has been adding market-linked courses and driving out unconnected courses. "We must accept that we have a new mandate," George Mason University's president Alan Merten declares, "and a new reason for being in existence. The mandate is to be *networked.* There was a time," Merten goes on, "when universities weren't held accountable for much—people just threw money at them [—but today] people with money are more likely to give you money if you have restructured and repositioned yourself, got rid of stuff that you don't need to have. They take a very dim view of giving you money to run an inefficient organization" (*Atlantic Monthly* [March 2000], 51).

"Amid this whirlwind of change," Press and Washburn write, "degree programs in classics, German, Russian and several other humanities departments were eliminated. They were eliminated in the university president's point of view because there was a commitment prior to an education in values and meanings. 'We have a commitment to produce people who are employable in today's technology work force.' Students are seen as "good consumers," meaning they will pick products and services that give them the most value for their money, and value here is the eventual accumulation of wealth. "Students at GMU are 'good consumers' who want degrees in areas where there are robust job opportunities, and the university has an obligation to cater to that demand" (*Atlantic Monthly* [March 2000], 51).

If you estimate that this sort of educational mentality has already been around for about twenty-five years and has accelerated in the last several, then it's not by chance that we now face a generation of twenty-

and thirty-somethings who find most of the past, what Matthew Arnold termed "the best that has been thought and said," as irrelevant to this new high-tech, e-commerce world. Apparently it's irrelevant to running for the presidency. When candidate George W. Bush was unable to name some world leaders who had been in the news recently, a campaign spokeswoman attested that the American people didn't want to know whether a presidential candidate knew names, but only whether the candidate had "a clear vision of America's strategic interests around the world and can that candidate exert American leadership in the world" (*Washington Post* [Nov. 5, 1999], A1). The disconnect between knowledge, in this case based on keeping up with the news, and knowing what's in America's interests and exerting leadership, displays astounding stupidity, which can be attached to George Dubya's astounding ignorance. The appeal is clearly to a "conservative" constituency that believes knowing what's good for us and being able to impose that around the world is all the knowledge a president of the United States needs to have. Knowledge of other realities is superfluous, irrelevant. Why, indeed, know the "best of what has been thought and said" if all one needs in the present is a knowledge of what we want now—which is what the market wants now—and the continued power to get what we want now? It isn't just a corporate takeover of universities that has led to the grand deletion of "noncommercial" subjects. We are subscribing to a politics of authentic "No Nothingism" and are fully prepared to elect a man running on ignorance as president of the United States.

Presidents like this join with our new dot-com millionaires in standing ready to redo all of history—and we all know what a horror human history is—as if for the first time. Ideationally, conceptually, and imaginatively they are quite capable of doing what is comparable to re-inventing the wheel, not having known it had already been invented. Of course it's not the wheel they wouldn't know about, but "all the stuff you don't need to have" in a market-driven world. Intellectually, they are quite capable then of moving on from utopian notions of cyberspace and back to every debacle in the history of the human race—and do so as if they were encountering something brand new.

Besides not knowing what bodies a stock market crash can leave in its wake, these ecstatic dot.coms wouldn't recognize a demagogue if they heard one; have no qualms about living like aristocrats in the *ancien régime* while democracy is still breathing in this country; would be likely to do a double mouse click that would end in nuclear disaster since they've never had a lesson in real world accountability; and may, at the end of their cycle, wind up living like Thoreau, seeking to simplify their lives as if the spirit of that had not already been a living part of America. It had, but sadly not for them.

Back to Anthony Perkins's contribution to *The American Spectator* symposium: "Election 2000: What's at Stake?" "Just as the commercial world has had to accept the reality of 'creative destruction,'" Perkins writes, "where many old companies and ways of conducting business die and new ones emerge, allowing capital, ideas, and people to be reallocated, so must government. The next president should start re-directing government money into the hands of the social entrepreneurs who are working more nimbly and efficiently in the free market to solve many of our most difficult social problems" (Feb. 2000, 37). I don't know what I find more offensive: the cavalier "reallocating" of people in order to meet business's drive to profit or the notion that the free market can solve most of our difficult social problems and these dot-coms are society's saviors.

Incredible ignorance grounds both these presumptions. What they have in mind I suppose is developing some sort of Internet site to bridge the gap between rich and poor, or a site to get the money out of politics, or maybe a Mother Nature home page where we click flora and fauna in and out of existence, clean up oil spills, and clear the air in cyberspace. Perhaps we can stop building prisons and "creatively destruct" criminals; or perhaps we can find some way to market illegal drugs over the Internet without getting busted; or perhaps a nimble social entrepreneur can create a hospital site on the Web where the uninsured can go and get help; or maybe an even more nimble social entrepreneur can create a social security site where retired folks can browse on the first of the month instead of getting a Social Security check from the government; or maybe an ever-nimble social entrepreneur can create a Web site that will take you back to a world before there were dot-com social entrepreneurs and such a thing as the Internet and when you woke up in the morning the first thought you'd have would not be to go on-line and check your e-mail, because that wouldn't exist, but to look out the window at this glorious planet of which we are, perhaps for just a short time, the caretakers.

The Boiler Room

February 2000

> *Like Gekko, Jim and his conferees, who rake in millions ped-*
> *dling dicey stocks over the phone to suckers in the hinter-*
> *lands, represent the seductive power of unadulterated capital-*
> *ism. Not that anyone needs much seducing these days.*
> —A. O. Scott, "'Boiler Room': Sell Enough Dicey
> Stocks to Rubes, and You Can Buy Ferraris"
> *New York Times,* Feb. 18, 2000

Either you've got a wicked jump shot or you're slinging crack rock . . .
I didn't want to be innovative. I just wanted to get in, get the stock
options, make a million and get out. I wanted in. I heard stories about
secretaries working for Microsoft taking stock options instead of a
Christmas bonus and walking away millionaires in a year.

So goes the opening voice-over of the new millennium version of
Oliver Stone's 1985 film *Wall Street.* We're deep into caring for our
investment portfolios and very far indeed from thinking about caring for
our planet. Seth isn't telling any of his twenty-something peers in the
audience anything they don't already know; they know what gives in
New Millennium America, and it has all to do with making a million,
retiring before you're thirty, and spending the rest of your life buying the
latest toys and a top-of-the-line look. Seth has already dropped out of
the graduate program he was in; we don't know what he was studying
but he's given up in order to run a twenty-four-hour gambling operation
out of his home. He's being entrepreneurial, as he tells his father later in
the movie: "I've got employees, I'm running my own business and making a profit. I thought you would be proud of me." The dad, who is a
judge, isn't proud; his son is jeopardizing his judgeship by running an
illegal gambling operation. So when Seth gets a chance to work for the
unknown brokerage house of J. T. Marlin, he gives it a shot. It's his

escape from criminal entrepreneurship to legal entrepreneurship and thus back into the good graces of his father.

Will this legal entrepreneurship bring in the bucks? Well, according to Ben Affleck, who is J. T. Marlin's prospective employee pitchman, if they work their asses off, learn the trade as well as the senior brokers who teach them, they'll be millionaires by the time they're Affleck's age—twenty-seven. "I'm already over the hill at twenty-seven for this game," Affleck tells the new recruits. "We need guys your age with hardons for making millions now. And do millions buy you happiness? I'm a millionaire and just look at the smile on my face. Anybody who tells you money can't buy happiness tells you that because they don't have any money and never will. You got to want it."

Seth wants it. The story line about wanting it to regain his father's love and respect is nonsense; it's part of the same moral nonsense in which market conservatives like to wrap their own entrepreneurial priorities. James Dean and Raymond Massey played this father and son drama out in the mid-1950s movie *East of Eden*. Maybe then there was something to be said for Dean going out there and making money, buying beans low and selling high when a war breaks out, just to regain his father's love, to prove to his father that he was worthy. But you could see how in the 1950s a twenty-something could be more interested in a father's respect than "wanting in," more than wanting to make a million in six months.

But that's slapped on as a moral facade in this 2000 film, and when Seth is willing to go to jail just to protect his father's reputation, we as Americans can say that we may all want stock options in this ever-rising NASDAQ world, but the bottom line is we have other moral values that trump our entrepreneurial values. But I suggest that it's Affleck's credo that strikes a real note: "Your mother and father have problems with what you're doing here? Fuck 'em."

The Will to Wealth trumps any and all other intentions and values; Desire is totally fulfilled by being rich. Affleck's "You Got to Want to Be Rich" spiel takes me back to the mid 1980s when I and my family are being treated to a Christmas Eve dinner at top-of-the-line prices. I'm seated next to three twenty-somethings who are talking about a friend about whom they seem worried. One of them says, "You know what's wrong with him? He doesn't want to be rich anymore." And the three of them shake their heads in mourning for their friend's lost desire. I don't recall if I said something or not, but perhaps I was wise enough to realize that any word from me, who was past forty and not rich, would earn me nothing more than pitying stares. I have seen those looks over the ensuing years in my classes when I try to engage "counternarratives" to the reigning Will to Wealth. Regardless of what I transmit, it's all received through the filter that Affleck has presented: "Anybody who says money doesn't buy happiness just doesn't have any money and never will." And this film, in spite of the fact that the Feds come in and bust everyone at J. T. Marlin and Seth's voice-over now tells us, "I guess I'll have to get a real job," does not counter Affleck's money promo. Everybody in the audience, and especially the twenty-somethings, want in, and now that they've seen how it works in "the boiler room" of making bucks, they're probably more-than-ever anxious to "get in" and get theirs.

J. T. Marlin is a chop shop brokerage house, which apparently doesn't uphold the high standards of Solomon Brothers or J. P. Morgan or Merrill Lynch. They scam and spin people, break SEC regulations, and skip to a new locale before the Feds close in. Since brokerage houses are now rushing to "merge" with banks and other financial institutions, forming one-stop-shopping investment capital outlets, there's a pretty good chance that the film, *The Boiler Room,* has some of that money in its bloodstream. I mean, why make the effort in more than one very peripheral scene to separate the "Good Brokers" from the "Chop Shop Brokers"? The Chop Shop guys have offices in strip malls out on the Long Island Expressway and not Wall Street; they don't wear the right suits; they're loud, ill-bred, bigoted, racist, profane, and violent. On the other hand, the Ivy League brokers are offended by the very existence of these Chop Shop dudes. They besmirch the honorable trade of brokering. This is the second nonsense moral dimension in the film.

Every bit of training that Seth gets on how to make a cold call and spin whoever is on the other line into buying stock is classic, good sales training. If brokers don't use that approach in the Ivy League brokerage houses then they probably don't "want to be rich." Can we assume that the Ivy League houses are into the game not to win but to play the game fairly and honestly? Have there been no scandals of corruption at any of these respectable houses? What is it that J. T. Marlin is doing that is so clearly over the line? If I grasp Seth's explanation, J. T. Marlin is doing two things, one sort of semi-illegal and the other totally illegal. They are selling stock in companies not yet gone public, what Seth calls a "bridging" operation. These funds will enable a company to reach a level in which they can traded as an "initial public offering" (IPO). The second activity involves the selling of stock in companies that are not only not IPO, but don't in fact exist. So everyone in the boiler room busy making seven hundred calls a day is just doing a telemarketing version of the "I've got these thousand shares of Klondike Gold Mine selling at six that I can let you in on" that somebody like John Carradine pulls out of his pocket in those old movies.

Now that's clearly criminal activity. The company doesn't exist. It's a swindle. Is it more or less criminal than selling crack rock? Let me put it this way: if you can get your Ferrari selling legitimate IPO stocks, then why risk jail by selling phony stocks? I mean if you've got a wicked, legal jump shot and can get your Ferrari with it, why risk jail selling crack? The phony stock bit is just more smokescreen hooey. It wants to implicitly and by contrast legitimize the hard sell of the "reputable" brokers by focusing on these tacky "bridge-and-tunnel" louts. But right now we have hundreds of dot-com companies that do exist, and in spite of the fact that they are being traded at thousands of times their assets and profits, people are still being convinced that they should keep buying. Who's selling them? Why would J. T. Marlin risk jail when they could make a bundle just making cold calls to a population that's already convinced that buying stocks is the road to prosperity?

We are inches away from dumping the whole Social Security fund onto Wall Street and letting the brokers broker our retirement security for us, altering the word "security" to "speculative." Transnational logic fills our heads: we should not expect "security" in our lives because it tends to get in the way of profit. On the other hand, "speculation" is what the stock market offers, past performance being no indication as to future success. We've all got to gamble a whole lot more if we really want the big bucks, and we all do. So there's no need to make a hard sell in the current climate because people have already been softened up and are ready to get their portfolios going. Everyone wants to be a player, either through day-trading or through conventional brokering or through company stock options. As long as we keep the J. T. Marlins and the "bridge-and-tunnel" riffraff out of the game, it's all sweetness and light. Trust Hollywood to come up with an easy scapegoat; it's not these ruthless players over *here*; it's just these ruthless players over *there*. Get rid of them, and the darkness fades. There's light ahead.

Except for now when the darkness doesn't seem to fade the way it should.

East Lansing, Michigan

March 2000

Yesterday, in a town close to my own, a six-year-old boy killed a fellow first-grader by shooting her in the chest with a .32 caliber handgun. There can't be something wrong with just this kid, a headline reads, there has to be something wrong with our whole society. According to an Associated Press article, the kid lived "in a 'flophouse' where drugs were found and used a stolen handgun he apparently discovered loaded and lying in a bedroom there" ("Prosecutor Discusses Background of Boy in School Shooting," *New York Times* [March 2, 2000]). The boy's father was in jail and his mother had just been evicted from her home and had left her two sons with her brother. The police as of this moment have not been able to locate the mother.

"This boy comes from a very troubled home," Genesee County Prosecutor Arthur Busch said on the "Today" show. "He is really a victim of a drug culture and a house that's really in chaos." Sounds to me like these folks were among those Governor Engler has "liberated" from the welfare rolls—which means of course that they continue to exist, but the state no longer cares about them since they no longer exist as welfare statistics. Statistical or nominal reality is the only reality that counts in our new "tough on welfare" democracy.

The same day this news hits the Web, I read a *Salon* piece entitled "Two Million Americans Are in Prison." Pretty soon the Russians will have less people in prison than us, the society that touts itself as the "freest on Earth." "Our prison system has become the last resort for many of the ills which plague our society. The mentally ill. . . . The drug addicted. . . . The ill educated. The ill fed or poorly raised find a final home there. We won't pay the price to provide the means to alleviate these horrors but we don't mind building more prisons instead" (*Salon Table Talk* [Feb. 28, 2000]). Guilt is with the whole society; we're not only creating a society in which horrors occur, like a six year old shooting to death another six year old, but we're getting pretty horrible ourselves.

147

I know there are multitudes all over Michigan today responding to this new horror, one that even trumps the Columbine massacre, by focusing a narrow lens on the six-year-old murderer. Let's keep it personal; individual choice kind of thing; the culture of personality, of everyone individually expressing his or her free-to-choose mandate and willing to assume personal responsibility. So it comes down not to an increasingly dysfunctional society, but to the personalities of this six year old and his dysfunctional family. The kid should have already been spotted as a threat and should have been in some kind of correctional facility, with his evicted mom and his imprisoned dad. I find out that the kid had already been suspended from school for fighting and for stabbing a girl with a pencil. Maybe this kid is evil incarnate; maybe it's all true that there's an evil seed in people and no matter how perfect things are around them, they will do evil. In this story, evil is not just something we humans project into the world and ourselves but a reality independent of us. If there were no humans in the world, the world would still have evil in it. Or, if it disappeared when we disappeared, then we took it with us.

I come in close and focus on the six year old. "When he was questioned, the boy didn't seem to understand the gravity of the shooting, Police Chief Eric King said. Later, he 'sat there drawing pictures,' King said" (*New York Times* [March 2, 2000]). The conscience of Hannibal Lecter: no conscience. But where would his conscience come from? He has a "flophouse" conscience, on which the professors of ethics have not yet filled us in. "The father heard about Tuesday's shooting from a cell mate and 'a cold, sinking feeling came over him because he knew it was his son,' Pickell said. He said (his son) liked to watch the violent movies, the television shows." I can picture this six year old in his flophouse home digesting the values of a crack/gun exchange, hearing this or that said by the people who were around "just hanging out," not real sure about what a dad is or does, picking up an "I've just been evicted, goddamn it" vibe from his mom, and then turning on the TV for entertainment. Oh, yeah, he goes to primary school in Flint; if you don't know what the market did to Flint, rent Michael Moore's film *Roger and Me*. So the upstart is that the kid didn't understand the "gravity of the shooting" and took to drawing pictures right afterward. He's not feral; he's worse. He's a pure product of America's current creed: "I've got mine, get yours and don't anybody tax me to help the losers out." Winning is not totally winning unless you can see the bodies of the losers lying around. Winning leaves bodies in its wake. And America is deeply into that psychology.

～∞～

"If you say good and evil are not out there in Nature, would you also say that Hitler wasn't an evil guy or Christ a good guy? Can postmodernists point to who's good and who's bad or is it just 'that's their own reality' kind of thing?"

I get that question via e-mail. Is this evidence that Socratic dialogue is alive and well in cyberspace? This student wouldn't have called me on the phone to ask that question, or take time out to drop by my office and ask that question. He could have asked it in class, but what if he didn't think of it in class? I do my postmodern response—capsule version of what's in my "Meditating on Postmodern Ethics and Religion" in *A Primer to Postmodernity*—and e-mail it to the whole class, via a nice class list e-mail feature. But life and TV have recently pushed me off the abstract plane and into the mosh pit, and I'm rethinking good guys and bad guys from there.

Former President Bush called Saddam Hussein a "Hitler" and met with a Jewish response: such a comparison diluted the evil Hitler spawned. What Milosevich did to the Muslims in Bosnia was like what Hitler did to the Jews: it was another Holocaust. And our tardy mobilization to stop this latest Holocaust parallels our Word War II tardiness regarding Hitler's "Final Solution." We need to keep the memory of the Jewish Holocaust alive so that it can never be repeated in the future. At the same time, when we think it is being repeated—at whatever stage— we shouldn't compare it to the Jewish Holocaust because that diminishes our sense of what evil really is.

We're defensively bureaucratizing "evil" anyway. I think that if we mentally sequester evil over in the Hitler/Holocaust corner, then it's a whole lot easier to think of ourselves as *not* evil and a whole lot easier for evil things to be done every day and for us as a society to fail to recognize them. There's a peculiar blending of personalizing and bureaucratizing of evil going on here. If, on one hand, you can bureaucratize it, you can avoid a face-to-face encounter on each and every new outbreak of evil. You don't have to re-examine your conscience, you just see if it fits the profile. You can file *this* with *this;* and this is what Jews want to avoid in regard to the Holocaust. They want a continuous recollection of this evil's difference, not a reduction to sameness. On the other hand, we personalize evil—this guy or that guy—in order to detach it from ourselves and from the social order within which we groom ourselves. There's a diplomacy regarding the handling of evil; we focus the cameras on the one man, the evildoer, Hitler, in order to spare the "German people," who we still have to deal with in the present. But when we can reduce evil to our cult of personalities with impunity, we do so because it spares our present order of things. And since our present American order of things is a Dow Jones market led order of things, we do all we can not to upset that stability. We never have "political" prisoners in jail these days, nor are any of our bombings, sieges, or massacres connected with "civil disobedience." We're always dealing with evil individuals, from Bin Laden and Saddam to David Koresh to Ted Kaczynski and Tim McVeigh. And now this six-year-old kid and his family. We'll let him off because of age. In this special case, his "evil" is not his own but his class's—the underclass's. This is a class that can be smeared and demonized without upsetting social stability.

Let's go in close on this. That boy sitting there calmly drawing pictures after having shot and killed a six-year-old classmate is surely an opportunity to witness unconscionable human nature; consciousness totally devoid of faith, hope, charity, compassion, and love; temperament oblivious to the moral battle between good and evil. This is the perfect photo opportunity for an America boasting "the economy is the best ever!" but who is nonetheless caught off guard by repeated incidents of "civil disobedience," from the Waco siege to the Oklahoma bombing and the Unabomber Manifesto to "psychotic" episodes like a murder spree by a "disaffected" day trader to the Columbine massacre and now a killing of a six year old by a six year old.

How does this picture of a six-year-old boy calmly drawing pictures after killing a classmate distance our assertion ("the economy is the best ever!") from any link to the boy, to the murder, to evil? Certainly one person has here killed another person, just as Kaczynski personally sent those bombs, and the "trenchcoat mafia" at Columbine shot their classmates.

∽◦◦∽

When we read this description of the six-year-old boy unmoved by his murderous act we automatically hook-up with it within our cult of the personality mode. Look, if Bill Gates and Warren Buffet and the billionaire crowd are personally responsible for every dime they own, without any sort of social or cultural dependencies, obligations, debts, or connections, then we can't start looking for social and cultural connections in any of these headline atrocities. We've got to keep it on the level of personal responsibility so that Winners can be solely responsible for winning, and Losers can be solely responsible for losing.

Now as this kid is only six years old we can't go too far into that personality; there's no room to roam, not like the Unabomber or Tim McVeigh or David Koresh. So we jump off to his parents: the run-out mom and the dad in jail and the uncle with the drugs and the guns, and the drug-dealing, gun-running friends. We go from one personality to an entire class, the underclass. After all, if we want to see the worst dregs of human nature, evil incarnate as it were, we just tune into the "Jerry Springer Show" or "Cops" and see where the dark side of life hangs out.

Evil belongs to a class, the Underclass; evil also belongs to individuals, psychopaths, and sociopaths lacking "family values," and individuals like Bill Clinton who have "lost their moral compass"; and, finally, evil belongs in general all-serving bureaucratic categories like "Arab Terrorist," "Hitler-like," "Manson-like," "Mafia," Communist," "Serial Killer," "Columbian Drug Dealer," "Pornographer," "Anarchist," "Skinhead," "Cultist," and so on. If evil still seems unlinked, there is always "the Devil" to blame.

The entire Underclass can't seem to outrun the devil these days; Bill Clinton comes from a Southern revivalist tradition in which the devil has to be periodically purged; and there's no doubt in Pat Robertson's mind that the devil has gotten into "liberalism" somewhere along the line.

What if we jumped past the smokescreen scenarios of what evil is and tried to figure out how the excesses of American society and culture, what Marx called the "savagery of capitalism," will nurture evil acts and suborn the lukewarm and the innocent to evil. I want to argue that a six-year-old boy should be inhabiting mostly the realm of Innocence, and if he isn't, it's not because he didn't create and foster that realm but our American society didn't—and doesn't. Simply put, we're a society going for the money and leaving bodies in our wake as we do so. It's a dangerous game, but we've done nothing for the past twenty years but show that we're willing to play it. Here's where evil emerges.

Michael Moore made use of e-mail to get his linkage of the murder of Kayla Rolland, the six-year-old girl shot by a six-year-old boy, and the Hell this boy comes from.

> Isn't it enough that Flint suffers from the highest or near-highest per capita rates of murder, rape and theft in the nation? What else do the people of Flint have to go through while the rest of the country mouths the propaganda of the evening news claiming "the economy is the best ever!"? The top 10 per cent just get richer and richer and the next 30 per cent of you keep the CNBC stock ticker on your screens all day and toss out all sections of the daily paper but the pages that tell you how well your portfolio did yesterday. (Michael Moore, "Letter from a Friend of Flint" [March 3, 2000])

This six-year-old slayer was robbed first by a society rising and falling to the tempo of the market, to the tempo of deceptive mantras of "work not welfare," "assume personal responsibility," "family values," "tough love," "just do it!" "free to choose," "show me the money," "a zero sum game," "affirmative access not affirmative action," "creative destruction," "right to work," "money talks and bullshit walks," "compound interest requires self-interest," "market rule is good and social engineering is bad," and, the latest from presidential candidate George Dubya, "compassionate conservatism."

So many claptrap slogans that stand in the way of just reaching imaginatively into the lives of others, into Nature that doesn't know if it's true or false, right or wrong, into feelings of love that don't reckon profit or loss, into a world beyond winning and losing, into a world overspilling self-interest. Rational choice in the information age means nothing more than being wagged by spin and then yapping defensively about "free choice" and "rational choice." A six year old looks into the eyes of another six year old and pulls a trigger. Where? Not there in that school really. But in some spin in the kid's mind. A place where bullets don't produce holes in flesh and blood doesn't flow. Death is an actor who will show up alive again on another channel. If these six year olds live, they can sit before Ben Affleck in the boiler room and listen to the mantra of millions. That future dramatic scene awaits them. That's another possible role to play. Meanwhile, marketers discover a demand for "reality TV," a hunger to see raw, candid reality, where ordinary people like you and me find themselves in the Australian outback, or in boot camp, isolated from the fads, fashions, spins, and hype of our bubble America. How can we escape the bubble we're in and touch what's really there, what's free of our own hyperactive, out-of-control spin making culture? In other words, let's discard all human intervention in the world and start over again. And maybe some time in the future, a six year old won't shoot and kill another six year old.

It seems that I have always been trying to see outside what Keats called "the moods of one's mind," railing against the shadows his own mental disposition placed upon a Nature that fascinated him. He was, in a way, lucky; he had more personally to do with drawing that veil between eye and world than we are allowed today, as the age of spectacle reaches warp drive and fabricates a nether zone in which we are losing sight of each other, of other creatures, of the rocks and trees and water, of worlds outside our own orbiting.

Oxley Holl'r, West Virginia

Summer 1975

I remembered a time when newts, snakes, and rats broke through my own mental mood and reached me.

"Chicken snake only goes after chickens," Rev. John told me as we both were bending over the collard greens growing lushly in the chicken yard in front of the big barn (the Reverend had a hand with collards). "Swallow them whole. Whip snake be hanging in a barn, when you come in whip around your neck so fast you finished brother. Dem cabbage snakes get in there and you eat 'em whole, and then you finished brother. Rat snake gonna stand up as tall as you and go at yo' haid. But that snake keep yo' house free of rats. You ain't hearing a word I said."

Now here was something irrational run amok, I thought, but I just told him I heard him. A whole world of imagined creatures and their imaginary habits. He had just finished telling me to make sure I kept Elaine, who was pregnant, out of the gardens because she had what he called "milk leg" and that would ruin the crops.

I should have listened to him on the rat snake.

It was raining cats and dogs that day, and as I ran from my VW van to the house with groceries I noticed that the door to the spring house was opened. I dropped the groceries on the porch and ran, head down, through the long spring grass. About ten yards from the spring house a thick black snake that seemed as thick and black as a truck tire suddenly arched upward right in front of me. I leaped as high as I could. I didn't know if it had tried to strike me, but I didn't feel anything. I was already drenched; my heart was pounding so hard I thought I could hear it above the rain. I looked back and saw a snake with the biggest head I had ever seen on a snake. I ran into the spring house and grabbed a long-handled spade. Without thinking about anything but killing that snake, I stood over it. It raised its head; it was coming up as high as my own head. The Reverend's words had been meant for this snake and my head. I swept that shovel down across the middle of the heavy, wet body. The snake's mouth went wide, the lower jaw dropping like a suddenly released derrick scoop. The shovel squashed into the snake's body. I looked up, and through the wall of rain I could see Elaine at the picture window we had installed in the kitchen. She was looking at me. My heart was still racing. This was different. I looked down at the snake in that dark green, wet grass.

Later on, when I told Mr. Parker about the snake and told him how big it was, he said, "Close to the house?" I nodded. "Probably crawled out for water. Rat snake. Judging by the size might have been living under that house for a long, long time." He shook his head as if I had done a really stupid thing, but he didn't say anything. Years later I returned with my family to West Virginia and to that town of Athens and I found Mr. Parker standing there looking out the store window, older, but eyes still alert. "Sure, I remember you," was all he said, as we shook hands. "In the long run the sharpest weapon of all is a kind and gentle spirit." That was Mr. Parker.

That winter we found out more about the snake I had killed. Field rats took to nesting under the house where it was warm and then started to crawl up between the clapboards and the interior walls. It was Brenda's first winter and she lay in her crib in the front room, a room now filled with the sounds of rats scurrying and scratching. Dickens and Cissy, our two dogs, spent most of the night rushing from one room and one wall to another, sniffing, barking, and pawing the wall or the floor. They both had excellent noses and they knew we were being besieged. Something had to be done. I went to Mr. Parker for advice.

Mr. Parker had been the principal of the local village school, but now he was retired and running the hardware store that had been in his family for generations. It was 1975 but everything in there was priced at 1955 levels. He and his son, the fire chief, Joe Parker, had helped me already that winter when newts had gotten into the septic tank we used as a water reservoir. Using a brand-new septic tank as a water reservoir cached about halfway down the hill between the spring and the house had been Mr. Parker's idea. Mr. Parker had told me that there was a steady flow of spring water coming out at the base of an oak tree somewhere up on the hill behind the house. The Reverend and I had gone in search of it and the Reverend had found it, moving steadily up the hill from spots of soft, wet ground until we had found this huge old oak tree. And then the Reverend had "developed" it so that the flow of water was increased. Mr. Parker engineered a system of spring box, plastic piping, and a brand-new concrete septic tank about halfway between the oak tree and the house below. It was a gravity-flow operation. When the five hundred–gallon reservoir was filled there would be enough pressure and a sharp enough decline for water to come into the house at a good rate and pressure. Later Mr. Parker put in a Jacuzzi pump so that the washing machine would fill up in time and we could put a shower in our new bathroom.

Some time in the summer, when I was checking the spring box under the oak to clear out dead leaves and such and scrape the screen covering the pipe end clean, I noticed a pair of newts in the box itself. I tried to get them out but they sunk themselves in the bottom. I knew the newts were too big to get through the small holes in the screening so I didn't worry about it. That spring water was probably purer than any water we had had anywhere else, and I didn't think these newts would muck it up. It turned out that these newts were in love, were having sex in that spring box, and the eggs they produced did fit through the filtering screen. They all wound up flowing down to the reservoir and hatching there. We developed what we called "newt water" down at the house. If we filled the bathtub we wound up with tiny newts swimming in it. If we turned on the kitchen faucet, we would barely get a trickle. When we unscrewed the faucet filter, we would find a thick layer of crushed newt bodies. All this didn't happen until the winter. The newts were out of the spring box, but their progeny were enjoying themselves in the five hundred-gallon reservoir.

Mr. Parker had arranged for the reservoir to go into the side of the hill in such a way that you could get at the hatch, which conveniently had a thick iron ring sunk into it. All you had to do was pull. Trouble was, snow and ice covered the reservoir, the exposed hatch, and the ring. It had been below freezing for days, weeks, months. When you spent a lot of time digging out fence posts, slugging a powerful tiller around acres of fields, running a hedgehog over thickets, chain sawing, chopping and cutting by handsaw, dragging logs out of the woods, digging up wheelbarrows full of manure and pushing them out to the fields—and so on—your muscles get quite a workout. I couldn't eat enough to keep them replenished. I weighed about 190 pounds on a 5'9" frame; I could cut a full-sized tree down with an axe; I could hoist myself up to the barn roof with a rope; I could swing a sledgehammer to break concrete all day. But when I went out there and chopped through to the hatch ring and then scored all around the hatch with a sledge and chisel to break the ice, and then grabbed that ring, bent my knees, took a couple of dead lift breaths and pulled—nothing happened. I tried until my hands froze even in the double-layered mittens and my back wouldn't straighten up.

Next day when I drove out of the holl'r—by first putting chains on the rear tires because the 1972 VW van was not four-wheel drive—into town and into Mr. Parker's hardware store, I told him of my bad fortune. He heard me out and then said, "I'll come by with Joe." And he did. A couple of days later, his red pickup truck came down the road with him and Joe, both wearing baseball caps. Mr. Parker was about my size, Joe about twice our size. I shook hands with both of them.

"Let's get to it," Mr. Parker said, crowbar in hand.

He was spry for a guy who I figured was somewhere in his late sixties. He got up on the reservoir, bent over, and worked the crowbar along the hatch edge. Meanwhile, Joe took the ring in his hands, hunched his shoulders, pushed his rump down and lifted. I was just about to say we'd have to wait until spring, when the hatch lifted and Mr. Parker, with a deft movement of the bar, swung the hatch to the right. Then Joe pulled it completely off to the side so that we could look down into the dark, newt-filled reservoir below.

"Water's warmer than the air," Mr. Parker said. "Get yourself a net and you can go down there and scoop out newts."

As usual Mr Parker wouldn't take any money for his service, nor would his son Joe.

I did go down into that water with a bucket, a net, and a flashlight. I scooped out newts for the next three days. I scooped until the net came up newt-free and we could take a bath without the company of newts.

It was the same winter that the rats, who would have been kept off by the rat snake I had killed, were invading the house.

"Warfarin is all you got," Mr. Parker said this time, handing me a big can of stuff with a $2.95 price tag on it. "This stuff will get them real thirsty and they'll come looking for water. They'll head for your pond. Once they drink, they'll hemorrhage and die, out there away from the house. You don't want them dying under the house or between the walls."

"What do I have to do?"

"Get under the house and get this stuff where they're nesting. You got to leave it where they can all get at it."

"Okay," I said, taking the can, and guiltily paying him in 1955 dollars.

I took a hunting knife, a flashlight, and the Warfarin and went to the front of the house on a bright wintry morning. The more light the better, was what I was thinking. They seemed to assault the house at night, so I figured maybe they slept during the day. There was crawlspace in the front of the house because the house had been built against a hillside just so it would be partially off the ground. The sunlight backed off after I had crawled a couple of feet. Up ahead, toward the back of the house things looked pitch dark. And none too spacious. I had the knife in its sheath on my belt, but as soon as I heard some weird sounds—like Chip and Dale arguing—I pulled it out and ran the flashlight back where the sounds were coming from. Nothing, and then a couple of scurrying bodies. Way back there. Way back where the rough-hewn timbers did not rest on stone pedestals as they did at the front of the house but were sunk into the hillside. And there was only enough headroom for a rat. With the can of Warfarin in a side pack, knife and flashlight in the same hand, I crawled toward the sounds, which got louder and louder. The whole damn colony seemed to be aware of my presence. And the sounds were beginning to come from all around me now. I had on a wool jacket, jeans, and boots, but I figured if they started gnawing at me a little bit of cloth wasn't going to stop them. Now there wasn't any room to turn around; I would have to back out. I could barely raise my head without touching the floorboards. I could see the rats now in the light beam. I don't know what kept them from attacking me. The knife wouldn't have done me much good. Then I could hear my dogs Dickens and Cissy right above me scratching and whimpering. They had picked up my scent and knew I was there. They wanted to help, but I was alone on this. I was too far in and too wedged in to move quickly. In other words, I was dead meat for rats if they decided to rush me. Assured by the sounds that I was at their home base, I pulled the can of Warfarin out, pried off the lid that I had already loosened, and began to lay the stuff out. It was so close to my nose that I thought I might be breathing in its lethality; an hour or so from then I figured I would be joining the rats heading up to the pond looking for water. I figured since I had made that crazy crawl once and wouldn't do it again, I would leave the whole $2.95 worth of Warfarin on their doorstep. I moved as best I could laterally right and left, spreading the stuff. And then I went eyeball to eyeball with a rat and freaked out. I dropped the can and began to crawl backwards, making all the progress of a dead body being dragged out by its heels. I scraped the hell out of the palms of my hands and banged my head a couple of times, but I wanted out of there. All of a sudden I was claustrophobic; all of a sudden I couldn't breathe. All of a sudden if I didn't get out of that dark hole quickly the whole house was going to come down on me. When I crawled into the rays of sunlight filtering under there, I exhaled for the first time. And when I got out and stood up in that morning sun and took some deep breaths, I knew what resurrection was. And then I looked over at the spring house where I had killed that rat snake and I said a small prayer for forgiveness to the soul of that snake.

Killing that snake troubled my conscience, which wasn't used to being troubled that way. I mean, the Xaverian Brothers, a Catholic teaching order of men who had taken vows of celibacy, obedience, and poverty, had taught me the Catholic art of conscience review. And it mostly, or predominantly, focused on "sins of the flesh." Maybe sexuality was the hot spot of conscience because we were teenagers, and sex was what spun our lives. Anyway, there I was in my early thirties and wondering why killing that snake was troubling my conscience. More like, why was that murder lingering? Murder? Did I say murder? And why was it lingering when my conscience at the moment was absorbed with a sex matter, which I hadn't thought of as a "sex matter" until Rev. John pointed it out to me one night when I was working as a night watchman in the local college library.

I was sort of coiled up like a snake in that night watchman's office, old wooden chair on wheels tilted back to the wall, Frye boots up on the desk, Rev. John in a chair squeezed between the desk and the wall. Rev. John would stop by at night just to talk. Johnny Lee came in. Johnny was a student worker I had inherited. He knew everything there was to know about the place. He knew which keys fit in what door, who to call in case of this or that problem or emergency, where this or that tool was. He knew how to lock up and close the place down. And he knew how to go out for a pork barbeque sandwich which he did every night about ten. He picked up one for himself and one for me. Now he interrupted Rev. John, who had been telling me about what some folks might be saying about me and another student worker, a black girl named Ginny.

"You ready for some barbeque, Dr. Nat Lee?" Johnny Lee said, standing in the doorway.

"Yeah. Get one for the Reverend too."

"None of dat fo' me," the Reverend replied. "I done eating for today. You eat fo' yo sleep, yu gonna toss and turn. Be dreaming all night."

"Is that right?" Johnny Lee said, somewhat bewildered. "What you dream about?"

Rev. John looked him up and down.

"What yo say yo age is?"

"I'm twenty-three," Johnny said, straightening up. He was well over six feet.

"An' yo let folks call you Jack-off? Ain't yo' the one dat folks calls Jack-off?"

"They don't mean anything by it. Besides, I got a girlfriend now."

"Yeah, he's got a girlfriend now," I put in.

"Oh, he got a girlfriend now? She call yo Jack-off too?"

"She calls me Johnny."

"Yo most likely dreaming 'bout her," Rev. John told him.

"I dreamed about my mother once," Johnny admitted. "And she's long daid."

"Don't be telling me about yo dream'n 'bout yo muther," the Reverend said, putting up one large hand like he was blocking a shot Johnny was attempting to make.

Johnny looked at me quizzically.

"Get the barbeque, Johnny," I told him.

When Johnny left, Rev. John got back to what was on his mind. He was a shepherd and I was now one of the flock. And he was tending.

"You be letting that girl hang all over you. And I'm telling you that dey hear dat up there on the Hill, yo be gone and that girl ain't gonna be treated well."

"She's a lively kid," I said. "I can't talk to her?"

"I'm telling you that folks is noticing. Be best for you if you keep your distance."

Ginny had a sharp intelligence and a real curiosity about unfamiliar things. It's rare to find someone at any age testing the walls of his or her reality frame, jumping back on his or her own sense of realism and taking another look. Ginny was that kind of person. She had an eye out for the odd element in the familiar mix, and that was me. She had once asked me, "Dr. Nat Lee, you come from the old country, don't you?" "What old country?" I said. "You know," she said, flashing a big smile. "The old country. Over on across the ocean." "I thought you meant Brooklyn." "I know you a Talley," she said. Talley was what the West Virginians called "Eye-talians," the stone masons who had come years before and built the retaining walls that kept everything from sliding on down the hill. "I'm gonna be crossing the ocean some day," she told me. "Do you ever want to go back from where you came from?" I started to say, "Brooklyn?" and she said, "Not Brooklyn." "I'd like to go way back to the Garden of Eden before sassy Eve went for the apple." That made her laugh. "Dr. Nat Lee, you a funny man. Don't you ever be serious?" "That's the way people are from the old country," I told her. "I mean Brooklyn. We're funny in Brooklyn." She then turned away in disgust but quickly swung around, her eyes flashing: "Had to be one of dem was black. And I say it was Eve. And she was sassy cause she had to be." And then she walked off.

I was thinking about Ginny and going over whether I had crossed the line with her, even with that kind of banter. I could hear my Brooklyn buddies saying, "Yeah, right, you were interested in her *mind.*"

"Ain't no good for her to have folks seeing her running after a white man who already married," Rev. John said, interrupting my Review of Conscience.

Was my old Catholic moral compass working, or was it beginning to postmodernize? I mean, was time and place taking me beyond the kind of confessions I had made as a teenager:"Any sex?," the priest would ask. If the answer was no, your conscience was clear. Was I beyond that now? What? "Kill a snake? no. conscience clear? yes. conscience not clear" review? What about the field rats? I killed them. I poisoned them. What about the newts? I slaughtered hundreds of them. Fuck the lower orders. Creative destruction is called for. What the hell does destruction create? And what happens when the "lower orders" include the "lower classes"? And still . . . what about Ginny? I was pushing her to review her world and that just meant pushing her to become discontent with it. What part could I possibly play in the consequences of that? Slash and run is a bad pedagogical style. It haunts the conscience. I was heading for a conscience-haunted syndrome. In the wake, I guess, of Bill Clinton.

Eden

August 2000

There's a syndrome for everything now, and what's not a syndrome is a fugue, like "watch out, she's in a fugue state." She's liable to wander into you personally and then say, "Where the @#***@#@ am I?" Here's the cocktail party wisdom on Bill Clinton: he has a sexual psychopathology; he's obsessed with sex; he's a sex-aholic. He sees someone with big breasts, full lips, big hair, and a "come and get me" swagger, and he has to get some. He has no restraint, perhaps because he suffers from another disorder: moral insanity. Hillary, according to street wisdom, may be sexually inhibited; rigid control and restraint create her syndrome. People don't wander into her, the way Monica wandered into Bill. Bill's accommodating; Hillary's not. What was once called stereotyping is now only and always a "syndrome." The first rule of "syndrome" is that you personally don't have one. The second rule of "syndrome" is follow the money. The third rule of "syndrome" is follow the whiff of sex.

Back at the ranch, the last of the cowboys are taking their Viagra, e-commerce in pornography is showing the only notable profits in cyberspace, and money, power, and sex are marching arm in arm to the drumbeat of a rising Dow Jones. "First you get the money, then you get the power, then you get the women." Maybe an Arkansas boy like Clinton did him some observing of how the rich and powerful go about getting their sex and he just copied their moves. Any one who doubts that a horny middle-age crisis dude (some greying at the temples) won't use power and money to leverage a lay or a blow from a promising and alluring intern has suppressed his or her reason. This is a winners reap all their perks and profits kind of world, and sex with alluring women who are bombarded by magazines and advertising urging them to be sexy and alluring is high on the perks and profit list.

You have to figure that at a time when (1) the already wealthy have increased their wealth by one-third in this decade; (2) consuming pleasures at a voracious rate is the sign of a Winner; (3) "attractiveness, sexiness, and youth are power" and everybody wants them; (4) in our still puritanical America, Eve's naked body is the temptation, not the apple; and (5) advertising keeps us buying by keeping us titillated—why, you have to figure there are a lot of Bills in the boardrooms and corporate suites fondling a lot of Monicas. And nobody is asking them for public confessions.

Of course, I think either the president of the United States or the press or both should be discreet in these matters, as the press was with JFK, and Ike, and FDR. Truman, Nixon, Ford, and Carter seemed to have had a built-in discreetness. LBJ was just too plain ugly and gross to make anyone think of him having sex. Talking to young women when he was on the bathroom throne seemed to satisfy him. But Carter said he could look at a woman and have sex with her in his head; and what Nixon withheld from poor Pat and expended on his political manias only God knows; and Gerry Ford may have had sex with Mrs. Ford the way Ozzie had sex with Harriet—I mean you just don't think of them that way. Truman was a haberdasher and you can never know what kind of kinky sex haberdashers have, especially when they become presidents of the United States and drop atomic bombs on civilian populations. This was a haberdasher who didn't blink. The buck stopped with him. You just don't know.

I'm asked today by a student whether I think Mary Kay Letourneau was really in love with the sixth-grade student with whom she had two children, in addition to the four she already had. Her shrink and her lawyer see "syndrome" and not love. She suffers from an emotional disorder, or emotional instability, or moral insanity, or some sort of situational neurosis: she sees this kid and she wants him; he's her obsession; she has the kind of depraved appetite people on a steady diet of Jerry Springer display. Or maybe it's a regressive neurosis: she thinks she's a sixth grader too. Anyway, she's got a "syndrome."

Look at it this way, she's got four kids and all the financial wherewithal of a sixth-grade school teacher, so maybe falling in love with this kid is her escape route. It's a breakaway story planned by the Freudian id; this is a dream kid of tireless copulations and she made a grab for him and is holding on for dear life. My thinking goes back to the president of the United States staring at the backside of a sexy intern who has just popped her thong in his face. "Have her deliver the pizza back here," a little voice tells him. "But you're the president of the United States," cautions the same voice that tells Mary Kay, "But he's your student and he's only eleven." But teacher and president go for it and the rest of us wonder, "Can this be love?" and "Have we got another Johnson in the White House?" Syndromes are wrapping us up from high to low. What gives?

I stop channel surfing and pause at the Jabba the Hutt–like countenance of Larry Flynt on Rupert Murdoch's Fox News cable network. A rabbi, a shrink, a wife who's presumably lost her husband to pornography, and the show's hostess are taking turns ripping into Larry Jabba the "pornographer." They're fishing in the waters of his soul hoping to hook . . . what? A confession? An apology? A concession from the devil? An Oprah-like collapse into tears? But this Jabba is giving them nothing: he's imperturbable. The rabbi even admits to Larry's charisma: Larry has a Buddha-like posture and he's even-tempered. He could be standing before Pilate and keeping his cool. They can't rile him, although his attackers are jumping all over each other trying to make their points.

The shrink asserts that a steady diet of pornography isolates and dehumanizes, not to mention objectifies women. The wife tells a story about how her husband could be physically present but really not there. In his mind, he was collating memorable porn visuals. Like a drug addict or an alcoholic, her husband was lost to her. Larry calmly makes his response, making mild gestures with very small, delicate-looking hands. Pornography helps married couples re-invigorate their relationship, he says. And an interest in sex is just not for addicts; go into any house and you'll find a cache of porn. It's not illegal to rent or buy x-rated videos or purchase *Hustler* or go to a strip club or pay for a lap dance, yet it all continues to offend an always vocal segment of the population. The rabbi won't accept any positive role for pornography in marriage; the union is sacred and pornography is filth. They can't marry, Filth and the Sacred. The shrink is convinced that the simulacra of porn takes the place of real human contact, the hyperreality of porn spectacle replaces the reality of real love and sex.

What "real sex" is independent of how we image it and represent it in our heads, in our imaginative lives, the shrink doesn't say. All he knows is that if you masturbate to the spectacle of sex you become isolated, selfish, addicted, finished as a human being. Larry's only ally is a young attractive woman who acts in porn films; she insists that her life is fine; she knows what love is; she doesn't think being in porn films has robbed her of her humanity. She doesn't feel she's an addict or "lost to the world." She enjoys her work and thinks porn has a useful place in people's lives. The hostess probes to see whether or not this poised, well-spoken young woman might, after all, have all the mentality of Jerry Springer's guests. "I speak three languages, have a university degree, and studied at the Sorbonne," the porn star replies. Indeed, she doesn't look stupid and depraved; Larry looks composed and speaks rationally; the rabbi is getting hot and the hostess has to vent her moral indignation a few times; the shrink can't handle the porn star's comment that her work is fun. Doesn't she know that sex is a dark, sticky opium that corrupts your soul, destroys your peace of mind, and haunts you in the aftermath? Doesn't she know sex is THE syndrome inducer?

∽∾∽

Strangely that night I dream about my Xaverian High School days in Brooklyn, which began in 1957 when the Brothers of St. Francis Xavier built a very modern-looking building right on Shore Road near the 69th Street ferry to Staten Island. Shore Road real estate property was elite and I think by building that Catholic high school there the Xaverian Brothers were putting their place of business in a locale that could afford it. I bused there from Bensonhurst and my mother and father struggled to pay the monthly tuition; they did it because sending a kid to a Catholic high school was the right thing to do. I had never been in a Catholic school; saying prayers before class was new to me; taking classes in religion was new to me; looking around the room and seeing statues of the Virgin Mary, seeing a crucifix above the blackboard, watching the brothers finger the rosary beads hanging from the sash around their long black habits was new to me. Moral authority was new to me; you listened to Brother Christopher or Brother René or Brother Cyprian and all the rest not just because you wanted to do well and pass the course; there was something more. They had the Right Reasoning of God behind them. You didn't dare diss them, although some students still did and paid the price: slaps, shoves, ear pulls, knock overs, detention, dismissal.

These brothers took a vow of celibacy; sexuality wasn't anything they were prepared to handle. They lived in the penthouse, I suppose in private rooms. They were having their own problems dealing with sexual urges I'm sure. But they gave you textbooks to read that had a lot to say about sex: what I especially paid attention to was how far you could go before a venial sin turned into a mortal sin. In regard to masturbation, if you came, you went mortal; in regard to a partner, if you fondled below the waist you went mortal. Almost anything that was sexual was an "occasion to sin" and I suppose pornography lost any claim to social virtue at that point. You also had to be on the lookout for "bad thoughts," which was what the Fox News shrink was into. He wasn't claiming "bad thoughts" led to sin; what they led to was a neurotic or psychotic syndrome. You could go to him for a cure. Hillary Clinton's health care plan had proposed that the Feds pay to cure us of our syndromes. It would have been a far less expensive proposal if she had just proposed having her husband cured. That would have preempted Bill's need eventually to make a TV confession.

Back in my Xaverian days we could go to confession on school time. A sound mind in a sound body with an absolved conscience. I would walk into a classroom empty except for a priest sitting at one of the student desks; it was usually a Jesuit. I sat at a desk next to him and began my "Bless me Father for I have sinned." I always started with the non-sex stuff which wasn't hard to reveal at all: "I fought with my brother and sister: I disobeyed my mother and father; I used bad words; I got angry four times; I took money from my mother's purse; I missed Mass twice; I had some bad thoughts; I fought the law and the law won . . ."

"Wait a second. What was that? Repeat."

"I fought the law . . ."

"You had some bad thoughts? What kind of bad thoughts?"

"That's the thing. I had these . . . these thoughts in public school and I didn't think they were bad. Thoughts. But now I'm thinking maybe these . . ."

"About girls?"

"Well, yeah, not all the girls but some of them. You know . . ."

"Did you touch her?"

"Who?"

"You touched yourself then?"

"When?"

"Do you know if you give a bad confession it's a double offense to God?"

"I . . . I did some things to Betty Lou. And then some things when Betty Lou wasn't there. A sort of off and on again relationship."

"How many times?"

"To Betty Lou?"

"WHOMEVER," he thundered.

I had been hoping to conceal her sister and now he had given me the chance.

"Total: three."

"I do the totaling. You just give me the numbers. Do you know you have done moral harm to this girl's soul?"

I shook my head. I was then glad I hadn't given him her real name because I think he was close to asking me to bring her in for a confession.

"She's Jewish I think," I said.

"Did I ask you that? How often do you masturbate?"

"I don't . . . I mean, not really. I just . . . you know . . . have some bad thoughts."

"YOUNG MAN, DON'T PLAY GAMES WITH ME. DO YOU KNOW THAT YOUR SEXUAL APPETITES WILL DEVOUR YOUR SOUL? WITHOUT RESTRAINT YOU ARE NOTHING MORE

THAN A BEAST. SEX WILL TAKE YOU TO THE LEVEL OF THE
BEAST. DID YOU KNOW THAT?"

"I keep it to a venial level," I told him, trying to look up at him.
Many years later I read a memorable passage from Pierre Bourdieu's
Distinction in which he claimed that an overflowing dish of spaghetti
lacked the "distinction" of French *cuisine minceur* because the former
displayed an Italian lack of restraint, a sign of chaos and not order, while
the minimalism of the French dish displayed the admirable and civilized
qualities of discipline and order.

"Your sexual appetite is driving you away from God," he told me.
"Do you promise to leave these girls alone?"

"The movies are out?"

"Who's talking about the movies?"

"I like to take . . . ah . . . Peggy Sue to the movies. Some times."

"And by 'take Peggy Sue to the movies some times' you mean what?"

"Jeez, I don't know."

"Do you plan on marrying Peggy Lou?"

"Peggy Lou? I . . . I don't think so."

"Then you mustn't rob her purity from the man who will marry her."

"You mean Ricky Holley?"

"Betty Sue has a husband?"

"Betty . . . ? No. No, she doesn't."

"Her virginity is her gift to her husband, Nick Hollingsworth. Not
to you."

"Nick . . . ? Yeah, I see your point."

"Six hundred Pater Nostras and a thousand Ave Marias. Say a
prayer for me."

"You got it."

"Young man, did you ever think that sex was driving you insane?"

"Jeez, you mean I've got a syndrome?"

"I've got one of those syndromes," I said to myself on my way out.
My sexual appetite was the biggest pain in the ass in my life; it was
totally eating me up, screwing me up, and putting me through hell. I
decided to master that appetite for no other reason than to end this shite
in confession. I would walk into that room the next time, look that old
bastard in the eye, and tell him I robbed, fought, lied, cheated, cursed,
got drunk, forged my father's signature, fought the law and the law won.
And that was it. None of that stuff became personal to me; he could
probe all he wanted about any of that and I would be glad to give him
the particulars. All you had to do was delete sex from your life and you
could avoid being humiliated; you could keep that dark cloud from
entering your soul. Only something intrinsically bad could put you

through so much misery. Bill Clinton could have done all the damage Reagan did to our egalitarian democracy and NOT mess with Monica and Bill would be a poster boy right now for Pat Robertson's 700 Club. Al Gore would have run on Bill's moral coattails and it would have been a clear victory over Dubya. A little stain of sex goes deep into the heartland of America. The savings and loan scandal which should have tainted the name "Bush" forever was not a SEX scandal so it didn't play. The Iran-contra affair displayed more contempt for our constitutional democracy than Watergate, but it was not a SEX scandal. The "sin" didn't register. You have to remember that "politics" bores Americans while SEX titillates them. As soon as "Deep Throat" came on the scene, Nixon's fate was sealed. Somewhere in the American cultural imaginary Linda Lovelace was lurking. The grounding reason why the Puritan crusader Ken Starr got nowhere with Whitewater was because it wasn't a SEX scandal.

When I dreamed that night I was totally back into that sixteen-year-old mind-set and I got up shivering. My dark night of the soul was grounded in sexuality; there was something radically and drastically wrong with this. There was something terribly wrongheaded with this whole approach to sexuality. I had no idea what the right approach was, but I knew the Xaverian days approach wasn't the right one.

And I had been terribly wrong to think that all transgressions not of a sexual nature were innocuous, were untroubling, to me and the rest of the world. That mentality has persisted; while sexuality has taken the brunt of our moral focus and filled our moral sensibility, we have lost our sense of how dark and terrible injustice is, presumptuous power is, greed and selfishness are, dishonesty and bigotry are, thievery and uncharitableness are, how estranging and heartless prudery is, how terribly we treat the "lower orders," and how the sins of omission—what we fail to do on each other's behalf—erode our compassion and love.

∞∞

It doesn't take very long in discussions—I mean screaming sessions—over whether gay marriages should be permitted, or gay partners should get medical coverage, or gays should be allowed in the military, or gays should be allowed in the classroom to talk about being gay—and all permutations of such discussions—before someone gets explicit about just what homosexuals and lesbians are doing to each other in the bedroom. "Look, if they want to make love to their own sex, that's their business. But why should we extend any legal rights or social recognition to them? Or lower the moral bar to accommodate them?" Pederasts and sadomasochists and sex fetishists of all kinds have *their* sex lives, but they're not a part of civil society; the social order is neither enhanced by their presence nor compelled to admit them.

Somehow the nuclear family and heterosexuality reinforce the order of things and promote a stable atmosphere in which profits can be made, while same-sex marriage and homosexuality upset order and stability. If moral sanctions were dropped in regard to sexuality, we'd all lose our moral sense and direction. It seems that a moral compass, then, is no more than a sex gauge. But if I remember my Dantean circles in hell, there was a whole lot more to evil than illicit sex. Of the Seven Deadly Sins—Pride, Covetousness, Lust, Anger, Gluttony, Envy, and Sloth—we seemed to have made pride a necessity for political and social identity; covetousness and lust marketing devices; anger a second-half motivational device; gluttony an issue of saturated fat content; envy the by-product of believing self-interest is a grounding virtue of human nature; sloth, what the Underclass exhibits and makes them "natural losers."

I have my own list: Deceit, Arrogance, Selfishness, Meanspiritness, Closed-mindedness, Prudery, and Greed. These are not the Seven Deadly Sins of our new global market order, but rather they have become the "virtues" of our American culture.

Advertising seduces us deceitfully: what was previously unrepresented in our minds suddenly appears as a desire, that desire quickly becomes a need, that need can be met by the market. You can buy it. I see arrogance from an arrogant class which corrupts our democracy in order to preserve its elite status, which has no incentive to change our society on behalf of countless millions simply because such change may damage that class's portfolios. Selfishness is the ultimate destination of a creed grounded in self-interest. Meanspiritness is another inevitable by-product of "market values are the only values" creed. Closed as we Americans now are in a "show me the money!" reality frame, we have no way to imagine other configurations of reality. A closed-minded person is not necessarily a prude. But a prude also suffers from a lack of imagination, or, as in the case of those who can imagine same sex sex, draws back in horror. Prudes bind energy of all kinds and project their inhibitions onto the world in the form of laws and protocols and rules and advisories and behavioral guides. Prudes are nurtured in our "to be is to consume" reality because their senseless armor becomes an easy target for advertisers. Pitch an implicit or explicit sexual message to a prude and you will draw them in. Attach sexuality to product and the prudes pull out credit cards. What they suppress and repress is forever a way to reach . . . into their pocketbooks.

What needs to be said about the importance of greed in our "Who Wants to Be a Millionaire?" world? Every contestant on that show affirms the "need for greed." If we all weren't ever greedy, ever desirous of having more and more "things," more and more comfort and convenience, why, our profits would not maximize, the economy would not "grow," and "jobs would be lost." So be greedy for the sake of America. Greed is not just an American Dream but an American reality. It's elsewhere but we are the major exporter of this mentality. Greed is our true pathological syndrome. And who speaks out against it?

Not Seattle

November 1999

"High Coaches' Pay Irks Some" reads the headline today on our campus newsheet. The guy on record as being irked is a university trustee and he thinks the $780,000 the basketball coach is making is a bloated salary and represents "a losing battle academia is waging against athletics." Another trustee, who happens to be a multimillionaire entrepreneur, dismisses the criticism, stating that supply and demand determine salaries. "People get paid based on what the marketplace calls for."

Two days later the headline announces the departure of the football coach. He has had a winning season, taken his team to a bowl game, and as a result has received a "big offer" from an even bigger football school. The headline now reads: "Job Means More Cash for Former Leader." He'll get 6.25 million dollars in cash over five years. What the football coach had as part of his salary at the job he leaves behind was radio, television, and shoe endorsement contracts, and an interest-free million-dollar loan for investment purposes. "Money isn't everything to a true Spartan," writes a student in the newspaper's letter column. But there are strikingly few letters; there is brief, subdued chatter about this in the locker room, students don't mention it when I ask, as I always do, "What's breaking in the headlines?" There's no easy handle on this. You want to come out censorious. You feel you've got reasons. A guy who asked a losing team to bleed for him and gets them to do that and makes them a winning team jumps ship in less than twenty-four hours. And when asked if he did it for the money says, "No." "What other reasons then?" "I don't know," he says, looking like someone who needs to confess something but can't find any reason to.

This is the guy who most likely called upon his players time and again to reach deep inside themselves and find the motivation to win, to put aside their personal hurts, their failing enthusiasm, their personal peeves, and "do it for the team." Don't let your teammates down, don't

170

let your university down, don't let yourself down. Go the extra yard, give 110 percent, give beyond what you think you can give. You want to say winning in football is a capitalist thing, but it's really more of a socialist thing. The great and winning team is a team in which everyone leans on everyone else, depends on the other guy while themselves doing all they can to justify the others depending on them. The hotshot in there for personal glory, the hotshot pursuing self and not team interests, is a drawback. It takes teamwork to win. Presumably, a winning coach elicits that teamwork from his team; he makes them see how interdependent they are and gets them to think twice about referring only to their self-interests. Don't let the team down interlocks with don't let yourself down.

Then this coach leaves for a "sweetheart deal"—and why not? He wants to be a millionaire, or more precisely in this case, a multimillionaire. A TV game show of that name has swept the ratings, followed closely behind by an even more in your face title: Greed. You can't come out censorious because you want to be a millionaire too, and because you agree with the trustee who says the market rules. Supply and demand is an incontrovertible law. And pursuing self-interest compels you in the most natural way to seize every opportunity to place yourself in greater and greater demand. Why wouldn't students thrown into an America which knows no values but market values be speechless at a time like this? How could they be critical? What counternarrative of values would they be drawing upon? What countermemory before Reaganite economics can they draw upon?

I'm fascinated by the silence, by the speechlessness, by the incapacity of students to put into words, to find a discourse, to narrate a response to this notion that the market steers our lives and we should bow to it without a murmur of dissent. This failure to narrate has been going on throughout the country with this generation. At this university there have been three riots which have gotten national attention. The last one involved numerous fires, cars overturned (including police cars), an ambulance stopped, and private property destroyed. A presidential task force on alcoholism was the administrative response. Students rioted on all these occasions because some had been binge drinking. Why were they binge drinking? Because they won or lost a game? Because their drinking privileges—kegs, open field tailgating, fraternity and sorority parties—had been terminated? Why were they drinking so much? Because their freedom to drink so much was being eroded? The stupidity of this circular reasoning doesn't make the headlines. For their part, students have no reasons to give; no narrative, no tactics of revolt, no ideology of revolt, no self-reflexivity, if you will.

They cannot be hyper-conscious about their own awareness and actions. When questioned, they adopt the discourse of the administration: some students binge drink. Maybe, some say, they binge drink because their binge drinking rights are being infringed upon. And the police, city and campus, are harassing students because they've profiled all students as binge drinkers, as always just seconds away from being unlawful. So the campus police are dosing the students with "tough love" because they drink and riot, and the students are drinking and rioting because the campus police are dosing them with "tough love" because they drink and riot. Thus, the student's apologia, another circle of stupidity that doesn't make the headlines.

The stupidity here is doubly stupefying because this is a university crammed full of academics who teach on the average of six hours a week for about seven months of the year and who, ostensibly, "do research and publish" the rest of the time, and students who are here to . . . to do what? To learn how to maximize their value in a supply-and-demand market-driven society. For the last twenty years they've been demanding faculty and courses that enable them to maximize their value in the marketplace. And except for a small enclave that is more involved in "political correctness" than in "critical thinking," this university gives students what they want. It's a matter of supply and demand after all. Why should the university be fostering and implementing any other values? Why would we expect that this privileged academic elite, privileged because they have time to read and think, privileged because they get a chance to communicate what they think to the coming generation, would be presenting to students a countermemory, a counternarrative to market values? Why would we expect that this university education itself would supply students with the narrative means to tell us why they are rioting? Why are students un–self-reflexive and uncritical at the very moment when they are acting as if something is oppressing them, something is rotten in the state of Denmark and they don't have the means or the inclination, the wherewithal to see and say what it is?

The protests in Seattle against a meeting of the World Trade Organization (WTO) make the important headlines, pace football coaches with sweet deals. In dramatic contrast to the rioting university students, these protestors know what they are protesting; they have a discourse of protest; they have brought their anger and frustration to a sayable level. They have critiqued this new move toward globalized trade and found it to be without sufficient safeguards and consideration of worker's safety, rights, benefits, and wages, and environmental concerns of all types and magnitude. When I ask, "What's breaking in the headlines?" expecting the WTO riots to be mentioned, no one says anything. This protest is caught in the same bind as the coach's departure for more money. If you're protesting trade you're protesting market values; you're protesting the free play of the global market. "Trade is freedom," Republican presidential candidate George W. Bush affirms, giving us yet another hook-up with the signifier "freedom." When you equate "freedom" with "trade," anyone bringing up things like workers and environment, matters which themselves should be settled by the law of supply and demand, is trying to constrain freedom. Transnationals will go where the labor is cheap; the environment shall be a constraint upon free trade when and if and where science says it should be and not until.

This is not a generation shaped to be rebels; this is a generation shaped to be consumers. So when they read that their basketball coach makes $780,000 a year and their own humanities professor makes a whopping $49,000, when they read that their beloved football coach has taken a job that pays him twice his present $650,000 a year salary, and when they read that a board of trustee member says that this is just the law of the market—implying an irrefutable, incontestable Law of the Land—this is all swallowed by this Cool Beans generation. It's all as it should be. Consuming at the top of the food chain and doing all you can to get there is what it's all about. No one can be blamed for looking out for Number One. What Thomas Carlyle called the "cash nexus" is the connection that trumps all others. Already consumed by the market's logic of unrelenting consumption and the pursuit of even greater and greater consumption, members of this generation have no recourse but to continue to shape themselves—their thoughts, their perceptions, their present and future—within this "to be is to consume" ontology. Something like the protest of a WTO's continuing policies and activities which benefit only those positioned to profit at the expense of those positioned to be victimized, including the environment, comes across as nothing more than an incomprehensible obstruction of the "freedom to consume," or, as Milton Friedman referred to it, "the freedom to choose" . . . which I take to mean choosing products off a shelf, out of a catalog, off the Internet.

At the same time that the young are caught in this vicious circle of knowing the world as something to be consumed and producing that world within that way of knowing, sporadic acts of rage, mayhem, and riot reveal feelings of abuse, exploitation, victimization. This is a generation targeted by the same market that gives them no special place: in the market view the young are not the future of America; their worth is restricted to their buying capacity. On the debit side is the huge cost to educate and the perennial restlessness of the young which always threatens the status quo. Order, not democracy, is what corporations, including transnationals, require. Order is grounded in redundancy not critical thinking; in a constrained imagination not a rebellious one. Left out, sold out, demoted, trashed, angry, anxious, mystified, frustrated, bitter, resentful, the young on this campus riot and break stuff with no words to express or explain what they are about.

And why should they have the words? Consumers aren't shaped to be skeptical, to be self-reflexive. The football coach who makes greed shape his needs, in line with the hottest new TV show "Greed," doesn't inspire my students to dig deeply into this gospel of greed and into their own lives and its effects upon them. It just makes them more cynical; a cynicism that doesn't know its source. It's rather like stepping into a dark room and not being able to see who's hitting you or where it's coming from.

The first casualty of the creed of "Consume or Be Consumed" is the consumer: their ways of knowing and being are consumed; their hearts and minds and perceptions are consumed. Most tragically, it's their potential to be in the world in ways that have nothing to do with profit which dies on the vine.

Elsinore Castle

November 7, 2000

> *By God these votes are being counted by people and not machines! What finality can come of that?*
> —A Bush spokesperson on the occasion of the second recount by hand of Florida presidential votes

Predicted as a low turnout election that you could nap through and one that would be very close because George W. and Al Gore had been locked in a statistical dead heat throughout the campaign, this election drew a huge turnout of voters, and one day after, is still undecided.

No one is napping now. Early in the evening of November 7 every network announced that Florida was Gore's. An hour or so later, Mary Matalin on CNN declared that that was a premature call. The Bush camp demanded the networks throw Florida back in the undecided pile. The networks complied. Now at 2:43 P.M. November 8, Florida votes are being recounted. A ballot box has been found in a church in Dade County, Florida, in a minority-filled district. Overseas ballots have not yet come in. Gore has a slim lead in both the popular vote and in the electoral college, but a win in Florida for Bush will give Bush the electoral college and the presidency. But will it? Jesse Jackson has flown down to Florida alleging that "It's not just a recount, it's about investigation." He's gotten a whiff of voter intimidation. First count of the Florida vote put Bush ahead by a mere 1,784 votes. A second count is underway. The country waits.

Foundationally, the battle here between Republicans and Democrats in this election is between profit margins uninterrupted and unimpeded, and cuts into those margins on behalf of those who have been left out of the Dow's Golden Age. It's all an economic deal, a market matter. Neither side wants to kill the goose who's laying the golden eggs. Ralph Nader and the Green Party want to put the market on the back burner on behalf of environmental protection, worker's rights and safety, consumer protection and rights, and the poor. Nader's message is so dangerous to the "We All Want to Be Millionaires" mentality of the moment that it's kept out of the debates. If we put environmental concerns before profit concerns, profit margins stand to be clobbered. If we let workers do more than just wet their beaks in the reservoir of profit, profit margins stand to be clobbered. If we put consumer protection and rights before profit concerns, profits stand to be clobbered by lawsuits. If we redistribute the wealth downward through a progressive income tax, inheritance tax, luxury tax, and capital gains tax—all with shark teeth—personal fortunes will take a hit.

New Democrats are "new" in this way: they're for passing on some of the winnings of the market to those discarded by global capitalism not by tempering the savagery of the global market but by finessing a concession here, a compromise there, a redefining, a playing along to get along, a Slick Willy piggybacking on the market train. Old Democrats are "old" in this way: they're looking for some way to knock the market engine off the track and put the engine of egalitarian democracy back on track. To do that they have to solve the transnationalization of the market problem—the first problem being that neither the Democrats who won the presidency in 1992 and 1996 (the New Democrats) or the Republicans deem a problem at all. The Old Democrats have to prove that the road to wealth is not democracy's road; that in the battle between capitalism and democracy, capitalism has to be remodeled and not democracy.

Global capitalism is already seeing itself *beyond* nationalism, *beyond* egalitarianism, and *beyond* democracy. What's wrong with plutocracy, with oligarchy? Academic economists tell us that there is no economic repercussion to the huge gap between rich and poor in this country. Of course, they don't leave their Ivory Tower offices to take a stroll through the inner city at night. Those are not stock market consequences; those are easily avoidable consequences—unless the discontented become nomadic and sneak through your gated community and show up when you're "home alone." There are bloody consequences then, and loss of property.

More people showed up to vote than expected, a lot more. Why had all the network and cable chatter pushed low turnout? Were they relying on the same sort of statistical sampling that so egregiously let them all down on election night? It's legend that high turnout benefits the Democrats and low turnout benefits the Republicans. When the bottom 40 percent of the population—the working poor and barely working crowd—turn out to vote they are more liable to identify themselves as "workers" rather than "shareholders," more liable to rely on big government working on their behalf, less enchanted by the glamour of corporate downsizing, less likely to be hanging breathlessly on the rise and fall of the Dow Jones, more on the lookout for a reliable safety net, and not ready to get rid of the minimum wage because it's a burden to employers. Some well-planned, deliberate effort has to be made to spin this crowd away from voting.

You can hear the spin all around you: "There's no choice here. Two boring candidates." "There's no difference between these guys. It doesn't matter, so why vote?" "One guy is as corrupt as the other. I wouldn't waste my time voting for either one." "Two millionaires fighting it out; nothing to do with me." "President doesn't mean anything because he can't do anything. He's not running the country. So why vote?" "When they say something in my language that affects my life, and they say it straight and simple without the politics, then I'll vote." "No vote ever helped any poor man out of his poverty." "Politics is a dirty business. I wouldn't dirty my hands with it."

As the country becomes increasingly divided between the very wealthy and the wannabe wealthies treading water with sixty- to eighty-hour weeks and maxed-out credit cards, the job of spinning the Have Nots into believing that government won't help them or shouldn't help them, and not seeing that the Haves are enjoying the status quo and therefore have no incentive to change things (making them the least appropriate choices for political leadership in a democracy) becomes increasingly difficult. The old reliable phrase since Reagan's days—Big Government is the problem—is now moving from easily mouthed shibboleth to scrutinized "signifier."

I, for one, would like the various regulatory agencies to protect me from toxic food, water, air, pharmaceuticals, dangerous working situations and so on, safeguard my Social Security not as a speculative Wall Street investment but as a secured retirement savings, protect and preserve the natural beauty and resources of this country from the driving force of short-terms profits. I want the Department of Justice to jump on monopolistic mergers; I want those who fall by the wayside to know that we do not live in a "war of all against all society" and that blame for their plight is not as easily assigned as our present understanding of "free to choose," "assuming personal responsibility," and "rewarding bad behavior" would indicate.

Look at the demographics of spinscapes, starting with the twenty-somethings at university. They're nodding "yes" when they hear Ben Affleck in the film, *The Boiler Room,* tell them that they can be millionaires in three years, and if anyone tells them money isn't everything, what they're telling them is that *they* don't have any money. "There's power in the dollar." They certainly are not busy taking apart terms like "free to choose," "assuming personal responsibility," "contingency," "having a moral compass," "relativism and absolutism," "determinacy and indeterminacy," "the view of non-correspondence," "explanation vs. interpretation," "realism and nominalism," "intentionality," "materialism," "consciousness," "faith and reason," "ontology and epistemology," "political and economic equality," "self-interest and mutual aid," "competition vs. cooperation," "individualism vs. socialism." The list could go on until it exhausts a two-semester philosophy course, and even that course would leave no one with any sense of closure. Certainly there is a sense of how conflicting interpretations are slyly transformed into grounding principles.

You might say that while all varieties of socialism, from anarchism to communism, appealed to the best in human nature—a giving up of one's self-interest on behalf of others—our regnant form of global capitalism appeals to the worst in human nature—an amassing of personal wealth accompanied by an indifference to the plight of others, a blatant indifference often hiding behind "philanthropy," which has more to do with tax write-offs than a charitable feeling. While governmental intrusion on behalf of the Losers is labeled "social engineering," allowing the market to rule is allowing "individual freedom and choice" an opportunity to make us all rich. This translates into a red flag for applying critical interrogation to social, cultural, and personal issues and a green flag for allowing the casino logic of the market to rule in all these areas.

After hundreds of years of trying out various ideologies amid the often disastrous play of Chance and the tyranny of despots, we now have decided to let the rise and fall of the Dow Jones, the toss of the dice of speculative investment, to navigate our society. History is as dead as yesterday's Dow Jones report; creativity pays off only as entrepreneurial innovation; philosophy may have its uses as a Prozac-like palliative; science is measured in patents pending; religion is the retreat of the Losers; ethics guide the Losers; medicine underwrites drug company profits; and public education from K to 12 wanders in a maze of cultural legacy and market demands. University education aspires to neutrality and objectivity while being increasingly sabotaged and redirected by market demands. Academic economists provide the needed alibis posing as rational and statistical evidence to support market values. At the same time they fail to step back and examine the frame of their own spin.

What spinscape is the Entrepreneurial Class in? They are the brokers at the wheel, New and Old Economy entrepreneurs, those both in the captain's quarters and increasingly distinguished only by what they own and how well they play the game. They are not distinguished in any way in spirit, in mind, in imagination and vision, in heart, in compassion.

George Dubya latches onto this word "compassion," he's a "compassionate conservative." Why, except to mock our lingering attachment to it in a dog eat dog world forged by our privileging of market values, of profit margins, above all else? Clearly there is no place for "compassion" in our entrepreneurial wars of all against all: Winners win and take all and Losers go out of business. But this word "compassion" is sounded now in this election as a defense against the masses awakening to a world robbed of all compassion. The more a signifier gets flapped about, the greater the chance that its meaning has vanished in society.

Within what spinscape are the masses ensnared? They are distracted by issues like gun control and single sex marriage, issues that arise from America's long time fixation with sex and violence (fixations that legislation will not detour). There is endless worry whether this person or that has or has not a "moral compass," whether I have or you have lost our moral sense, whether that sense is vanishing because "family values" are vanishing. Is it a collapse in "family values" that is the root cause of our moral decline? Do I lack conscience? Do you? Does the whole country? I think of these doubts in the same way I think of Hamlet's doubts and concerns: could he act and yet preserve his integrity? Lose or not lose his peace of mind? Was a personal sin rotting the soul of all of Denmark? These are not trivial concerns; they are eternal concerns. They don't vanish if a president is impeached for his sins. They don't vanish if his political party is denied success in future elections. But fingering any state of "family values" as the arbiter of personal and social conscience is a gimmick, a device, a trick, rather like the magician pointing over *there* as he pulls something from up his sleeve over *here*. Sure, Claudius's murder of Hamlet the King precipitates a decline in "family values." But the murderer and the murder is who and what you've got to keep your eye on.

Corporate greed, local, national, transnational, and personal greed, in every class, murders all our values, not simply "family values." We value within the compass of "power in the dollar" and thus lose sight of how and where are lives are devalued and diminished. What divides a family more than a need for both husband and wife to work forty hours and more a week each, leave their children in day care or with a neighbor down the street, have time only to order a pizza or drive through McDonald's, believe that the more stuff they buy the better the quality of their family life, dream that somehow the Internet will do the child rearing for them, and that Madison Avenue and Hollywood celebrities are the role model for themselves and their children?

Karl Marx didn't foresee the soma tablets of the future, the dis-
tracting, exploiting, victimizing, seducing spinscapes of our postmodern
world. He saw religion as an opiate keeping the masses from perceiving
the plight they were in, the boot soles on their necks. The state would
crush religion. Political ideology would take its place. But he underesti-
mated human greed and self-interest. I mean the pervasiveness of it. It
saturates the slaves as well as the masters, owners as well as workers.
Let's look at this split right down the middle in this election as not only
an old-fashioned Marxist split between Haves and Have Nots, but one
in which both sides share a psychology of desire and suppression. Desire
is spun in the direction of market profits; what gets in the way of that
spin is suppressed, dis-remembered, vilified, demonized.

The Haves, as always, have no incentive to change a status quo that
serves them well; unlike an aristocracy built on bloodlines, our American Haves cannot rest on their laurels. Their portfolios must be ever
expanding. "Enough" is a word that has no meaning for them. If they're
observant, they have fear of the Disaffected and understand the usefulness of "tough love" crime laws and tax money spent to build prisons.
If they're observant, they do all that they can to insure and secure their
privacy, their possessions, their own safety. Money will influence legislation; the presidency is no more than a position that must be kept from
anyone who would use it to "social engineer"—that is, push values
other than corporate values. Everything must be privatized and brought
to the level of "pay as you go" so that profit can be made everywhere
and in everything; profit to be made from the sick, from schoolchildren,
from the old, from workers, from the imprisoned, from the land, water,
and air. Water once free is now bought; air once breathable now must
be "conditioned." And the earth must be taken from the family farmers
and turned to real estate profits.

The philosophical underpinning of all this is a naive and simplistic
notion of free will. The Winners choose to win; they are totally and personally responsible for their stock market successes, for their seven-fig-
ure bonuses. Why should any part of their winnings be taken away by
the Feds? Why should any part of their winnings be used by the Feds to
help the Losers? Chance is not a factor; neither are all those social, bio-
logical, and cultural constraints that were brought up in the days when
the argument between free will and determinism hadn't been set aside by
consumer capitalism's mantra of "free to choose." We're more ignorant
than we used to be, ignorant of the penetrating critiques made against
naive views of free will, personal responsibility, winning and losing,
what liberty is, what equality is, where and what we are in Nature, what
social justice is, what the American Dream may be, defined beyond

stocks and toys. This class capitalizes on such ignorance. It protects their niche at the top of the food chain. If you raise a wealthy man or woman from the dead from any century, he or she will become acclimated to our times swiftly. They will know how to preserve their privilege and will soon see what the threats to that well-being might be. Raise the dead Haves from four hundred years ago and they will as surely vote for George Dubya as the living Haves have done.

But today we have a more divided plutocracy, a schizoid one. Here's what I mean: take a baby boomer from the working class who has taken advantage of the post-WWII state or city university expansion and has now "professionalized"—become an accountant, chiropractor, broker, engineer, etc.—and has married someone also professionalized. They were both radical hippies in their twenty-something years; they have a warm place in their hearts for liberal causes. Now it's the year 2000 and they have to vote for George W. or Gore. They understand what Clinton meant; they understand what Gore means. But they've had a combined salary of over six figures for the past fifteen years. They have a portfolio and a financial consultant. They watch the "Nightly Business Report" with Paul Kangas. They'd like to see a drop or an elimination of the capital gains tax; they'd like to see an annihilation of inheritance taxes. They'd certainly like to pay less income tax. They're schizoid; they're drawn in two different directions at the same time. They're split right down the middle. How will they vote?

Let's compound the scenario: the guy is a professor who also writes for different magazines; the wife is a lawyer who wants to take pro bono cases but has to disappoint paying clients to do so. Both are on the neighborhood council where all decisions are based on the preservation and enhancement of property values, including a tough love view of crime and criminals. Fifty years ago, a less well-heeled, un-portfolioed intellectual class would speak out and write on behalf of social justice while deconstructing each seductive spin as it came into view. Now this class is divided between tending their stocks and speaking out. The least reprehensible thing they do is to do nothing in the face of injustice, inequities, privilege, corruption, and exploitation. The mediate reprehensible thing they do is to vote to preserve their portfolios and property. The most reprehensible thing they do is show up on cable TV and spout alibis for the privileged class.

Who then will speak for the Disaffected? Certainly not this year's candidates. George W. Bush is running on a ticket of not speaking to or of the Disaffected but merely hoping to continue a politics of extermination. And since Gore refuses to acknowledge the part our trust in the casino logic of the global market plays in disenfranchising some 40 percent of the population, while another 40 percent are already on the discard pile, he too is not speaking for Losing and Losers. These folks are caught in a spinscape that they themselves have not the means to get out of.

The concept of the "Disaffected" is itself an accusation made by the Haves: these people over here, in this trailer park, on this "Jerry Springer Show," are "disaffected." They have lost their capacity to connect with anything, certainly they are not connected with the demands of competition and entrepreneurship. Their disaffection is of their own making; they can remedy it but they choose not to. They refuse to assume personal responsibility for their own disaffection. We owe them nothing but tough love if they bring their disaffection to the point of rebellion and criminality.

What do the Disaffected say for themselves? Will they get out and vote? Neither George Dubya nor Gore made any special pitches to the bottom two-fifths of the population. No sense in transmitting when there are no receivers. For the Republicans, the United Auto Workers (UAW) having election day off and spending the day "getting the vote out," is a problem because the UAW will try to herd in this bottom two-fifths. Jessie Jackson "getting the vote out" among blacks is a problem, too, because he will try to herd in this bottom two-fifths. But in a world in which this bottom two-fifths share the same spinscapes as their more solvent fellow citizens, there is no guarantee that these Disaffected will vote in their best interests.

From the Reagan era on until the mid 1990s, an increasing number of minorities caught in an unmoving pre–middle class existence saw entrepreneurship and not government intervention as a way out and up. But that has reversed with this 2000 election. Clinton's popularity among blacks during his eight-year tenure was not simply the result of his expressing the words "I feel your pain." Blacks saw real change and improvement during his administration. And this split election indicates that for blacks, at least, government rather than entrepreneurship is more liable to ease the conditions of their existence. The idea that blacks would be better off today if they had never followed Dr. King and his fight for Civil Rights in the 1960s, and instead started businesses and gotten into the arena to compete, was for a brief moment an "idea" and is now just a spin, one of the more ludicrous, insulting ones to come down the pike.

Our election is split down the middle because positions are finally clarifying, finding shape, and though any number of spinscapes blur these lines—a well–stock-optioned homosexual votes for Gore; a long-term Democrat born again votes against Clinton and for Dubya; a trophy wife votes for Hillary because she's a woman; a poor man fearful of losing his gun to the government votes for George Dubya; a husband and wife with four jobs between them always come running to the sound of "reduced taxes"; a lower-class racist votes against liberal entitlement programs; a heavy smoker dying of emphysema salutes the mantra of "assume personal responsibility"; a downsized worker rises to the corporate call to downsize the federal government; a middle-class family enjoying camping in the national parks rises to the call of "privatize public lands out West"; a husband and wife with a young asthmatic child decides to buy a huge, air-polluting SUV; a man whose grandparents were immigrants to the United States rises to the Conservatives call for anti-immigration legislation of all kinds; a professional liberal couple making six-figure salaries offer neither health nor retirement benefits to their illegal immigrant nanny; former liberal bleeding hearts of the 1960s instruct their broker to get them into socially concerned stocks only if their profits are not affected; a millionaire whose own father's union provided death benefits which brought financial security to his mother now votes as an anti-union Conservative; a woman brutalized by her own father and now her own husband votes Republican because she hates the sight of Hillary Clinton; an eighteen-year-old kid heavily into sports votes for the party with the slogan "Let the best man win!"; a pregnant eighteen year old wanting desperately to abort votes for the party seeking to end legalized abortions; a black sharecropper's son who gets into college through affirmative action and goes on to become a medical doctor votes for the party seeking to end affirmative action . . . and so on endlessly.

I listen to words coming out of Dubya's mouth that sound as if they had been part of a telegraphy message game, and Dubya is the last to have received the message. I listen to the sentences he forms and my mind wanders in his stochastic pauses; he pauses as if he were wondering if this was where the sentence ends. I move with him toward an ending that never comes and drift back to another try at saying what he thinks he might have already said. When the left eye wink comes and the mouth twists into what looks like a smirk, there then is the end.

I yearn to hear some fool from my educational past rave about how much progress the world has made, how greatly things have improved, how startlingly brilliant and overwhelming our technological future will be. Victory through chemicals; progress through plastics; the future from General Electric; a transnational corporation paying its top executives salaries higher than the gross domestic product (GDP) of half the countries in the world, "bringing good things to life" for the privileged few on this planet. And then I listen to Dubya's muddled connecting of word and world.

You've noticed that Nature doesn't extend the model of progress; you don't pick it up from the seasons. You can of course say that you preferred the winter of 1969 in upstate New York to the winter of 1982 in Los Angeles—maybe because there is no winter in Los Angeles, ever— or you prefer the reverse—exactly because there is no winter in Los Angeles, ever. You might like the spring of 1963 better than the spring of 1999 because young love filled the former and divorce the latter. This autumn was the absolute tops and you don't know why. Probably because you can't remember other autumns. And the summer when you were twelve went on for twelve years, or so it seemed. And last summer was over it seemed before it began. We fill the seasons with stories, some fact based, some all fiction. These seasons repeat, not ever the same, but within generous boundaries we never fail to recognize.

We're heading for winter now; Thanksgiving is on the horizon. There is a soothing solace to the come-again quality of seasons and their holidays. Winter especially. Perhaps because it is the death that summer falls into, clearly showing us that all progress made ends here, and what begins again next spring is neither a continuation offering the promise of progress, nor a new beginning, also offering the promise of progress toward some end. Nature offers something radically different and incomprehensible to us; the orbit of this planet has not yet made an impression on our mental orbiting. We are orbiting elsewhere, I fear.

In the Ring

October 1999

> *We really have no freedom about creating our identities,
> because we are trained to want what we want.*
> —Foucault

> *These men, disenfranchised by franchise-mad America, are
> the rabid battalions Starbucks hath wrought; zonked by
> malaise, they can feel alive only when they hurt . . . we men
> are all living in a toxic dump, and it's called America. . . .
> We've all been deluded by advertising . . . we've had no great
> wars or Depressions to preoccupy our testosterone. What's a
> poor guy to do?*
> —Peter Rainer, *New York Magazine*, Oct. 25, 1999

"I hope this film isn't going to be given the brink-of-the-millennium treatment by deep-think commentators," Peter Rainer writes about *Fight Club* in *New York Magazine* (Oct. 25, 1999). In his view the film "has about as much going on in its head as an afternoon with Oprah. Actually, Oprah may have the edge." But Jerry Springer is more in the Fight Club world than Oprah. You join the Jerry Springer Club or you join Fight Club kind of thing.

⌒◡⌒

As a participant in the Jerry Springer Club you don't catalogue shop; all the credit cards are maxed and no credit card company is sending you any more. Still, you've been trained by Madison Avenue to want what you want: a lot of top-of-the-line stuff, to be a millionaire, to have the lifestyle of the rich and famous, all your toys fully loaded. You want them to show you the money. In the way of collateral assets and future potential you show your ability to read at a fourth-grade level, the critical thinking capacity of Cro-Magnon, a moral sense shaped by Gangsta Rap or Melrose Place, and a grasp of why you're in the spot you're in that begins and ends with the word "fuck." The closest you come to solidarity is maybe your posse life, or your support group on the Inside. America is your neighborhood, your turf; nothing worth anything is outside that world. Nobody knows you but you know them. If you listen to them too long, it will erode your self-confidence, suck out your strength. People who think they are better than you only want what you have. You're proud of your life; you're in control. So when you're asked to join the Jerry Springer Club as a participant and tell your story, you say why not? You get your shot on TV; you get your fifteen seconds in the spotlight. They don't like it? Who cares?

❦

A participant in Fight Club? A long distance, my friend, from a participant in the Jerry Springer Club. You have to jump the grand canyon between assuming you want what you want because it's what you want to looking around to see who and what is feeding you your wants. Why and how come next. Why would you first begin to doubt you're in charge? What would be your first clue? What would give away the game? What Edward Norton does in the film is first cruise support group meetings. Looking for what? Propelled by what? Let's just say it's an Ishmael-like cold and rainy November in his soul, and instead of going to sea for relief he attends these meetings in which the grieving and dying, the hurt and shamed, try to find comfort in numbers. He seems numb to the perks of his catalogue-furnished apartment and his "symbolic analyst" level job. When he gets smothered in the arms of Meatloaf in a testicular cancer support group he finds the tears flowing. The crying does something for him; it's a real expression of his state of mind.

❦

He needs to grieve first for what he is, for his own life. Crying is more authentic than trying to know why he is crying. Knowing tells him that he's on a fast track to career success; that he has the means to buy what he wants. Somehow he has to break outside the boundaries of that knowing. He has to follow the grief because he feels that's the right track. He should be grieving for what he has become. What he is has somehow gotten away from him; he is a function of a kind of thinking that begins to seem alien to him; he begins to separate from that kind of thinking. He begins to separate from himself, or more precisely, a self that he now suspicions is caught within a constructed way of knowing that forces him to continue to create himself within that way of knowing. His IKEA furnished and designed apartment is symbolic of this designed self. What is interesting here is that the IKEA self has no conscious motivation to strike out against itself. This self can't make the grand canyon jump from self-assurance to doubt, interrogation, revolt, and rebellion. Thus, Tyler Durden, Norton's alter ego, shows up and slowly leads like the Freudian id leading the ego.

Schizophrenia, or a loss of a controlling image of oneself, a giving over to what one's present self-image cannot admit yet can no longer hold off, is the catalyst for change. And the change is not merely personal but extends to the social and cultural. First, the mass-produced consumer self that has become Everyman has to be severed from its human-to-product connection and reconnected human to human. Fight Club is born; the *mano a mano* is a way back from something artificial to something human, a Lawrentian struggle of body and blood so intense that it wipes out the steady staccato of "I shop therefore I am." Norton takes an obvious pleasure in showing up at work with bloodied shirt and bruised face as if to say "Everything here is fraud, but this blood is real." It's sort of simplistic ontology of authentic being-in-the-world provoked by a relentless simulacra assault. If you have become nothing more than a consuming machine created to fill the maw of the gross domestic product, that GDP bound to a future of exponential increase in the service of a Dow Jones promising all of America to be forever bullish, then maybe your blood is all that you have that's truly yours. Your blood is your metier, your salvation; it will lead you to who you are when you are not wanting what you have been shaped to want.

With the taste of your own blood in your mouth, you begin to look around and see what does not pulse with the same realness and authenticity of your blood. Indeed, what is it in our America that has forced us into Fight Club? Fight Club members can now recognize each other; they have a bond now; they see their mutual connectedness in their mutual bruises. And they recognize what lacks the authenticity of those bruises and how and on whose behalf inauthenticity is perpetrated. The Haves of the world are holding the Have Nots in mental shackles, filling them with desires to consume that lead to their perpetual exploitation, disenfranchisement, and dehumanization. The serving class that fills Fight Club were already on or heading for the Jerry Springer Club. They were detoured into Project Mayhem, a Tyler Durden campaign against corporate control of their lives.

The film ends with the massive bombing of the headquarters of various Manhattan credit card companies. Freedom begins now in 1999 with freedom from credit card debt. It's a beginning. It's a freedom that at century's end trumps racial freedom and freedom for women and freedom for gays and freedom to choose and all the other varieties of freedoms with which the twentieth century has been filled. This is a freedom from not being poor, a freedom from not being exploited by the rich, a freedom from being inescapably targeted as a consumer and not a fellow human being, a freedom from desires created for us long before we had the chance to create our own desires, a freedom from becoming consumer selves that we have no means save schizophrenia to escape.

Brooklyn

Thanksgiving 1953

"Stuff that you own winds up owning you."

I quote Tyler Durden, a guy who doesn't really exist, a split-off from a really disturbed individual, a guy who just dissolves, disappears once you do the craziest thing a crazy guy can do: shoot yourself just to show this figment of your crazed imagination that you don't need him anymore, that you're together, that one is enough and two is crazy. So what about anything that comes out of the mouth of a figment, of a delusion, of a hallucination that vanishes as soon as you "assume personal responsibility" and stop looking and leaning on somebody outside yourself, especially somebody that really isn't there? Wouldn't you say the stuff that comes out of that delusion is delusional stuff? The stuff that Tyler Durden tells us about stuff owning us is clearly insane in a world that believes you can't individually, personally, privately, on your very own, just for you, all your own, EVER get enough stuff, EVER get too much stuff. How could you have too much stuff? Doesn't the guy with the most toys in the end win? Aren't we presently living in that kind of society? Why be surprised that *Fight Club* won no awards, received no great popularity, never reached the mall theater crowd and stands now as one of the underrated films of 1999? I mean, if you browse the Web and find movie lists compiled in basements of houses like the one Tyler Durden lived in by Tyler Durden types.

How can owning top-of-the-line stuff be bad? What's better that owning a lot of stuff? What's the counter to owning a lot of stuff? Being "stuff-less"? Being poor? Durden is an antimaterialist. He's against materialism; blood is spilled in an effort to get beyond all that, to get to rock bottom and then rebuild. Find what's lasting, true, authentic, real. Not the stuff that you own but what you are as a living creature among other living creatures on a planet that breathes, that takes a long breath in the spring, grows to luxurious life in the summer, and then fades, goes into a long, cold sleep of regeneration only to rise up and breathe again in the spring. We're somewhere in there, not driving smelly SUVs or walking with cell phones glued to one ear, or walking with ears muffled with Walkman earphones, or sitting long, long hours looking at an icon-filled computer screen.

It sounds like I'm ready to do that sixties thing once again and drop out, return to the land, and live "naturally." Back to the holl'r. But I go back further, in my memory. I go back to a time when my immigrant grandfather sat at our table, to a time when that first-generation feeling of finding success in America was couched in a stuff-less surround of much older and different protocols than America offers us at this moment. No one was aware, or was only remotely aware, of what a shareholder was, or aware of shopping as an ontological act rather than a grocery-buying chore, or aware that your friends were your psychic "support group," or that stopping on the street and listening to a neighbor's tale of woe was profitless "networking," or that eating together every night as a family or indeed as an extended family, would soon be an extraordinary and unusual display of "quality time," or that the security enjoyed on a job and the secure medical and retirement benefits and the overtime paid for work beyond forty hours were all forms of bondage that in the coming years your descendants would be liberated from, allowing them to become freelance entrepreneurs with options.

Going further would put me into novel writing mode. There was a difference in how the world was known and perceived and therefore in how lives were shaped and lived. But there also had to be a seed of what was to be. The stuff that would wind up owning us was not there, surely, but the desire was birthing. You could perhaps see it in a look, catch it in a phrase, smell it in the air, hear it in people's dreams, see it on your plate. If I can find through memory the nuances of my family life when we were liminal, on the threshold of becoming American in all the ways which Tyler Durden eventually sets himself against, perhaps *I can find what there was when there was no stuff.*

࿊࿊

"We pray Lord that we will never forget the faces of those who have broken bread with us and whom we have loved and that they will know we still love them and miss them and wish they were sitting with us here today. Amen."

Strangely, there's no turkey at this Thanksgiving meal. It's not a bird that's familiar to Sicilians; it's not part of the culinary lore that my mother's father, Benjamin, who sits at the head of the table, took with him when he left Sicily at the beginning of the twentieth century. Our

Thanksgiving meal reflects the hold Sicily still has on us. We will do antipasto, pasta, meatballs, sausage, bracciola, salad, capons, potatoes, pears, apples, oranges, figs, fennel, nuts, and then, hours later, black coffee and Italian pastry from Luigi Alba Bakery. Those pies from Ebinger's Bakery are our American connection; the bakery is run by Jews displaced from their homes in Europe, yet they put out masterful renditions of quintessential Americana: apple and pumpkin pies. The capons also represent our first, tentative moves toward culinary Americanization.

The logic of the connection goes something like this: the capon is bigger than a chicken and in this way like a turkey, but tasty, something no one in the family thinks a turkey can ever be. The idea of celebrating a holiday with an untasty bird as the centerpiece is a concession that, in 1953, my family is not yet ready to make. Instead our *prima piatti* is pasta, what we called then "gravy," which on a Sunday and holidays was invariably some type of macaroni, here ziti, and meatballs, sausage, bracciola, and spareribs. The antipasto is superb: everything is of a quality that will be, for me, in the coming decades gone with the wind. But in the years ahead Elaine and I never give up pursuing the real presence of a pecorino romano grating cheese, a fennel sweet sausage, a sesame seed encrusted bread, a creamy, end-twisted mozzarella, an olive cured not canned, a canoli filled with fresh ricotta. For the next forty years these are only absent signifiers roaming our linguistic memory banks.

Now, here in 1953, the cheese has been cut from a well-aged, hard provalone hanging in a kitchen closet; the dried sausage, soppresata, cured olives, artichoke hearts, mozzarella, stuffed hot peppers, pepperoni, roasted red peppers, and huge anchovies are glistening side by side in an oval platter of many compartments. The crusty round Sicilian breads from Three Star Bakery—where neighbors line up between four and five everyday to buy bread just out of the oven—have been sliced and are in wicker baskets on both ends of the table. Wine bottles with wicker bottoms are within everyone's reach. The formalist qualities of an aesthetic order not built on order, restraint, and discipline, and therefore lacking the "distinction" defined by Bourdieu, was nevertheless a feast for my eyes. The table overspilled anyone's sense of order, for here was neither restraint nor control, neither pattern nor theme, but only a clash of color, aroma, appearance, texture that slipped by a Martha Stewart sense of arrangement.

At the head of the table—really two tables connected by an acre of tablecloth made by my paternal grandmother—sits my grandfather Benjamin. He took little with him when he left the seminary in Sicily and headed for America. He, in fact, took very little besides one of the maids in his father's house, my grandmother. Moments away from ordination into the Church, he took his clandestine beloved and escaped to America, refusing to fulfill his role in his father's promise to the Church that this son, Benjamin, would belong to the Church. It is almost impossible to see the Church Latin that my grandfather knows or his ability to say Mass or hear confessions or baptize or perform any of the priestly functions. But if you look close and long you can see the vestiges of his patrician upbringing. He is one of two at the table wearing not only a suit jacket but a vest, not only a tie but a removable shirt collar; later on he will remove this stiff starched collar and his suit jacket and unbutton his vest. There's a gold chain that goes from one vest pocket to another; at the end is a watch and a gold key shaped like the Bergdorf Goodman building. It was a retirement token given to him after some thirty years working as a presser, an elite presser at that. "It was my father's job," my mother, who also worked for Bergdorf Goodman in the 1930s, would say, "to take the cloth a designer had folded and pinned and press it into the shape it needed to have. He was an artist." He is a silent man, a man of few words—so few that I don't know how many English words he knows. But I do know that like my father, who had been educated in Sicily but born in upstate New York, my grandfather spoke Italian and Sicilian. My own father, whose father was killed in the First World War, is only able to speak Sicilian to his mother because she cannot speak either Italian or English. She's not stupid; there's a politics of usurpation here that she's fighting: Italian usurping Sicilian; English usurping Sicilian. She's going out with the language she came in with. Grandfather Benjamin would be dead of pneumonia in a few short years, but now he is here sitting at the head of the table.

He says grace and when I pick my head up and make the sign of the cross, I see my brother sitting across from me, Pete, twenty months older than me. Sitting on one side of him is Uncle Dick whose name is always modifed by the title "Black Sheep of the Family." Why he is a black sheep is hard for me, a ten year old, to comprehend, but somehow it makes him more exciting. To me he's like the Black Knight of the Family, vastly different than my own father who goes to work, comes home, eats, smokes a cigar, reads a paper, watches some TV, goes to bed. Or any of the other adults I know who lack the exotic mystery of Uncle Dick. And Uncle Dick has a missing finger. He lost it because he wasn't paying attention on the job, my mother had told me. I conjured up a job that demanded unrelenting attentiveness and a brief glance elsewhere and then . . . Tragedy! But even with nine fingers Uncle Dick can juggle walnuts or oranges or apples—which he will do at the end of the meal to Pete's and my applause—or pull a coin from behind your ear or make that same coin disappear. To the normal conversation Uncle Dick provides a spark; he takes the banal down a different path. His difference from the norm is what I find intriguing. Clare, his ex-wife, is Jewish, which seems to be something inexplicable, like Uncle Dick being a black sheep.

At a time when a Sicilian would think twice about marrying an Italian who wasn't Sicilian, think three times about marrying a Catholic who wasn't Italian, think four times about marrying a Christian who wasn't Catholic, and think marrying a Jew sent you into a mosh pit of wailing and weeping, my Uncle Dick had married Clare, a Jew, always referred to as "Clare the Jew." Only when I step out of the Catholic world of Xaverian High School and enter the secular world of Brooklyn College in 1961, with a student body at that time predominantly Jewish, and I begin to see the world through the eyes of many professors who are themselves or who have family who are escapees from Hitler's concentration camps, do I begin to see the alienating and ostracizing tactics of language itself. When I spend a summer at a friend's cottage his grandmother, a Calabrian, refers to me as "the Sicilian."

I am nervous about and wary of waxing nostalgic over my New York Sicilian-American separateness. We didn't have "stuff," but we had family and the beauty of the family lay in its ethnic insularity, its distancing distinctions. The further it appears in my mind from the IKEA furnished world of Edward Norton in *Fight Club,* the more appealing it seems. Although there were qualities to be found in that ethnic difference, and ample reasons to cherish our cultural distinctiveness, and our difference then rose to an excluding identity, we could justify neither privileging our distinctiveness nor our exclusions. This is difficult to accept emotionally, because what my memory so much now aches for as it wanders back to a Thanksgiving dinner so long ago is precisely that difference from our IKEA world of the present.

This was ground I had covered in the first volume of this cultural history of the 1990s, in *Hauntings* (SUNY Press, 1994). It was Derrida's notion of *differance* that provided a key to my thinking, but not my feeling which I orbit back to a decade later:

> *Identity deferred into/toward difference.* I am trying to construe Derrida's notion of *differance* here: "[W]ithout a trace retaining the other as other in the same, no difference would do its work and no meaning would appear." *Differance* thus takes the starch out of an unrelated difference as well as an unrelated identity. (P. 88)

⌦∽⌫

In every homeless man I see, I see Uncle Dick. Sometime before he came to sit at our table that Thanksgiving he had left Clare and his two children, a Down syndrome child named Harriet who was just a bit younger than me, and a newborn baby. He had left them and wandered off, the way black sheep do. Now he was back living with my grandfather, or living off of him, as my mother put it. What the years ahead held from him remained mostly a mystery in regard to the details, but not in regard to the life itself. My mother would hear from him once or twice a decade. The Salvation Army periodically rescued him; he was a dishwasher in a boy's camp up north; he showed up at my grandfather's funeral and a black suit and shoes were bought for him; he appeared at my parent's home just before I was married and it seemed as if he were back in our lives—but he wasn't; then he was in a hospital dying. When my mother and her two sisters went to his bedside he looked at them and then died, and my mother said it was as if he had waited to see their faces before he let go. You know that if I could crack the mystery of his life, his failure, as we now say, in "assuming personal responsibility," a whole politics would emerge, an entire ethics, a new way of seeing.

Sitting next to me at the table is Mr. Wooten, an Englishman with whom my father worked. He is wearing a dark, pinstriped suit with a vest; he is not portly and bald like my grandfather Benjamin, though, but thin, with hair, neatly parted and greying at the temples. I love to hear the inflections of his speech; to me it's as if one of those crisp character actors right out of old British movies were here sitting with us, here at our Thanksgiving dinner. Next to Mr. Alex Wooten is Floyd Johnson, florid-faced Floyd, like Mr. Wooten, a bachelor. These were the bachelors with no family to go home to and no family awaiting them on the holidays. Mr. Wooten had left England after the war and had not returned. Did he have family there? "No, I'm afraid not." This in itself was an inexplicable mystery to *ma famiglia* and reconfirmed my father's observation that the Brits were "cold eggs." It confirmed my mother's intent to remedy that fault by having him join us for holiday dinners.

My father liked Mr. Wooten because he expressed the kind of loyalty and gratitude that a Sicilian could understand. An Englishman among the many Irish who worked on the waterfront, Mr. Wooten had, I think, received the support and protection of my father, for whom Mr. Wooten and Floyd Johnson worked. The man "over" my father at that time was Jack McGinty, a hard-working, hard-drinking Irishman who would be dead in his forties. I remember one summer that one of his many children stayed with us for weeks. I don't know why, but I remember that she made some comments about Italians and I think we had already been packaged stereotypically in her mind. Jack had a liver problem and his doctor told him he had to stop drinking beer; he compromised by drinking whiskey, which was, according to his doc, better for his liver. My father liked Jack, but I sensed early on that there was an uneasiness between we Italians and the Irish. Maybe it all started with the story that an Irishman had come to an Italian house for dinner, had been served pasta and had asked for ketchup to "spice up the sauce." Now I do believe such a culinary transgression would precipitate hostilities.

Floyd Johnson was the perennial eligible bachelor for whom we felt sorry because his notion of family extended no further than to a hooker he would engage for a drunken weekend. I only knew this because of a late-night phone call that sent my father out of the house in a rush. When he returned and my mother asked what was up, he had said something like, "They were both drunk and she wouldn't stop screaming that his money was hers." I must admit that that scene in my mind has stayed with me and has been attached, in Laconian fashion, within my linguistic unconscious so that the words "Floyd" and "Johnson" declared to be "American" by my father forever represent the "WASP Way of Life." There are no children, all meals are eaten out, it's always cocktail hour, and there are no joint accounts.

My uncle John and my aunt Gladys were also at the table. He was my favorite uncle and I had taken his name as my confirmation name. Aunt Gladys was Puerto Rican and had worked with my uncle in some factory, I think it was a shoe factory. She spoke English with a heavy Spanish accent and he spoke English with a heavy Italian accent. He was the youngest son of three, and the only one born in Sicily. He had come to this country just a few years before. He had black-marketing talents he had honed during the war and he applied them almost immediately here in the States. He bought jewelry at economical prices and sold them at high prices to fools who didn't know they could go to the diamond center in lower Manhattan and pay half the price my uncle charged. He was more than something of a con man; was an excellent poker player and could count on cards as a source of income. Rather than drive a car he was at this time going about on an English racer. By the time he died peacefully in his chair after a good meal many years later, he was bloated and J & B Scotch–soaked and had lost all his money in a South American gold deal run by con men smoother than himself. It was an ironic collapse, to say the least. The glimmer of gold was ever in his eye, even then at the Thanksgiving table. His favorite coup de gesture was to take a thick rubber-banded roll of bills out of his pants pocket and hold it in front of your face. He'd tell you, "This is what talks!" Not very attractive, and yet this humane mantra was to become the exclusive mantra of the whole country. I know now that the attraction he held for me then was the attraction of the con man, the man outside the margins of business as usual—the man, in short, who was strikingly attractive compared to my law-abiding father. By the time I was out of my own rebel-without-a-pause youth, his luster had lost its sheen and all I began to see was a man hoarding stuff. Perhaps it is the destiny of all immigrants from impoverished countries to want here in this country all that was denied them in their home country. And those desires pass on to their offspring: the houses must be bigger, the cars bigger, the lawn more vast and magnificent, the vacations more grand, the colleges more expensive, the wardrobe more varied, the toys more plentiful.

My father sits at the other end of the table; my mother sits closest to the doorway leading to the kitchen; my three-year-old sister Linda sits next to her. After dinner I'll amuse her by putting a pillow on my head which I pretend is a hat and a head of hair and calling myself "Captain Hairy Harry." I'll run after her, which gets her squealing, till my mother orders me to leave her alone. Now, a half-century later, I talk to my sister seldom on the phone; distance erodes connections of the heart in a more deadly way than time. If I think back to what she was then as a child I relive her presence warmly; when I drove hundreds of miles to see her in Florida and got there, all that we had was that distance between us and we never overcame it. We never thought space would undo us.

For years after I am married and living far from home, my mother will call up and say, "Out of sight, out of mind." And I always protest that it isn't so. Somewhere always just beneath the surface of an everyday awareness is this other awareness memory incites. Whether good or bad, significant or banal, happy or sad, this awareness provides for me an image, a feeling, a desire by which I gauge everything.

Now at dinner's denouement, Uncle John makes his traditional toast in a twisted syntax that somehow covers family, ambition, and the future: "Keep and go. We live to be a hundred." Keep striving: the immigrant ambition that, in the view of some, a repeal of an inheritance tax may destroy. But also keep guard on what you already have; don't jeopardize the family for a bird not yet in hand. Stay close to home but at the same time go as far as you can go. It's a primordial toast, a timeless toast about surviving, about being the one who doesn't die but lives, who doesn't lose but "keeps." Keeps what? Health? A stock portfolio? Wisdom? Memories? Your IKEA stuff? It's primitive and atavistic, a celebration of the maintenance of the life force, of the will to live in the face of all obstacles. I heard Uncle John expound his world-view often enough to know that this was also a toast mindless of morals, of love and friendship. In the end, the one who lives the longest wins. The one who accumulates more days above ground wins. Your flesh becomes like a piece of earth, your consciousness is in your appetite, your thirst is for life-extending blood, your hope is that though all may fall by the wayside, you will be the last man standing. Beyond all ideas and visions, beyond riches or poverty, beyond all dreams and hopes, there is this one fundamental drive: to survive and live, to endure. You don't have to observe and you don't have to contribute and you don't have to share. All you have to do is continue to live. "Keep and go." Maybe this is the credo of my ancestors; maybe it's just Uncle John's. But I remember it. It's indelibly impressed in my memory. I don't know yet what to make of it. But I know that it's more than Uncle John's obsession with "stuff."

My grandfather Benjamin doesn't heed the toast, maybe because he's been educated as a priest and this toast is before religion, a toast that worships the possession of life and not the giver of life. There's nothing charitable or loving about the toast. We are in fact excluded, expendable. We are being told that our death ends everything and yet means nothing to any one. So my grandfather Benjamin is artfully peeling and slicing fruit; I'm fascinated by the way he peels one continuous peel from an apple. The fennel, which is refreshing and is meant to facilitate digestion, is also being eaten. Figs are eaten along with the fruit. Uncle Dick picks out a tune with a couple of walnuts in his fist. Later on the table will be cleared by my mother, and the men, except Mr. Wooten, will play cards. Pete and I will sit on the sofa and watch the TV in the corner of the room. The table takes up so much of the parlor that the back of the folding chairs on this side almost touch the sofa. Pete and I have to keep our legs up. In four or five years we will move from this apartment to a house up the block, a house with a backyard and a front yard and a driveway, a house with a basement which Uncle Neil will "finish," following the strange fascination of the fifties for "finished basements." We are beginning to prepare the house for "stuff." We are turning off one road and starting down another.

Orbiting in a Time Machine

October 1, 2000

> *We can see this crisis in the growing doubt about the meaning of our own lives and in the loss of a unity of purpose for our Nation.*
> —Jimmy Carter, The "Malaise" Speech, 1979

> *I think the American people will be shocked by such contempt for their intelligence. This isn't Ivory Soap versus Palmolive.*
> —Adlai Stevenson, 1952 presidential campaign

> *Presidential campaigns will eventually have professional actors as candidates.*
> —George Ball, 1952 presidential campaign

> *As a Man is, so he sees.*
> —William Blake, Letter to Dr. Trusler, 1799

On one of the big fall football weekends that this town and gown go at with all their hearts, a twenty-four year old, drunk and vomiting, was beaten to death in front of a buffalo wing and beer joint. It was the day after Rosh Hashanah, the Jewish New Year, a time to begin examining the wrong turns made the year before, a time to plan amendments for the coming year. A time to re-see. I don't have the scoop on "buffalo wing" significance. It's such a fast food it flies—the faster the better.

The twenty-four year old suffered a fractured skull and a blood clot in his brain, the kind of injuries you'd get if you fell off a two-story building. Doctors induced coma, hoping the brain swelling would go down. It didn't. For about ten days Brandon was somewhere a cell phone couldn't reach him, and then he died on October 11, the same day

Al Gore and George W. held their second presidential debate. His father, who flew from Bend, Oregon, wants to get the guy who killed his son. "There must have been a lot of people out there who saw something going on out there."

I've taken my walks into town after midnight on the weekends; I've stood in front of BW-3. There are always a lot of people out there. Did they see something going on the night Brandon was beaten to death on that sidewalk?

Time travel with me. Go back fifty years to October 1, 1950.

Times are not that fast yet. But you can now make rice in a minute. Sugar Pops have just come on the market and Kraft has just taken the ancient process of cheese making and converted it to deluxe processed cheese slices. Women this year who don't want to make cakes from "scratch" can now buy cake mixes for the first time. Hounding Joe McCarthy launches his Soviet witch hunt. A coffee shop in Quincy, Massachusetts, changes its name to Dunkin' Donuts and in five years they franchise. The population is a hundred million less than on the day Brandon is murdered. There are only ten million homes with TV. Ozzie and Harriet haven't even come to TV yet; you still have to listen to them on the radio. Ninety million folks are listening to "The Shadow" and "The Lone Ranger" on radio. The comic strip "Peanuts" debuts October 2, 1950; its creator Charles Shultz draws the last one in 1999 and dies a month later.

I'm standing in front of the BW3 of its day. They're not serving "buffalo wings." Maybe it's Pleasantville and Jeff Daniels is the counter-terman, paper airline stewardess hat on his head, white shirt and bow tie. Waiting behind the counter to serve.

It's after midnight on a weekend night. There was a football game the day before. The team won, the team lost. Whatever. But it was vital then, that day, consequential, significant. Not as vital and consequential as an Aztec football game where the losers got hacked to death. But it's the allegorical 1950s: this football game is really the American team vs. the Soviet team. It's the place where the Cold War can heat up without Americans having to go through all the horrors of real war. Fifties films like *War of the Worlds, The Day the Earth Stood Still,* and *Invasion of the Body Snatchers* are all thinly veiled Cold War allegories. Movies theaters and football stadiums are places where you can work out and work through your antipathies, your prejudices, your anger, your need to be the winner and see the other guy the loser. You can still clearly see the face of your enemy in 1950; you can conceive of real opposition, of a real force set out against you. That antagonist may strike at you at any moment; you have your fallout shelter in the backyard, fully provisioned. No matter that a toxic death awaits you when you do come out. The point is that safe shelters are Real, enemies are Real, there is a Real fight to be won or lost. Seeing the world in such clearly drawn lines projects down there onto the football field, or up there on the movie screen. And then you realize how much reel is in your real.

I can join in on that way of seeing. I can feel its pressure, its claim on me. I can walk in those moccasins.

I'm in a local bar now listening to the buzz about the game that day. Everyone is into deep analysis of every minute of the game; they're all doing psychological profiles on every player. It sounds like this game was as significant and consequential in their lives as a football game fifty years later. Same place, different time, same intensity. But there's no Cold War in 2000; why does the intensity linger? The outcome of a Big Ten football game in the Midwest is as consequential in 2000 as it was in 1950. What gives? I mean the outcome of a football game is about as consequential to American society as Yuppies treating themselves to a cruise, or a dot-com entrepreneur building himself a sixteen-bathroom retreat with a view of the bay, or a new six-carat diamond on a trophy wife's finger, or an Ivy Leaguer getting a "fully loaded" SUV for his twenty-first birthday, or Mrs. Shoptillidrop paying Dr. Showmeyourmoney six figures for a facelift, or Mr. and Mrs. Weonlycatalog collecting every Hummell figurine ever cast.

In whose interest is it to keep us so distracted? What are we working through now so intensely that we are all eyes for a football game and ready to jump out of our seats and get into it ourselves and yet cannot see Brandon D'Annunzio being beaten to death, cannot act, cannot conceive that there is consequence here and not in that football game? The football game and what it means in our lives is very real; a beating on a public sidewalk in front of one of the busiest bars in town is a blank space, an empty happening, a Web site you don't want to or care to surf. It's not yours or in your plan or in your life or in your field of vision. It's a distraction.

There are a lot of people out there. There's a lot going on out there. Someone must have seen something.

Everything "out there" is there to be seen. But what do these people around me here in 1950 see? Now I see a tall man with shoulder-length hair rushing over to a young man vomiting at the curb. The tall man rushes up to him and begins to beat him, smashing him to the ground.

At once, people around me rush up to the man and restrain him, helping the beaten man to his feet. And the sense behind the scene rushes over me like a flashlight from a streaking saucer—this is not a computer screen, a cold call from a telemarketer or a "Real World" episode, not your Walkman in your ear or a job for your Palm Pilot or a chat on a cell phone or an e-mail session. Not for these folks around me here in 1950. Their heads are not on-line; they don't experience that glitch I just got when I looked up from my computer screen and out the window at this rare beautiful autumnal day with classic clear blue sky.

I'm back in the present.

In a couple of minutes I'm going to be walking into that scene. That scene—not into what's "out there" but that "scene." That screening of the world that Nature has transmitted today. I'm going to be biking to the gym and that requires me to renew my relationship with the unmediated, untransmitted, unscreened world. Cursors here can collide; you can really die here. Here, in what we now see the necessity of calling "real time." And something can happen that requires you to give up seeing the world as hypertext on a screen in front of you that you can click on if you want to and see the world as coming at you, a hand on your shoulder drawing you in, your fortune, good or ill, in the wind in your face, everyone around you, like you, capable of bleeding. I've been in the middle of a raging fire rushing in one direction toward my house and in another direction toward my barn: I've seen one minute in time open up to all the minutes I've ever lived and one thought fill all the space around me: save my family. Everything to be done is clearly visible before you in such a moment.

When was this kind of seeing not merely personal but social? A half-century before?

I'm orbiting back again to 1950.

I'm trying to look closely at how these people around me look at things. What kinds of interpolations are automatically made here in 1950? What is inserted between the perceiver and the perceived? This is pre–Born Again fever; charismatic Christianity hasn't hit the headlines. Everyone is Sunday churchgoing; the protocols and liturgy of Catholicism seldom extend beyond Sunday and when they do, like eating fish on Fridays, they cause no ontological crises. The Cold War, fear of a nuclear attack, the atomic bomb whistling overhead, the Communist threat—Hollywood and football and Joe McCarthy are taking care of that. Advertising jingles fill the radio bands and people's heads. Catchy product tunes and slogans stand in for thought at stressful and empty moments. But Madison Avenue and Wall Street are not calling you at dinner time; credit card companies are not pitching you during your "quality time." There is no "quality time" here in 1950. Or, equally true, all time is quality time; all time is "real" and all time offers all the qualities that humans can invest in this notion of "time." This is the same as saying this is a time in which time has not been given qualities.

No one here in 1950 is interfacing the world in any intrusive way through technology. But fifty years later, everyone who lives long enough is set up to become a "choosing machine," a seeker of speed and comfort maximization, of more stuff and quicker access to it, of less "sparking over the garden fence" palavering and more networking toward fixed goals. There are no "human resources" in 1950. Human resources for who and for what? "Resources" are what humans have and manipulate; the idea that humans are the resources of something greater than themselves—corporations—that has and manipulates them is not yet acceptable usage. You can have small jobs for small lives not seeking fifteen seconds as celebrities. "Winners" and "losers" are found in sports; no one here is categorized that way. People are "having a tough time of it," or "living high," or "getting over a tragedy," or "trying their best," or "making a mess of their lives," or "hoping for a better day," or "just getting along," or "thanking God it's Friday," or "fair to middlin'." Greed hasn't become good yet; it's still one of the seven Deadly Sins. No one has any idea that the epitome of what humanity can be will be expressed in the word "Player."

Ronald Reagan has been on the screen in a couple of—movies; no one thinks he will be the president of the United States—except maybe playing that part in a B movie—or that there will be a serious campaign to put his face on Mt. Rushmore, alongside Washington's and Lincoln's. Politics has to become a product campaign, a contestation of images, a discourse of sound bytes, an orchestrated pageant before we're all ready to see that a man playing the part of a president is just like a man qualified to be president.

In whose interest is it to replace the direct handling and delivery of the world with all sorts of interpolations? Well, as a postmodernist I deny that we've ever in any age or time had a direct handling and delivery of the world. We're talking about degree, purpose, quality, and effect of interpolations. For instance, the Cold War mentality is like a virus that has to be nurtured to survive. "Better Dead than Red." Free enterprise can't be free under Communism. What had become increasingly clear by 1950 was that when the Soviets took control of a country, everything private became public, including property. Private property was held to be theft; not a definition that went down well in the manor house. Private investment and entrepreneurship built a firewall in the minds of Americans between itself and the "Red Threat."

Fifty years later, the free play of the global market espoused by transnational corporations dedicated only to short-term profits to shareholders reshapes the American mind to suit the new exigencies of a post–Cold War world. The political notion of what a "citizen" is has to be redefined as a busy consumer boldly using the credit extended to him or her, augmenting their sense of personal freedom by augmenting their choices of products and services, referring to the compass of self-interest to guide them through, replacing an interdependent civil order with networking toward self-empowering, self-aggrandizing goals and objectives, and structuring a "timescape" tolled by quarterly earnings reports.

The world has to become an "as if" place merely to offer endless opportunities for the maximization of consumption and profits. Advertisers package the world into nothing more than a myriad of buying opportunities or catalogue the scene in an interactive way. But if the world remains unpackaged by the advertisers, then every potential consumer is caught in the limited scenario of events as they happen on the street, in the home, on the job, at sea, in the woods, in the skies, in holes in the ground.

We'd have no choice but to see on October 1, 2000, Brandon D'Annunzio being beaten to death. We couldn't surf to another channel or Web site, or keep the Walkman headset on, or keep our ear to our cell phone. Or simply not see what was before our eyes because it's only *as if* Brandon were being beaten to death, and in that case it's not real and we can walk on, or turn away and choose another "as if" scene, one that better fits our design of this night and this place.

I now see the significance of the Bush and Gore debate held the same day Brandon dies: we see this presidential campaign "as if" it were an Ivory Soap or Palmolive commercial and we've learned not to pay any attention to it. The price of our marketing and advertising, of our spinning as if scenarios in order to buy and sell the whole world, has narrowed our lens, our field of vision. We do not see within a wide range of as if stories, but only as if we were the consumers we have become. An awareness of that crime extended to more than one-half of those who showed up to vote in the 2000 presidential election, but they didn't win.

∞∞∞

I fall back on my postmodern view of awareness: there is something clearly to be seen out there in the streets, as clear as Brandon's murder. We're standing by; we're the onlookers but no one is seeing neutrally; no one, in fact, is seeing what there is to be seen without filtering it. What there is to be seen meets our expectations, or, more drastically, is already erased, elided, absented by those expectations. Given that this is yet another part of the world as I know it, this scene here now, whether it be Brandon's murder or America at the new millennium, simply reproduces and reinforces and reiterates how and what I know of the world.

Radically split are we right now on how we know the world, on what we see.

Long Island

July 1999

I go to see Stanley Kubrick's film *Eyes Wide Shut* twice in two weeks, once alone and once with Elaine. She falls asleep on part of it: the part when Victor Ziegler is explaining to Dr. Bill Harford all that has really been going on. It's the denouement, the unraveling of the mystery, if you felt there was a mystery. The scene is supposed to answer the question, "What the hell has been going on?" Immediately following this scene, Bill returns home and tells all to his wife Alice. Then the last scene, a Christmas shopping scene, and a final bit of closure dialogue between Bill and Alice. What they've both learned from it all. It's even less interesting than Ziegler's calm, rational explanation of what everything we had seen meant. I don't care for either metanarrative. I've seen the film; I don't need the cover-up alibi for what I've seen. Ziegler's tone is patient, more than slightly condescending and patronizing, cloyed with the dominating manners—from the way he handles the pool balls on his custom-made red cloth pool table to the way he caresses his tumbler of twenty-five-year-old Scotch—of a man who lives in a house the size of the Metropolitan Museum of Art, has a billiard room the size of my house, and can summon and dismiss people according to his mood. Bill and Alice's final-scene review of what's happened to them lacks all that upscale élan, but they are equally rational and composed. "No one day or night can capture the full complexity of life." "Reality and dream have both taken us on paths to recognition." To roughly paraphrase the lessons they've learned, and which I suppose we should have learned also. But these seem to me to be bullshite analogues for a film that has already expressed itself in ways that have nothing, or very little, to do with either Ziegler's directive as to what went on or Bill and Alice's rush to thread their marriage back together—with words.

Resentment propels this film and directs it, the kind of resentment that fills Edward Norton's alter ego, Tyler Durden, in *Fight Club*. Tyler resented a society that lays a veneer of apparently sensible discourse on a ruthless war of all against all. He resented how that veneer of the "right and the reasonable" had already been shaped in such a way that while it shackled the Have Nots, it could never constrain the Haves. Indeed, we are all being rational, right, and realistic within the wealthy's configuration of these; we're brought up within an order of things that confirms and assures a lopsidedness that favors those like Victor Ziegler and all his hooded friends out there at that orgy on the Somerton Estate. And meanwhile, the new generation, represented by Bill and Alice, are taken on an initiation journey into the reasonableness of this order of things.

Put aside your focus on the "theme of jealousy" or the "theme of women's desire" or the "theme of men's desire" as having only personal scope, that is, of everything in the film being there in terms of Bill and Alice's relations, their marriage, their lives. Now pan back as Kubrick did in *Barry Lyndon,* where Barry's personal exploits are part and parcel of eighteenth-century English life; as he did in *Dr. Strangelove,* where whatever is personal explodes immediately into the cultural vibe of America at that moment, as he did in *2001: A Space Odyssey, A Clockwork Orange, Full Metal Jacket,* and even *Lolita*. What do you see? You see a filmmaker obsessed with working from the personal to the broadly social/cultural; a filmmaker trying to capture the cultural imaginary of the moment; a filmmaker who takes his source text and films it to bring out its widest implications and extensions into the social/cultural milieu. All personalities and personal dramas are played out on this panoramic staging; to get at the social/cultural he takes a close focus on the personal, to varying degrees in his films. There is less of the personal focus in *2001, Full Metal Jacket,* and *Dr. Strangelove* than there is in *A Clockwork Orange, Lolita,* and *Barry Lyndon.* Nonetheless, Kubrick's *Lolita* captures the repressions and obsessions of the 1950s as well as *Dr. Strangelove; A Clockwork Orange* captures the anarchy of the 1960s; and *Barry Lyndon* plays into class issues still extant in the present. The scope of Kubrick's *mise en scène* is never narrow. Why now, in his last film, should we treat *Eyes Wide Shut* differently, as if this is a film to be seen and judged as if it were Bergman delving into the "lyricism of obsession"?

If we pan back to reveal the intersections of the film's *mise en scène* and our own American cultural one, we in essence see the film with eyes wide open. To see it with eyes wide shut is to not only keep oneself masked but to agree to keeping the masks on those "who if we knew who they were we would lose sleep." Perhaps it is better to remain asleep with our eyes wide shut if we wish the order of things portrayed in this film to continue. But let's say we were like Tyler Durden, full of resentment and wanting, Ahab-like, to break through the mask and see what's really there. Imagine, if you will, Dr. Bill Harford with the temperament of Tyler. Replace if you will Alice and Bill, young upscale consumers who have the manner of the jejune Dan Quayle at the moment of his vice presidential selection—not one real life experience—with Tyler, around the track too many times and on the wrong end of too many real life experiences. In other words, instead of seeing the film as if you were Bill and Alice—who don't laugh in the Hungarian seducer's face and tell him to go back to his own century, who crumble when a comedy of masked orgiasts try to get tough, who say nothing when a friend is called a cocksucker and a prick, who teach their daughter how to figure who has money and who doesn't—instead, in short, of seeing the film through the eyes of people who have position and things but no depth—see the film unmasked. Because clearly Kubrick is sending up not only Bill and Alice but a whole society which not only tolerates a new order of oligarchical decadence but is incapable of seeing it, of critiquing it. The means to critique remains since the 1980s in America less significant to the new generation than shopping, cell phoning, investing, collecting, networking (in pursuit of self-interest), e-mailing (avoiding face-to-face contact in an increasingly "disaffected" society), surfing the Net (to shop), listening to your Walkman, and generally doing all you can to increase your net worth while doing all you can to avoid profitless time spending. What the latest fad is for spending and displaying your wealth is a major pursuit. Everybody is looking for it.

And so is Dr. Bill. His journey into the night is set off by the image of his wife with another man, but the journey soon goes down familiar paths of self-gratification. Maybe he goes with Domino the prostitute because he wants to do what the over-the-top Hungarian seducer says all married couples should do: cheat on each other and so keep the game even. But it seems like Bill is the same way with Domino as he had been earlier on with the two models at Ziegler's party, before Alice had introduced jealousy to him. Here's an enjoyable titillation, his actions seem to say; ditto when he's with Domino. Only Alice's unexpected phone call brings him to a reconsideration of what's he doing. Later, when he returns to Domino's apartment and finds her roommate Sally there, he hits on her fast enough. And it doesn't seem like he's doing it to get even with Alice. It seems like he's doing it for the sheer pleasure of it. Recall Ziegler's party at the very beginning of the movie: they don't know why they're invited. They don't know anyone. This isn't their "set," but they're thrilled to be there. Alice knocks back champagne so fast she's tipsy right off the bat, and vulnerable prey for the old seducer. Ziegler's party is a Christmas party: Contrast his tree with the two other trees in the film: the one in the Harford apartment and the one in Domino's apartment. There's a study in class divisions. Who's really celebrating the spirit of Christmas? The old lecher trying to get Alice upstairs for a quickie? Victor Ziegler, who sneaks out on his wife to get naked with an ex-beauty queen, Amanda Curran up in a bathroom only half the size of my house? Bill, who forgets about his wife and enjoys the attentions of the models trying to seduce him? Clearly, if jealousy is what the film is all about, we spend a good deal of time amid a disturbing decadence, a lot of time contemplating the Winners feeding all their appetites.

Pursuit of pleasure and not a motivating jealousy is what Bill's journey is all about. The matter is sealed as soon as he looks Nick Nightingale in the eye and says, "If you think I'm going to let you go to that party without taking me, you're crazy." What Nick has told him is that he's seen a lot in his time, but he's never seen women like he's seen at these parties. That's enough for Bill. He's on that like the Hungarian gigolo was on his wife. It's not, then, a question of needing a Bergman to direct the finer subtleties of jealousy; Kubrick just isn't interested in that. It's just something he's picked up from Schnitzler's novel. And jealousy has its place in his *mise en scène* of 1990s wealth and decadence: jealousy is sure to crop up in a marriage when both are first pursuing their own gratification, are always in the market for upscaling their pleasures. What, indeed, keeps Alice from going upstairs with her charming seducer? His approach hasn't caused Alice to laugh in his face, which seemed to me the first and most obvious response to such "come up and see my etchings said with a foreign accent" line. She hasn't gotten angry at him for treating her like meat in a meat market, as if beautiful women were just prey who expected predators to come at them. She shows him her wedding ring. It doesn't mean a thing to him because he already surmises that the self-indulgent do not indulge in any bond forever, that when given the opportunity to indulge, they indulge. There is in this new world of old decadence only a skin-deep understanding of the word "fidelio."

"Fidelio" is the password that gets Bill into the Somerton Estate orgy. Here's how the ritual of Christmas is now celebrated, how it has been restaged in the 1990s. The enormously wealthy—the peers of Victor Ziegler who attend the orgy—are engaged in constructing a new mythos that gratifies their palate much more than the existing ones, like Christianity, for instance. Instead of a priest in sacred garb at a decorated altar with incense and organ-playing, what we now have are cloaks and masks, a ceremonial conductor with a staff, chanting, and organ-playing. And, beautiful naked women, also masked. Communion is now not the eating of Christ's body but the coming together in every way possible of an enormously wealthy and powerful man with a beautiful woman—or man. There's no mystery as to who these masked people are: Ziegler tells us that they are people he does business with, his friends, his associates, his ilk, his class. And lest we underestimate their wealth and power, Ziegler tells Dr. Bill, who would seem to 80 percent of Americans to be living extremely well, that he was way out of his league. Masked and behind iron gates. When Bill returns to Somerton, curious about Nick's fate as well as the woman who has interceded for him, he never gets past the gates. A message warning him to stop asking questions is handed to him through the gate. What do they look like? Kubrick shows us in the early scene, when we see Ziegler putting on his pants and hooking up his braces over a naked torso. They look like Ziegler: aging dudes lusting after young bodies. Aging dudes with lots of money. But at the same time, while we know them, we don't know them, just as the bulk of Americans today don't know how life is lived behind the Somerton gates, or in the Ziegler mansion, or in any of the places Nick Nightingale has been taken to blindfolded. Every time it's a different place, Nick tells Bill. We are not just dealing with one degenerate billionaire throwing an orgy. This is indeed a Hellfire Club. Our lives are totally infiltrated by the rich and the powerful, but when we look to see who they are and to identify them, it is as if our eyes were wide shut. Cloaked, masked, behind high gates, and served by minions who follow us, lead us around blindfolded, and, when necessary, chastise and reprimand us.

Bill and Alice are only different from Ziegler and his fellow masked orgiasts in degree, not in kind. They have, after all, been invited to the Ziegler Christmas party; but they're not ready yet to join the orgy. Bill has been presumptuous and precipitous. He's not yet in the right league: he has a nice Central Park West apartment, but he doesn't live in a mansion like Ziegler; he likes good Scotch but he can not yet give cases of twenty-five-year-old Scotch away in a casual gesture, he's not yet a Ziegler who can casually say, "I'll send you a case. Come on. Why not?" Bill refuses because while he knows he's not in Ziegler's league, if he accepts the case of Scotch, he drops out of his own league. He can afford to *buy* a case of twenty-five-year-old Scotch is the league he is in. Nick Nightingale is not in that league. Nick would take the case and confirm his lower-league status; Bill confirms his by refusing it. In a class-ridden society, the finer points of class distinction become vitally important. Who is in the same league as Nick Nightingale, who has four boys in Seattle and has to go where the work is? Now he's in New York at Christmas time, a long way from Seattle. He's being led blindfolded to play at the ritualized orgies of the decadent rich. Why, I would say that almost everyone in the theater at both the showings I attended were in Nick's league. There were certainly some Bills and Alices, but I doubt if there was a Ziegler or any of his masked friends sitting next to me munching popcorn. Maybe I'm wrong; maybe there was a Hungarian gigolo standing at the refreshment counter waiting for some young prey.

The rich and powerful today are masked and hidden away behind protective gates and surveillance, but they are nonetheless leading us around blindfolded. Catch Ziegler's pronouncements on poor Nick, who has done nothing more than tell an old friend where the orgy is going to be that night. "That prick piano player, Nick or whatever the hell his name is." "Of course it was Nick's fault. Little cocksucker." "He's back with his family banging Mrs. Nick." Then Ziegler tells Bill that the masked crew at the orgy weren't just ordinary people. Why, who then are the ordinary people? Nick Nightingale for one. And Nick's a little cocksucker, a prick piano player who's back home banging Mrs. Nick. Americans haven't heard that kind of disdain since slavery days, when you could imagine a white overseer talking about "a little black cocksucker in his slave quarters banging Mrs. Black cocksucker." Ziegler abuses Nick like this because he thinks privacy, his and his friends', is a super sacred thing. Nick's life isn't sacred; that's not worth a thing. But the privacy of the wealthy is worth everything and Nick has violated that. He's let someone who's not in the right league past the gates and into the sacristy of the wealthy.

How contagious is this decadence of our global nouveau wealthy? More contagious, I would say, than the HIV that Domino the prostitute picks up. Take for example Bill's dealings with Milage, the owner of the costume shop. Bill establishes his class status as usual by pulling out his board-certified credentials and flashing them. He does this over and over again in the film. He's a doctor; don't go thinking he's just ordinary people. He leads with bucks but Milage is all about money and he wants more. Bill offers more: 200 bucks above rental price. But Milage will go a lot further to make a buck. When Bill returns he discovers that Milage is pimping his own underage daughter. "If there is anything you need, doctor," Milage tells Bill, "and it doesn't have to be a costume, come and see me." As Milage says this he puts his arm around his smiling daughter's shoulders. She gives Bill a shy smile, eyes twinkling with more knowledge than she should have. Depraved innocence and a father willing to turn a profit on it. It's not hard to image Milage's daughter in a few years with a mask and nothing else on serving the licentiousness of the wealthy just as Amanda Curran has.

Ziegler has as much compassion for Amanda as he has for Nick. "We didn't do anything to her. She just got her brains fucked out and then driven home. When we left her she was fine. She just overdosed. It was going to happen with a girl like her sooner or later. You knew that. You remember what you told her the night of my party when she overdosed? It was just a matter of time." How then does a girl like Amanda become "a girl like her"? Does she start out with a parent like Milage willing to rent her like a costume? Here's something else you can try on, Milage seems to be telling his customers. My daughter's body. And Ziegler's tone clearly shows how Amanda Curran is nothing more than a body he can buy like a product and use. There's no human connection. She's got great tits, is how he describes her to Bill. At the time Bill is called up to check on Amanda at Ziegler's party he tells Ziegler not to move her for about an hour and then have someone drive her home. "An hour?" Ziegler responds, glancing at this wristwatch, an annoyed look on his face. "Okay," he finally acquiesces. He's finished with her and he wants her out. He doesn't want her hanging around. Even if she's half-dead he has to think about allowing her to rest for an hour. Maybe he fears detection, but I doubt it. Mrs. Ziegler is most likely the masked figure standing alongside him at the orgy.

"Life goes on until it doesn't," Ziegler tells Bill. "But you know that, don't you?" Perhaps Bill only knows it the way a doctor knows it, but Ziegler means something else. He means that he acts within the measure of his own lifetime. There are no considerations beyond the span of one's own interest in one's own life. Apparently he'd find that Native American wisdom, consider the impact that what you do now will have seven generations from now, a stupid one. It's hard to imagine how a society can have a future when the members of that society gauge their actions by only the length of their own lifetimes.

Now let's put Tyler Durden in Dr. Bill's place at the Somerton orgy. I can't do the scene with Tyler and Vic Ziegler because Vic isn't going to invite Tyler into his mansion and Tyler's not ever going to get in, except in the way the French stormed the Bastille, the way they got in to see Marie Antoinette. But Tyler, like Dr. Bill, has sneaked into the Somerton orgy. Now the background music that we hear when Bill is summoned before the masked tribunal is apt: "Strangers in the Night." Bill is not really a stranger here because, like the masked revelers, he is pursuing his own pleasure as "the highest good." He's just in the minor leagues, whereas these folks are in the majors. Dr. Bill already implicitly accepts the logic and the rightness of the orgy; he respects their right to privacy; he's not offended by old money feasting on the body of young women. He respects the Law of the Cash Nexus. Everybody is being paid, and probably paid well, including his friend Nick. Money buys them the right to do what they want. Dr. Bill has no problem with this. He readily accepts the role they put him in: intruder without any rights. He's the trespasser, not they. They must forgive him his trespasses; the matter of their trespasses is not an issue because they have not sinned against God or Man or Woman. Wealth and Power give them the right to do anything they wish; it gives them the ultimate freedom to choose. And in a society in which "free to choose" is the foundational guiding principle and the criterion to be applied to everything, from abortion to sex, these orgiasts are Philosopher Kings, not sinners. So Dr. Bill meekly steps into the role of transgressor and trespasser. The masked Grand Inquisitor puts him into a sweat. Dr. Bill is tongue-tied. He becomes as much a victim as the naked women. "Mea culpa," he pleads, but that won't do. "Get undressed," the masked ringmaster commands. Bill begins to beg. "Take your clothes off or we'll do it for you." What do they intend on doing? Fucking his brains out as they have Amanda Curran? We don't get a chance to find out because Amanda intercedes and Dr. Bill makes a quick and grateful getaway. He promises not to utter a word about what he has seen. He is so grateful for his release, you get the feeling he would go around the room and kiss the feet of every masked figure there.

Now it's Tyler Durden's turn. He is truly a stranger in the night because he's not only critical of the Have and Have Not order of things, he's angry and full of ressentiment. His eyes are not wide shut but wide open. Tyler goes to the orgy because he's curious as to how far along in their decadence the super-wealthy and powerful have gotten. What does he discover? It looks like it's at a pre–French Revolution level. It looks like the entire *ancien régime* has been brought back in a time machine. Droit du seigneur is alive and well. Tyler arrives on his Harley, as quick a giveaway as Dr. Bill's taxi. If they really belonged they would have driven up in a limo. A masked servant tells Tyler somebody wants to talk to him about his motorcycle. Then he's led into the Court of the High Rollers and their high clergyman of orgy games tries the same approach he did with Dr. Bill. Only this time Tyler tells him to back off. "Let's get it on," Tyler announces, crisscrossing both his arms under his cloak. It's a Fight Club move, a street move; you're outnumbered but you're packing something. Or are you? Who wants to step up and find out?

Maybe they roll over him and crush him; maybe they kill him and dispose of the body so that no one ever knows what happened to him. And maybe they don't. Maybe that unexpected defiance leaves them stunned, just long enough for Tyler to get out. Maybe they don't have to get their hands dirty and just let the servants take care of Tyler. Maybe Tyler takes care of the servants. Maybe everyone sees a weapon and they run for cover. Whatever. Whatever it takes and whatever ensues when you stand up with your eyes wide open.

Halls of Valhalla

1999

There's every indication today that I'm hitting my peak, that like Jean Brodie I'm in my prime: I've just run through the Sanford woodlot for an hour and followed that up with an hour of weightlifting. Last week I turned fifty-six; an hour ago I had about that amount of weight in each hand and was doing "flies" on an inclined bench. I'm feeling good.

But I'm not sleeping well. Not like Proust didn't sleep well. I fall instantly to sleep and don't wake up until morning, but I've been doing a lot of fighting in my dreams. I've been facing a lot of violence and doing a lot of violent things—with my hands, with a bat in my hands, with guns in my hands, with a chair in my hand, with my West Virginia buck knife in my hand, with my black sheathed Commando knife, with everything but the jawbone of an ass. I've got to break heads, all of a sudden, or I can't get out of someplace. I'm meeting resistance down the street; I hear a noise downstairs and go down with my Louisville slugger in my hand, and then as I walk through the dark living room in my pajamas with the bat, I get jumped from all sides and I go down. It's hard to get up again but I manage to, and then I'm swinging that bat. I'm bleeding. I can't catch my breath. The bat flies out of my hands. I keep fighting. I can't be stopped. I won't go down again.

I'm fighting so hard I have to turn over on my other side in bed with a deep, anguished sigh. Maybe I've watched too many action movies.

One night I return from a movie I went to just to escape the heat, a movie called *The Thirteenth Warrior*. I knew nothing about the movie, but when I return I can't stop telling Elaine about it. I tell Kent and Rob and two nights later I go with them to see the film again. The next day I chew Elaine's ear off talking about it. She lets me talk; she listens in a way I recognize. She listens therapeutically. She's not interested in violent movies, but she's interested in my interest. She's never heard me talk so much about a movie before, she tells me. And I'm a guy who writes about movies. But I have no intention of writing about this movie. I don't see where it intersects this year 1999. It's a film that's been on the shelf for two years. The novel it's based on, *Eaters of the Dead,* by Michael Crichton, was written in 1976. This film could have been made any time after America developed a "multiculturalism and diversity" discourse. So why am I so attached to this film? What gives? "What do you think is going on?" she asks me.

∽◦◦∽

I read a review on the Internet that pans the movie; it was a movie that was put on the shelf for two years before release and the reviewer, after seeing the movie, knows why. It's an unredeemably bad movie. Only a jerk would like a movie like this. I'm that jerk; I can't stop thinking about the movie. It has a hold on me; it has potency, what Jung called mana value. In some way this film now connects with me.

Violence and death are the links.

A few months before, I returned from Europe, where twenty-four university students and my two teaching assistants joined with me on yet another "Is This a Postmodern World?" study abroad journey. I come back thinking that this was the best trip yet. But the "glitch" I wrote about in *Postmodern Journeys* upon returning from the 1997 program has become a gargantuan glitch. I am having a most difficult time readjusting to my small-town Midwestern life, where in the evenings Elaine and I take long walks through an antiseptically clean and orderly neighborhood. I'm Lester Burnham on Robin Wood Trail. You never see anyone on a front lawn or porch; the lawns are to be mowed but not used. No one is to be seen; the bigger the house, the less chance you will see an occupant. Only the noise of mowers handled by lawn care service personnel can be heard.

I don't like this neighborhood. Yet I have no reasons to dislike it here; I have no reasons not to like it. It's not noisy, littered, crowded on the sidewalks, with sirens going on at all hours, cars screeching outside, parties out on the lawn in the middle of the night, a rash of robberies, or gangs on the street corners. In short, it's not like where I grew up. And yet I'm nostalgic for my Brooklyn life, a life that if I could go back to in a time machine, I'd find no place I'd like and would be anxious to leave after a week.

I miss being in Europe—but I don't know what I mean by "Europe." Is it all the good times I remember and none of the bad? Is it mostly what I've already imagined Paris, Rome, London, Dublin, Madrid, and so on to be? And having lived there, is it now the same unreliable nostalgia I have for Brooklyn? But do we prize nostalgia for its reliability? Is there a clear past, a clear "surround," waiting for us if we just break through nostalgia's orbit? Not for this postmodern traveler. I've sought the orbit of memory and imagination my whole life. I've read an enormous number of novels: for all my traveling I've still traveled more in fictive worlds than in the real world. "Europe" is a signifier that strikes my imagination like a bell for round one and in I go, leading with the left. Somehow Europe for me resonates with archetypal dreams of "home." Who doesn't invest magical power in points of origin? And Sicily to me is endlessly alluring when I think in terms of origin. But I'm postmodernist: I'm suspicious of the idea of origins.

The way you cook is "Moorish," a woman from Tuscany tells me. "The red hair and blue eyes in your wife's family goes back to the French occupation climaxed with the Sicilian Vespers on Easter Monday 1282." This woman from northern Italy is a fount of information on Sicily; in order to distinguish what northern cuisine is like as opposed to Sicilian, she repeatedly uses words like "delicate," "refined," "subtle."

"You said in class that you come from a Sicilian background," a young black woman, surrounded by her black sisters, tells me after class one day.

"My wife too," I tell her.

"Do you know then that Sicilians have black blood?" she asks.

She's got it together but her sisters have been made uncomfortable by the question. They don't know what I'm going to say. "It's a part of what I am," I say, smiling at them. They smile back. But I know from observing how my relatives in Sicily avoid the sun and court paleness that they believe the Carthaginian blood in their veins is something to hide. I also remember how the Sicilians in my Brooklyn neighborhood would shop at Harry the Greek's while the Neapolitans shopped at Mastelone's. Harry's Greek confections suited my grandmother's palate; there was very little distance between what Harry's wife, Dora, could do with flour, butter, and honey, and what my grandmother could do.

Am I nomadic because of that Sicilian blood? Some seven hundred years before Christ's birth the Phoenicians had also inhabited Sicily. Maybe those nomads of the sea were my connection with the Vikings in *The Thirteenth Warrior*. I was nomadic in my soul because it flowed in my blood since ancient times. Pure irrationalism, the kind we reason within always.

My dislike of this Midwestern neighborhood comes from this: a battle between fact and fancy, between imagination and the real world. And not unsurprisingly, the real world loses. I have no legitimate, rational critique; it is all irrationalities, animus, strangeness, peevishness, complaint. I can't see or appreciate the grassy weave of life that enthralled Whitman. What I can catalogue are my antipathies.

Living here in this small Midwestern town is like undergoing sensory deprivation. I don't go to Red Lobster for a dining experience; I don't think suburban malls represent fashion, culture, and a fine social setting; black youths walking in my white 'hood don't frighten me; I don't think use of profanity is a sign of anything but accentuation; I don't wither when I meet a disagreeable person; I don't give a fuck if homosexuals, lesbians, blacks, Latinos, dwarfs, fat people, divorced women, students, or generally "strange types" move into the neighborhood. The neighborhood at the moment is unsettled by a burglar who only burgles women's undergarments. A shrink profiles him for the police: this is a lonely guy who has replaced other people who might love him with underwear. Maybe he finds the underwear more interesting. As soon as the police get their hands on him they'll fill him up with lithium and end his loneliness. He can start walking a dog after dinner past chemically cared-for lawns. He'll learn to find these people more interesting than underwear.

Just before classes start I get the last signals of an early-retirement offer. There's a couple of players involved besides me. One of the players wants me to go "off-salary" for two years with my medical benefits paid. The other player wants me to teach full-time at a "standard temporary adjunct" salary. One is offering me the carrot of starvation and the other the carrot of semi-starvation. I'm flattered. Are all early retirement offers so appealing? Elaine thinks it's just a joke; it's the university's way of saying, "Don't ever leave us!"

I blow the whole thing off: I've got a "non-career" and always have. This is just more of the absurdity that has filled my life from the beginning. It's a small matter. Meanwhile, I wind up listed in the "exciting 2000 millennium edition" of *Who's Who in America*. I find it in the library and discover, for the first time, what my occupation has been all these years, what career I finally went for: "Natoli, Joseph, English language educator." Fascinating. Is the whole book this reliable?

It's a small matter; all of this "career" stuff is coming to an end now with my "early retirement" offer.

❧

"It's a small matter," one of the Vikings tells the Arab who has supposedly written the account upon which this movie, *The Thirteenth Warrior*, is based. Someone has just said that the battle the Vikings now face would go better if their leader were with them and not over there dying in a hut. It's not a small matter, I think, because the leader, Buliwyf, has been the brave heart of this Viking group. Without him they seem doomed. But this Viking thinks it's a small matter because he believes in Fate, in a destiny long ago writ, in a thread long ago spun and whose end will be reached regardless of what humans may do or not do. If they are destined to win this battle, it will not be because their leader is with or not with them. It will play itself out and they will not step back from playing along. They plunge in and ahead with laughter; their fear will not alter things, so why fear? But they do not give up thinking their way into what befalls them, for thinking is what is required if they are to grasp the destiny that is mapped out for them. This is the thread of time, of their lives, and they will follow it with all their instincts. It is this ready and willing grasp of destiny that distinguishes these Vikings from their horses and their dogs, from the meat they eat, from the trees that grow, from the sun and moon.

I don't have this sense of personal destiny, a thread of my life woven by Odin that I will live through by fully embracing the challenges before me, by not wasting time on fear and regret and sorrow, by finding that destiny by ready acts and not by maximizing choices preliminary to acting or not acting. There's no need to worry about what are the choices, or whether my choices are limited and can be expanded. In the Viking world I see in this movie choices are not ours; and if I persist in seeing them as mine, I'm just spinning my wheels. It doesn't matter. What I choose is a small matter. How I take up what has already been laid down for me is what matters. It's vital to plunge ahead without concern for the consequences because the consequences are fated. What life throws in front of us is what is to be done, and one must do it with all the energy and enthusiasm at one's disposal.

Instead I live in a "civilized" world, where our present sense of "civilized" is defined by market values. You display such "civilized" behavior today by "looking out for number one," by playing a "zero sum game" where someone—you—wins and someone else loses, by believing that "you did it your way" without any intervention of Chance, that life is like a Monopoly game that you're going to win because you've made the right and opportune purchasing decisions, that consuming on the highest levels is the noblest expression of human will, choice, and volition.

⚭

Which world is crueler—the world of the Northmen or the world of the entrepreneurs? Let's look at the ultimate test: how you die in each. The Northmen in *The Thirteenth Warrior* fear dying in their beds. They want to die in battle with a sword in their hands, die with valor and glory and take their place in Valhalla, where they fight and feast in a never-ending cycle. The worst thing someone can say at their funeral is

"He died like a cow in the straw." And the Viking funeral is pyrrhic: not only the body goes up in flames but property, too. Entrepreneurial death? "The guy with the most toys in the end wins." And the battle over who inherits those toys makes lawyers rich. If you get "downsized" before your physical demise, you must take it as a "liberation." You are now free to "assume personal responsibility" and become entrepreneurial. Free of the encumbrance of a salary, you can stay at home and do a Homepage on the Internet advertising your readiness to "become rich." If someone is available to do your job at a lower salary, then you are one of the "liberated." Why should a business world anxious to respond instantaneously to the vagaries of a global market shackle itself by giving workers any form of security? Everyone is on continuous "acting" status; everyone is needed until they are no longer needed. Everyone is dispensable, discardable. Ever-increasing profit has tenure, not people. If you are dying in this civilized entrepreneurial world, you had better have medical insurance. But why should a business be paying for medical benefits? Are they philanthropists? Are they in the business of giving away something that the market does not compel them to give away? Can you find workers who will work without any kind of benefits? If you are sick and dying and have no benefits you are indeed dying *"like a cow in the straw,"* because you may find a stall in a barn but certainly not a bed in a civilized hospital in a civilized world.

I don't want to go out like that; I don't want to die like that. I'd rather die with a sword in my hand. Didn't Tony Curtis or Kirk Douglas say that in a Viking movie I saw as a kid in the Fortway? How else does the inveterate moviegoer die? How else do you die in a postmodern world, but within some Hollywood fantasy? The bell clangs and you step into the ring and lead with that left again, your imagination. And at this moment, I imagine whom I'd be fighting. I know why I have been in battle night after night in my dreams: I choose to fight the way we are civilized now. But then again, consider that it's not a choice but an inevitability for me; and that the way I imagine our American cultural imaginary to be—the way we see ourselves as civilized—is the only way I can imagine. My dissenting orbit is not outside of that cultural imaginary but part of it. I am in an orbital path of mind, heading toward the furthest orbit from birth. I'm seeing from there. And I'm not alone, nor the first, nor the last.

Leiden, The Netherlands

Spring 1999

I've already seen *American History X* but most of my students haven't and it is now playing here in Leiden, The Netherlands. It's an American film about racism in America and I'm doing this program in Europe so that we can, for awhile, step into what I call European "reality frames." But we'll be seeing it here in Leiden in a Dutch neighborhood theater; we'll be viewing as Americans; they'll be viewing as Dutch. And I already know that it's the kind of film that will produce a detectable vibe in the audience; racism is our quintessential American "birth defect," one we can't seem to overcome or wipe out. And the Europeans are more consciously aware of this than we are. It's part of our suppressed American cultural imaginary. Everybody over here knows what we've done and do to blacks and Native Americans. Since the 1980s the prevalent attitude of American students toward all this has been axiomatic: Why should I assume personal responsibility for something that happened a long time ago and which I had nothing to do with? Minds now consumed with creating an enviable investment portfolio and networking a major corporate job with stock options have no time to waste over issues about which Losers fret, such as racism. It only comes into play with something like affirmative action, which seems to guarantee the Losers an advantage in the "competitive arena." Everyone knows that the playing field is level and that everyone enters the competitive arena without any unfair advantages. Rather like the way the Bush brothers, George and Jeb, entered it.

Thus, the audience for this film: the Europeans put racism center stage when they think about Americans; my students think it's a dead issue from the past that has nothing to do with them. It's not a big surprise that the film got scant distribution and response in the States; it couldn't really be shown in the Pleasantville mall theaters. And here in the Midwest no one likes a muckraking film; no one likes unpleasant, disruptive, disconcerting, angry, divisive, NEGATIVE films. Most of these reactions get hidden under the word "violence." Why? I suppose because "violence" is what is too prevalent in our society; the "violent" need to be dealt with. If someone were to object to this film by saying it was "disruptive," the response may be "of what?" "Disconcerting" to whom? And why? But if someone were to object to the film by saying it was "too violent," any interrogating comment would normally be cut off. This is an after-Columbine society. Tag anything with the word "violent" and you have immediate censorship. Anyway, the glass in my neck of the woods is always completely filled, even when it's cracked. All this film can do is stir up racial tension, which would ultimately prove most economically devastating to blacks, who always wind up destroying their own neighborhoods and livelihood. So I suppose not paying too much attention to this film is a benevolent act. But it's going to run in this small local movie theater here in Leiden for a couple of weeks. The European have heard about it; they're interested.

During the intermission we all go down to the bar and unwind. We're unwinding because the first half of the film has been . . . moving. In fact, it was disruptive, disconcerting, angry. The students are in a shocked/mulling/silent mode; the Dutch, however, want to talk. And they want to talk to these young Americans who are the same age as the guy on the screen, the neo-Nazi skinhead, Derek, who has just "curbed" a black guy. They want to know if it's really like that in the States. My students deny it; it's just a Hollywood movie; it's not "real" life. They're on the defensive too because they thought skinheads were like Goths, both being into dark dress styles and dark music. The politics eludes them. They don't pay attention to politics because it's a "dirty business" and all politicians "are the same" and it doesn't matter who gets elected. What matters is getting that internship, that job, those stock options. They look to me to bail them out. Where would the French be if we hadn't saved their asses? The European economy sucks compared to ours! If it's so great here, how come they all want to come to the United States to live?

I'm silent; I'm dealing with this film in other ways. This second viewing has caught me by surprise; something is quaking below the surface. It's warp-driving my memory into orbit.

Everyone sees the final part of the film differently than the first part. What went on during intermission has something to do with it; what ensues in the film has something to do with it as the film continues to shock and unsettle. But I think we are now all aware of each other sitting there watching the film. The Dutch are unnerved by what they are seeing, maybe horrified. You can feel their disapproval in the air; their response is palpable, as palpable now as what we are seeing on the

Memory's Orbit

screen. What we are seeing on the screen is filtered through their response. And it's joined by the response of my students; by the way they are now looking at the film. This is now the context of our seeing. At first defensive of their Americanness, of their sure knowledge that they are not racists, that racism is not the issue back home that these Dutch think it is, that this film is showing it as, you can now sense that they are, in the words of Derek in the film, feeling a "little inside out." There are "things around here that don't fit." They are, in fact, in motion. You can sense that too as you watch the film reach its tragic conclusion. They've taken the journey that Derek has. But first they had to recognize that racism wasn't just Hollywood bullshite, that racism wasn't part of a dead past but a living part of the present, that not everything in America fits because the Dow Jones was bullish, that they too were living within stories of hatred, and that personal responsibility, like everything having to do with what we deemed "personal," was inevitably infused with the social and cultural.

The hating part of Derek's story hit home with me. The film traces the beginning of his hate to his father. The installation of this hate is most likely stretched over all Derek's growing up, but in the film, his brother, Danny, recalls one memorable dinner scene. Derek is talking about a tough English paper he is writing, a paper about the novel *Native Son*. And then his father unleashes a tirade against "affirmative black-tion." It's everywhere he looks. He drags out two of the stories that show up over and over again as affirmative action is debated in the States. In trying to present the black side of things in the classroom we've traded in great books for black books. On a level playing field, black literature can't compete with the white classics. Then he hauls out the story I hear every time we discuss affirmative action in my classes: unqualified black workers are given jobs and promotions over more qualified white workers. Do you think I like having a guy giving me orders who I know isn't as qualified as I am? Derek's dad asks him. And then the coup de grace: I say the best man for the job! He warns Derek against getting sucked into "nigger bullshit." There's a hidden agenda at work here. He's not sure what it is but it's there.

The dad isn't sure but Derek finds Cameron, a neofascist who knows what the non-white hidden agenda is. "We'll let the Niggers, Spics and Kikes grab for their piece of the pie," Cameron says. "We can't blame them. But they'll have to fight to get it." When Derek's dad, a fireman trying to put out a fire in the home of a drug dealer, is shot and killed by the drug dealer, Derek stands before a questioning local reporter and mouths the same kind of racism his father had. The drug dealer who killed his father was probably collecting a welfare check, Derek tells the reporter. Isn't this a result of poverty? the reporter asks, to which Derek responds that they aren't products of their environment. White immigrants faced poverty and overcame it. There's something intrinsically and inherently corrupt about blacks, brown, yellows in Derek's opinion. His hatred is unleashed at races; individuals within those races have no individuality. They are all branded alike, they are all hated equally, regardless of who they are as individuals. And regardless of who a white person may be as an individual, they are, in Derek's creed, essentially right, moral, superior.

I don't have a difficult time distancing myself from Derek's hatred, his particular brand of hatred. It's not my brand. But the words that come out of his mouth only fuel my own . . . I want to say anything but hatred: anger, dissent, edge, rant. Derek's racism gets more than a little help from the Conservative attack on Liberals: it's the Feds who are playing soft with a lazy and violent Underclass, who tax those who work in this country with the burden of providing welfare for the undeserving, who endanger the hard working by not playing hardball with the undeserving, who ultimately cause the death of Derek's dad because he's forced to care about people he shouldn't give a shit about. Ever since Reagan spoke of "welfare queens" and George Bush attracted racists to his campaign with his Willie Horton strategy, conservative ideology has targeted Underclass minorities as our "problem," as an "evil" which must be addressed. Internationally, Saddam and the Arabs would serve. Here at home, where a vicious and cynical campaign is being waved by the Haves against the Have Nots, it is vital that the Have Nots are confused, divided, and undermined by a continuous appeal to racism. Just as dissent is sidetracked as "violence," racism sidetracks class warfare. And the convenient aspect of racism is that, like violence, everyone can deplore and condemn it, including racists who, like believers, know that they have a religion and a faith while those Others have a cult and are brainwashed. Racists never see themselves as racists. And while the excesses of racism, as shown in this film, are clearly observable, the excesses of the Haves are not, especially in a society that has made the American Dream synonymous with the lifestyles of the rich and famous. When I'm at the top of my rant, I say what Cameron says in this movie: we're all after a piece of the pie. But I add: those that have most of the pie engage in a politics to insure that those who want a piece of what they have are denied, are defended against, are deceived, seduced and traduced.

∾◦◦∾

You see clearly the kind of hatred from which I have a difficult time in distancing myself. Does my rant have personal roots? Haven't I been writing my "memoirs" in and around and through my dives into "film and culture" in the 1990s from *Hauntings* to this book, which has expanded the "personal" into the title itself? In fact, you can find my personal wrestling with the racism displayed in my old Bensonhurst, Brooklyn, neighborhood in *Hauntings*. My essay there was triggered by the Yusef Hawkins murder and the Reverend Sharpton march through Bensonhurst. Were we brought up to hate blacks? Or Puerto Ricans? Or Jews? Or Asians? I mean is there a personal story I can tell as in *America History X* where we were at dinner and my father or someone else preached racism? Did I hear avowals similar to the one Danny makes at the end of the paper he titles "American History X" that he has been writing throughout the film?

Danny has already been murdered by a black classmate, but we hear his voice read the paper's conclusion: "My conclusion is: Hate is baggage. Life is too short to be pissed off all the time." And then he ends with a quote; it's a Lincoln speech made in 1861. It's the "better angels of our natures" speech. Maybe the nation is torn by economics: the industrial North vs. the agrarian South; maybe it's more torn by the moral issue of slavery; maybe it's a "devolution" issue with a strong federal government being contested by those who want power to devolve to the states; and maybe with each and every one who ultimately fights in that war, it is predominately a personal issue, a matter of personal honor and integrity, a matter of personal duty and obligation, a matter of personal vendetta and revenge. Did the Yanks personally hate the Johnny Rebs? Did the Johnny Rebs personally hate the Yanks? Can you separate the permeation and saturation of Southern stories and Northern stories into the fabric of what is personal from something that yet stands forth solitary and unmediated as the "personal"?

It is true: I have recurrent dreams in which I am always fighting. When the violence reaches a nauseating pitch, I wake up. Am I defending myself? Am I clear about who I'm fighting? Am I fighting in my dreams because I grew up on Western movies, went around the house firing my cap guns? Or because I spent all my teenage years as a "rebel without a cause" fighting a father who wanted me to become a "clean-cut American"? Or because I should have stood and fought that gang so many years ago on that hot summer night? Or because through the kind of bureaucratic screw-up that most often works against you I was not drafted in 1966, did not fight then? I discover years later in surfing the Internet that a Lt. Joseph Natoli died in Viet Nam in 1967. Am I fighting so that I can correct the wrong and take that Joseph Natoli's place?

Am I fighting in my dreams because I waged that union battle at the very beginning of my academic career and lost, and have been trying to refight it and this time win? Am I fighting the way my lifelong intellectual mentor, William Blake, fought, seeing myself—in cinemascope—as a "prophet against Empire"? Am I fighting because I've made all the rebels in history my study and know the world only as a rebel? a radical? Am I fighting because former beatniks and hippies left at the end of the century without stock portfolios can only fight in their dreams? Am I fighting the war that the Big Lebowski tells the Dude is over? "I have a message for you, Mr. Lebowski. Your side lost."

Is all this inextricably mixed up with a real politics and social policy, a real cultural divisiveness, a real environmental crisis in which the lines are drawn and one must take sides and fight? And not far behind the call to fight is the call to hate.

What finally brings Derek out of that world of hate is another person, the black man who Derek is assigned to work alongside of in the laundry. Derek refuses to speak to him. "I'm the most dangerous man in this prison," the black man tells him. "I control the underwear." Even though he calls Derek "a bad ass peckerwood with an attitude," he practices humor and not hatred. At one point, he tells Derek that Derek's anger and attitude is making the tedious job they have to do even more unbearable. What he hopes for is that they can both "ignore each other in peace." Laughter finally breaks Derek down; the black man does a kind of Richard Pryor routine on what he calls "make-up sex" and the hilarity of it is just too much for Derek. He knows that this is a black man in front of him and he knows what a black man is in his racist way of knowing. What he discovers is that this *particular* black man defies that way of knowing; he can't be an object of hate. He's too funny; he has the kind of personal style that occludes the hate in Derek. And when Derek leaves prison he realizes that this black man is not only too funny to hate, he's too decent and caring to hate. Derek realizes he owes him his life.

ᴄᴠᴏᴄᴧᴆ

"The mystic cords of memory," Lincoln says in the Gettysburg Address, "when again touched will swell by the better angels of ourselves." I recall that the young Lincoln was known for his wit and humor, and though that became less noticeable under the ever-darkening clouds of that war between the states, who can say that his defense against hatred did not always lay there, in that wit and humor. Maybe it's an antidote to any brand of hatred.

Re-orbiting

1975

If you went out the back door at night and climbed up the slope against which the house had been built just about two hundred years before, and looked up, all the constellations of the heavens lit up the sky. It could make you dizzy, looking, slowly turning to see what you could name, as if in the naming you got closer. There are no lights and the nearest house, Kell Petry's, is around a turn about a quarter of a mile further into the hollow.

Kell had a beagle dog, maybe a year old, who came down the road hobbling because his front two legs had been cut off in a fox trap; one above the knee joint and one below so when he walked on the stumps, he walked unevenly. That dog was always cross, eyes kind of dazed with continuous pain. Elaine had to ask Kell why he didn't put the dog down because it hurt her bad to see that dog, or even hear it bark in the distance. Kell didn't understand the question. I mean he culturally didn't understand the question. The beagle had survived the trap; he was crippled and in continuous pain, but he was still alive. Kell wasn't going to shoot him. Or pay a vet in town to put him "to sleep."

After seeing that dog, Elaine had me tie up our dogs, Dickens and Cissy; tied them up on a big runner on the slope just behind the house. Their doghouse was out there and bowls of water. She brought them in when it got too hot and every night so they could sleep in the kitchen by the wood-burning stove. Dickens was named Dickens because when he was a pup and could fit in the palm of my hand, he looked like a Dickensian caricature of a dog, the kind of dog Dickens would describe: unusually big black rubbery nose with a spot of pink at the tip; long thick beagle body covered in black terrier hair; short, stumpy front legs with big paws; longer, thinner back legs. A woman in New Hampshire, where he was born, remarked how distinctive he looked. "What breed is that?" she queried.

"Pootergle," I told her. "I've never heard of that," she replied. "He's wonderful." Poodle. Terrier. Beagle. A hybrid in Yankee country.

Nobody asked about Dickens down in Oxley Holl'r but Cissy caught folks' eye. Especially when they saw her chase after squirrel, so fast she could get out front and nip at their noses. "That dog can hunt some I bet," somebody would say. Something accrued to my reputation by having a blue-eyed beagle whippet mix. Good nose, agility, and speed. But she didn't know how to hunt and she was neurotic and if we didn't tie her up she would have wound up in a fox trap herself. Or, following one scent after another in endless orbits, she'd finally drop down dead of exhaustion, her nose still sniffing a scent. But those two dogs would get loose and go on wild junkets, returning tired, dirty, and hungry. I would go after them and stay gone while they were gone because there was no being with Elaine when the dogs were loose and lost. There was only that one dirt road that wound down into the hollow and only the few pick-ups of the six families living in the hollow that ever went in or out, but Elaine imagined Lower East Side Manhattan traffic. It was where the traffic was in her mind. And in my mind, I ran with them. There was something about seeing them on the loose and heading across the corn field and then gone out of sight that had me running with them.

In my Oxley Hollow constellations, Dickens and Cissy are always running, short bodies in tall pasture grass, making the sign of the Running Dog in the household of the Heavens where even now when I look up, I see them just breaking free.

Index

AEJ-1566

WITHDRAWN